Volume 42

TRANSACTIONS OF THE CHARTERED ACCOUNTANTS STUDENTS' SOCIETIES OF EDINBURGH AND GLASGOW

TRANSACTIONS OF THE CHARTERED ACCOUNTANTS STUDENTS' SOCIETIES OF EDINBURGH AND GLASGOW

A Selection of Writings 1886–1958

Edited by
THOMAS A. LEE

Routledge
Taylor & Francis Group

LONDON AND NEW YORK

First published in 1984 by Garland Publishing, Inc.

This edition first published in 2021
by Routledge
2 Park Square, Milton Park, Abingdon, Oxon OX14 4RN

and by Routledge
52 Vanderbilt Avenue, New York, NY 10017

Routledge is an imprint of the Taylor & Francis Group, an informa business

British Library Cataloguing in Publication Data
A catalogue record for this book is available from the British Library

ISBN: 978-0-367-33564-9 (Set)
ISBN: 978-1-00-304636-3 (Set) (ebk)
ISBN: 978-0-367-50081-8 (Volume 42) (hbk)
ISBN: 978-0-367-50090-0 (Volume 42) (pbk)
ISBN: 978-1-00-304875-6 (Volume 42) (ebk)

Publisher's Note
The publisher has gone to great lengths to ensure the quality of this reprint but points out that some imperfections in the original copies may be apparent.

Disclaimer
The publisher has made every effort to trace copyright holders and would welcome correspondence from those they have been unable to trace.

Transactions of the Chartered Accountants Students' Societies of Edinburgh and Glasgow
A Selection of Writings 1886–1958

Edited by Thomas A. Lee

GARLAND PUBLISHING, INC.
NEW YORK & LONDON
1984

For a complete list of the titles in this series
see the final pages of this volume.

Material from *The Accountant's Magazine* is reprinted by permission of that journal. The *Transactions* are printed by permission of the Glasgow and Edinburgh C. A. Students' Societies. The *Memorial* to F. Sewell Bray is reprinted by permission of *The Accounting Review* and R. H. Parker.

Library of Congress Cataloging in Publication Data

Main entry under title:

Transactions of the Chartered Accountants Students'
Societies of Edinburgh and Glasgow.

(Accounting history and the development of a profession)
1. Accounting—Addresses, essays, lectures. I. Lee,
Thomas Alexander. II. Chartered Accountants Students'
Society of Edinburgh. III. Glasgow Chartered Accountants
Students' Society. IV. Series.
HF5629.T7   1984   657   83-49441
ISBN 0-8240-6308-2 (alk. paper)

The volumes in this series are printed on
acid-free, 250-year-life paper.

Printed in the United States of America

Contents

ACKNOWLEDGEMENTS

I am grateful to the editor of The Accountant's Magazine for permission to reproduce the relevant obituaries and lectures from the Transactions; and to the editor of The Accounting Review for permission to reproduce the memorial of F. Sewell Bray. Mr Touche, Professor Baxter and Mr Leitch also provided relevant biographical details and, again, grateful thanks are due to them.

INTRODUCTION

The CAs Students' Society of Edinburgh commenced its activities in 1886 with an address on 3 November by its first President, George Auldjio Jamieson. Its membership was open to students and members of The Society of Accountants in Edinburgh, and its affairs were managed largely by the qualified members.

In 1887, a debating society for qualified members of The Institute of Accountants and Actuaries in Glasgow was formed, and this was the basis for the creation of the Glasgow CAs Students' Society in 1889. A Students' Society was formed in Aberdeen in 1904, but the major Societies proved to be those of Edinburgh and Glasgow.

The focus of the activities of the two Societies were the lectures given by prominent speakers for the benefit of the members of the Societies - particularly the student members who had few alternative opportunities of being made aware of accountancy and related issues of the day. These lectures were given by invitation and were published in the Transactions of the two Societies.

The Transactions of the CAs Students' Society of Edinburgh were published in 25 volumes from 1886-7 to 1913-14. The Glasgow CAs Students' Society Transactions commenced in 1903-4 and ran for 12 volumes until 1914-15. Following the First World War, the two Societies produced the Joint Transactions of the CAs Students' Societies of Edinburgh and Glasgow for the first time in 1919-20. These comprised 29 volumes until they ceased in 1956-8.

This text is concerned mainly with papers published in these various Transactions, but it is interesting to note some of the other features and activities of the Students' Societies. The latter were constituted originally to organise a series of lectures on contemporary issues. But

1

soon their activities extended beyond this function. For example, in 1906-7, the Edinburgh Society held a mock company meeting, and similar activities were held in later years in both Edinburgh and Glasgow. Indeed, joint meetings of the two Societies became a regular feature from 1912-13 onwards. The Glasgow Society had its first annual dinner in session 1902-3, and the Edinburgh Students' Society ball became a feature on the social calendar. The Glasgow Society held regular joint meetings with the Juridical Society from 1907-8 onwards and, in 1920, it set test examinations for would-be Chartered Accountants. The latter was a practice followed by Edinburgh in 1921, and in later years in Aberdeen and Dundee. Test exam papers and answers were published by the Glasgow Society from 1913-14 onwards, and by both Societies from 1920-1 onwards. Finally, in the early 1950s, the Societies organised visits to public offices and industrial undertakings by their members. In 1955-6 a week-end residential course was held - the forerunner of the present-day Summer School of The Institute of Chartered Accountants of Scotland.

Thus, the two Societies managed a series of academic and social activities for many years on behalf of the local accountancy community. The need for most of these activities has now disappeared but the permanent memorial remains in the form of the published Transactions, and it is to these that this text will focus the reader's attention.

The 66 volumes of Transactions from 1886 to 1958 contain 413 lectures of varying content, size and quality. Many of the lectures, particularly in the earlier years, were given by eminent accountants from throughout the UK (although the majority were Scottish Chartered Accountants). A list of all the lectures and lecturers is appended to this Introduction but the following is also given as a summary of the main subject areas in the periods of time 1886 to 1915; 1919 to 1940; and 1945 to 1958 (the gaps being due to War activity):

	1886-1915	1919-1940	1945-1958	Total
	%	%	%	%
Economics, business and management	6	15	3	9
Finance, investment and insurance	13	13	14	13
General legal matters	11	9	8	9
Company law	15	10	7	11
Trusts and bankruptcies	17	11	2	12
Taxation	5	11	23	12
Specific accounting systems	9	10	8	9
Financial reporting and auditing	13	5	19	11
Cost and management accounting	2	7	7	5
Miscellaneous matters	9	9	9	9
	100	100	100	100
Number of lectures	151	174	88	413

The published papers have thus been classified into the above areas of accounting and related activity. Over the entire period, the division of lectures has been remarkably even, no particular category dominating. However, there have been some obvious divisions and changes between periods. Coverage of non-accounting matters (the first three categories listed) was 30%, 37% and 25%, respectively, in each of the three specific periods. In 1886-1915, the proportion of lectures on specific accounting, reporting and auditing topics was 22%. In 1919-1940, this proportion fell to 15%, but rose again to 27% in the last period. A very small percentage of lectures in each period dealt with cost and management accounting (5% overall). In other words, through each of the three periods, a considerable proportion of lectures concerned non-accounting matters, and a similar minority dealt with external and internal accounting topics.

The remainder of the lectures in each period related to legally-based subjects - company law, trusts and bankruptcies, and taxation (37%, 32% and 32%, respectively). The most substantial changes over time are to be evidenced with these subjects - company law fell from 15% in 1886-1915 to

3

7% in 1945-1958; trusts and bankrupticies fell from 17% to 2% for the same periods; but lectures in taxation increased from 5% to 23%. These figures tend to reflect changes in the function of public accountancy between 1886 and 1958 - particularly the fall of activity in trusts and bankruptcies and the corresponding increase in taxation matters. What is surprising is the relatively low proportion of lectures dealing with financial reporting and auditing, and cost and management accounting. Indeed, the former category concerned only 5% of lectures between 1919 and 1940. The concern of accountants for accounting, reporting and auditing standards problems in the 1960s and 1970s were therefore not evident in earlier periods.

The financial reporting and auditing topics are the major concern of this text. They represent the one category of lectures given between 1886 and 1958 which have a continuing and international relevance and interest. The other main categories refer to economic, business, financial and legal matters which are either largely relevant to the Scottish situation or involve technicalities which demand a specific and detailed knowledge of the times and situations in which they were given. The remainder of the accounting topics dealt with specific business situations in detail but appeared to contain material of insufficient quality and interest to be worthy of reproduction.

Of the 46 financial reporting and auditing lectures given, 13 have been selected to reflect the contributions made in this area by leading accountants through the pages of the Students' Societies Transactions. 11 of the lecturers were (or are) distinguished Scottish Chartered Accountants; the remaining 2 were (or are) distinguished English Chartered Accountants. Their topics can be divided into three main areas - first, the nature of financial statements (Brown, Touche, Baxter and Lister); second, the specific financial reporting problems of goodwill, depreciation, and changing prices (More, Ker, Rintoul, McHaffie and Leitch); and, third, auditing (Hutton, Wardhaugh, French and Bray). Each of these lectures

4

reflects the practices of the times and changes that were then occurring. They all provide evidence of the strength of the writers concerned - they are uncluttered by the now conventional structure of footnotes and referencing; and with one exception (Baxter), they were written by practitioners who were dealing with the described problems from day to day. They are a permanent record of a unique academic contribution by leading practitioners to student accountants during periods when accountancy had not achieved a formal academic status.

TRANSACTIONS OF THE CAs STUDENTS'

SOCIETY OF EDINBURGH

Lectures Published 1886-7 to 1913-14

1. J.S. Nicholson, 'The Effects of Great Discoveries of the Precious Metals' (1886-7)

2. J.M. McCandlish, 'Accountants and Actuaries: the Work of the Actuary' (1886-7)

3. J.A. Robertson, 'Life Assurance' (1888-9)

4. R.B. Haldane, 'The Reform of the Law of Joint-Stock Companies' (1888-9)

5. G.J. Hutton, 'On Auditing Commercial and Company Books' (1888-9)

6. W. Graham, 'Recent Demand in London for Gold and for Money' (1888-9)

7. E.T. Salvesen, 'Bills of Lading' (1888-9)

8. G.M. Law, 'On the Tests by Which a Life Assurance Office May be Judged' (1889-90)

9. W.C. Smith, 'The Legal Interests of Married Women' (1889-90)

10. T.G. Dickson, 'Factorships (1889-90)

11. F.W. Pixley, 'The Investigation of the Accounts of Commercial Undertakings Previous to Their Conversion into Public Companies' (1889-90)

12. J.B. Nicholson, 'Valuation and Rating of Property' (1890-1)

13. F. More, 'Goodwill' (1890-1)

14. C.R.A. Howden, 'The Duties and Responsibilities of Gratuitous Trustees' (1890-1)

15. F.W. Carter, 'Trust and Judicial Investment Under the Trusts (Scotland) Act 1884, and Under Decisions of the Court of Session as at 1 January 1890' (1890-1)

16. A. Drummond, 'On the Mode of Conducting an Audit' (1891-3)

17. J. Muir, 'A Chat About Accounting (1891-3)

18. T.P. Laird, 'Trust and Executry Accounts: Their Preparation and Audit' (1891-3)

19. A.H.B. Constable, 'National Insurance' (1891-3)

20. T.A. Welton, 'Some Suggestions as to Amending the Companies Acts (1891-3)

21. M.C. McEwan, 'Income Tax' (1891-3)

22. J.L. Mounsey, 'The Law of Heritable Securities' (1891-3)

23. J.G. Watson, 'The Consideration of Securities for Loans' (1891-3)

24. E.H. Macmillan, 'Some Notes on the Silver Question' (1891-3)

25. J. Howden, 'The Profession: A Retrospect' (1893-4)

26. R. Brown, 'Recent Proposed Legislation Relating to the Profession' (1893-4)

27. J. Stuart, 'On the Realisation of Estates in Bankruptcy' (1893-4)

28. C.G. MacRae, 'Some Anomalies in Railway Law' (1893-4)

29. W.A.A. Balfour, 'Powers of a Company with Reference to Purchasing its Own Shares (1893-4)

30. J. Wilson, 'Cautionary Obligations' (1893-4)

31. R. Collie, 'The Working of the English and Scottish Bankruptcy Laws Compared' (1893-4)

32. G. McRae, 'Some Aspects of Municipal Finance' (1893-4)

33. W.C. Maughan, 'Indian Banking and Currency' (1894-5)

34. J. Cormack, 'Notes on the Mercantile Marine of Great Britain, France, and Italy' (1894-5)

35. G. Lisle, 'Solicitors' Book-keeping' (1894-5)

36. A. Oliver, 'The Death Duties' (1894-5)

37. P.C. Robertson, 'Public and Parochial Burdens' (1894-5)

38. G.W. Burnet, 'The Reconstruction of Companies' (1894-5)

39. K.M. Gourley, 'Bank Auditing' (1894-5)

40. J. Haldane, 'Proposed Amendments of Company Law' (1895-6)

78. J. Leishman, 'Town Finance' (1907-8)

79. G.W. Richmond, 'British and Foreign Insurance Methods' (1907-8)

80. J.B. Wardhaugh, 'The Legal Limitations of an Auditor's Duties and Responsibilities' (1908-9)

81. M. Macdonald, 'Shipping Accounts' (1908-9)

82. C.F. Whigham, 'Town Council Audits' (1908-9)

83. H.W. Haldane, 'The Examination of Securities' (1909-10)

84. D.E. Wallace, 'Building Societies' (1909-10)

85. J.S. Gowans, 'Trust Deeds and Deeds of Arrangement' (1910-11)

86. R. Brown, 'The Duties of a Secretary' (1910-11)

87. T.S. Thomson, 'The Practice of the Stock Exchange' (1911-12)

88. A.W. Tait, 'Reconstruction of Limited Liability Companies' (1911-12)

89. T.P. Laird, 'Trust Accounts and Apportionment of Dividends' (1912-13)

90. J. Leishman, 'The National Health Insurance Act, 1911, so far as Affecting Professional Classes' (1912-13)

91. J. Allan, 'Income Tax, With Special Reference to Recent Legislation' (1912-13)

92. W. Vickers, 'Company Registration' (1913-14)

93. J.B. Wardhaugh, 'States for Settlement with Beneficiaries in Cases of Testacy and Intestacy' (1913-14)

94. T. Cumming, 'Land Tenure in Relation to Trade, Commerce, and Finance' (1913-14)

THE GLASGOW CAs STUDENTS'

SOCIETY TRANSACTIONS

Lectures Published 1903-4 to 1914-15

1. R. Brown, 'The Joint Stock Company Code' (1903-4)

2. J.M. MacLeod, 'Exhibition Accounts and Finance, and the System of Checking Income and Expenditure' (1903-4)

3. W. Brunton, 'Trust Deeds in Scottish Bankruptcies' (1903-4)

4. R.N. Carter, 'Income Tax - Some Practical Points' (1903-4)

5. C.W.S. Jamieson, 'A System of Life Assurance Bookkeeping' (1903-4)

6. T.W.M. Watson, 'Trustee Savings Banks' (1903-4)

7. S.S. Dawson, 'The Companies Act 1900' (1904-5)

8. G.W. Wight, 'Burgh Audits' (1904-5)

9. J. Dalrymple, 'Glasgow Corporation Tramways' (1904-5)

10. W. Watson, 'The Law of Trusts' (1905-6)

11. J.A. Steven, 'Stock Exchange Practice' (1905-6)

12. A.H. Brown, 'The Use of Percentages' (1905-6)

13. T.E. Robinson, 'Municipal Debt and Accounting' (1905-6)

14. G.A. Touche, 'Reconstructions' (1905-6)

15. W. Nelson, 'Trusts: An Outline of the Course to be Followed in Their Administration' (1905-6)

16. F.W. Pixley, 'How to Read a Balance Sheet of a Commercial Concern' (1906-7)

17. M. Mitchell, 'Special Points Arising in the Audit of the First Balance Sheet of a Limited Company Formed to Acquire a Going Business' (1906-7)

18. H.P. Macmillan, 'Further Reforms in Company Law' (1906-7)

19. J.A. Todd, 'Fee and Liferent' (1906-7)

20. A. Moore, 'The Accountant as an Expert Witness' (1906-7)

21. V. Marr, 'A Card System for Friendly Societies' Accounts and Statistics' (1907-8)

22. P. Rintoul, 'The Treatment in the Accounts of Joint-Stock Companies of Depreciation in Value of Assets Arising from Their Employment, and the Duties of an Auditor Relating Thereto' (1907-8)

23. D.P. Fleming, 'Questions in Bankruptcy Arising Out of the Relationship of Husband and Wife' (1907-8)

24. T.J. Millar, 'Methods of Stating Accounts with Particular Reference to Trust Accounts' (1907-8)

25. B. Browne, 'The Economics of Socialism' (1908-9)

26. C.M. Aitchison, 'The Auditing of Public Accounts' (1908-9)

27. J. Wilson, 'Notes on Landed Estate Accounts' (1908-9)

28. W.H. Kirkland, 'The Law Applicable to Goodwill' (1909-10)

29. W.C. Smith, 'Citizenship' (1909-10)

30. A.F. Dodd, 'The Preparation of Accountants' Certificates for Purposes of Joint Stock Company Flotations' (1909-10)

31. A. Murray, 'Municipal Finance, With Special Reference to the Provision and Application of Sinking and Depreciation Funds' (1909-10)

32. J.S. Gowans, 'Company Liquidations in Scotland' (1909-10)

33. R.M. Maclay, 'Notes on the Audit of Accounts of Ships and Shipping Companies' (1909-10)

34. S. Fyfe, 'Bankruptcy Reform' (1910-11)

35. D.N. Sloan, 'The Companies Acts - Their Use and Abuse' (1910-11)

JOINT TRANSACTIONS OF THE CAs STUDENTS'

SOCIETIES OF EDINBURGH AND GLASGOW

Lectures Published 1919-20 to 1956-8

1. A.D. Nichol, 'Cost Accounts' (1919-20)

2. A. Cathles, 'The General Principles of Costing' (1919-20)

3. J.J. Cowperthwaite, 'Income Tax Law and Practice' (1919-20)

4. P. Rintoul, 'Excess Profits Duty and Coal Mines Excess Payments, etc.' (1919-20)

5. J.J. McLauchlan, 'Some Leading Principles of Life Assurance Bookkeeping' (1919-20)

6. H.R. Buchanan, 'Ranking in Bankruptcy' (1919-20)

7. G.J. Scott, 'The London Money Market' (1919-20)

8. A.C. Black, 'The Law of Evidence' (1919-20)

9. J. Girvan, 'Stamp Duties' (1919-20)

10. W. Annan, 'Profit Sharing' (1920-21)

11. J.H. Jones, 'The New Problem of Taxation' (1920-21)

12. W. Anderson, 'The Finance Act 1920' (1920-21)

13. W.A. Reid, 'Book-keeping for Farmers' (1920-21)

14. A. Murdoch, 'Farm Accounts' (1920-21)

15. A. Crawford, 'The Law of Property Title in Scotland' (1920-21)

16. H.P. MacMillan, 'Cautionary Obligations' (1920-21)

17. H. McIntosh, 'The Law of Insurance' (1920-21)

18. T.P. Laird, 'Insurance Companies' Accounts and Audit' (1920-21)

19. G. McBain, 'Hints to Apprentices as to the Tests to be Applied to the Figures in the Balance-Sheet of a Commercial Concern' (1920-21)

20. J.T. Rankin, 'Notes on the Voluntary Liquidation in Scotland of a Company Limited by Shares' (1920-21)

21. H.R. Buchanan, 'Voting in Sequestration' (1920-21)

22. N.M. Lindsay, 'Shipbuilding Cost Accounts' (1921-2)

23. J.H. Jones, 'The Problem of Foreign Exchanges' (1921-2)

24. W. Graham, 'Tests of Economic Progress' (1921-2)

25. W.E. Levie, 'Statements of Affairs' (1921-2)

26. W. Watson, 'The Law of Trusts in Scotland' (1921-2)

27. T.G. Wright, 'The Law of Shipping Documents' (1921-2)

28. J. McBain, 'Trust Deeds for Creditors' (1921-2)

29. C.E.W. Macpherson, 'Landed Estates' (1922-3)

30. T. Hart, 'The Audit of the Accounts of a Scottish Burgh' (1922-3)

31. Lord Sands, 'The Value of Money Since 1914' (1922-3)

32. J.H. Jones, 'Germany's Financial and Economic Condition' (1922-3)

33. A.E. Cutforth, 'Report-Writing' (1922-3)

34. H.P. Macmillan, 'The Duties of Directors at the Inception of a Company' (1922-3)

35. P. Rintoul, 'Finance Act 1922' (1922-3)

36. W.D. Lyell, 'Some Humours of the Scottish Bar' (1923-4)

37. D. Begg, 'An Introduction to the Study of Actuarial Science' (1923-4)

38. R.J.L. Hendry, 'Borrowing from Banks' (1923-4)

39. J.F. Rees, 'Economic Adjustment' (1923-4)

40. J.H. Jones, 'The Financial Condition of France' (1923-4)

41. J.L. Wark, 'Profits Available for Distribution by Limited Companies' (1923-4)

42. E.E. Spicer, 'Some Thoughts on Reparations' (1923-4)

43. J.A. Falconer, 'Notes for Examination Students on Apportionments' (1923-4)

44. C. Sarolea, 'The Present Position in Soviet Russia' (1924-5)

45. J.H. Jones, 'Credit Control and Unemployment' (1924-5)

46. K. Smellie, 'Practical Costing' (1924-5)

47. N.L. Hird, 'Some American Impressions - Banking and Otherwise' (1924-5)

48. C.F.C. Brodie, 'Notes on Loss of Profits Insurance for Professional Accountants' (1924-5)

49. J.A. French, 'Some Doubts on the Duties of Auditors Regarding Procedure, Grouping of Balance-Sheet Items and Verification of Assets and Liabilities' (1924-5)

50. J.M. Fells, 'Accountancy as an Aid to the Solution of Civic Problems' (1924-5)

51. H.G. Cree, 'Stock Exchange' (1924-5)

52. A. Robb, 'A Talk on the National Debt' (1924-5)

53. J. Girvan, 'Apportionments in Trust Accounts' (1924-5)

54. W.A. Robertson, 'Some Notes on the Business of Insurance' (1924-5)

55. J. Jeffrey, 'Parish Councils - Their Powers and Duties' (1924-5)

56. J.G. Scott, 'Modern Idealism in Its Relation to Industry' (1925-6)

57. C. Ker, 'Some Notes on Diversions of Capital' (1925-6)

58. A. Harrison, 'Machine Hour Rates' (1925-6)

59. J.H. Jones, 'The Return to Gold' (1925-6)

60. A.E. Sprague, 'Elements of Life Contingencies' (1925-6)

61. W. McLintock, 'Liquidations' (1925-6)

62. J. Drever, 'Vocational Tests for Clerical Work' (1925-6)

63. D. Begg, 'Pension and Superannuation Funds' (1925-6)

64. T.P. Laird, 'Investigations' (1926-7)

65. J.H. Jones, 'The Future of British Industry' (1926-7)

66. R.T. Haddow, 'The Finance Act 1926: In so far as it Relates to Income Tax and Excess Profits Duty' (1926-7)

67. W. Annan, 'Business Statistics' (1926-7)

68. W. Arthur, 'The Elements of the Theory of Probability' (1926-7)

69. W. Somerville, 'Income Tax - Administration in Law and Practice' (1926-7)

70. N.W. Duthie, 'The Accountant and Economics' (1926-7)

71. P.D. Stewart, 'Loss of Profits Insurance' (1926-7)

72. J.B.Wardhaugh, 'Intestate Succession' (1926-7)

73. W. Dickison, 'Stock Exchange Procedure' (1927-8)

74. I.F.C. Bolton, "Investment Trust Companies' (1927-8)

75. W. Arthur, 'Averages' (1927-8)

76. T.M. Cooper, 'Accountancy Evidence from an Advocate's Point of View' (1927-8)

77. J. Loudon, 'Reorganisation and Reconstruction of Limited Companies' (1927-8)

78. T.B. Simpson, 'Company Law' (1927-8)

79. J. Allison, 'Trust Deeds in Bankruptcy' (1927-8)

80. J.D. Imrie, 'Scottish Local Rating - Recent and Prospective Developments' (1928-9)

81. D.G. Prosser, 'Death Duties and Death Duty Accounts' (1928-9)

21

124. J. Loudon, 'Some Points in the Audit of the Accounts of a Testamentary Trust' (1935-6)

125. R. Browning, 'The Ascertainment of Total Income for Surtax Purposes' (1935-6)

126. A. Hogg, 'Preparation of Accounts from Incomplete Records' (1935-6)

127. A.H. McIntyre, 'Social Credit' (1935-6)

128. A.G. McBain, 'Income Tax Appeals' (1935-6)

129. J.L. Somerville, 'Administration and Accounting of Local Authorities' (1935-6)

130. J.A. Walker, 'Some Notes on the Audit of the Accounts of Local Authorities' (1935-6)

131. T.G. Robertson, 'Accountancy in the Law Courts' (1935-6)

132. W. McLintock, 'Creditors' Voluntary Liquidations' (1935-6)

133. W.L. Davidson, 'Building Societies' (1935-6)

134. W. Miller, 'Multiple Store Accounts' (1935-6)

135. J.W. Dallachy, 'Allocation of Oncost to Work-in-Progress' (1935-6)

136. W. Annan, 'Apportionment Difficulties and Inconsistencies' (1936-7)

137. J.G. McBurnie, 'Children's Settlements as Affected by the 1936 Finance Act' (1936-7)

138. I.W. Macdonald, 'Judicial Remits and Proofs' (1936-7)

139. A. Miller, 'Practical Cost Accounting' (1936-7)

140. H.G. Judd, 'The Investigation of a Business with a View to its Changing Ownership or Securing Additional Capital' (1936-7)

141. A. Gray, 'Index Numbers: The Value of Money' (1936-7)

142. J. Adair, 'Crime and Accountancy' (1936-7)

143. J.J.D. Hourston, 'Stock Control and Budgeting' (1936-7)

144. D. Witney, 'The Comparative Study of Farm Accounts and Costs' (1936-7)

145. A.H. Aikmen, 'Capital Expenditure for Tax Purposes' (1936-7)

146. A.S. Bilsland, 'National Development in Scotland' (1936-7)

147. A.R. Templeton, 'Fluctuating Currencies' (1936-7)

148. R.H. Forbes, 'The Profits Report on a Prospectus' (1936-7)

149. T.C. Currie, 'The Provisions of the 1937 Finance Act Relating to the National Defence Contribution' (1937-8)

150. R.H. Morrison, 'Some Features of Hotel Accounting' (1937-8)

151. A.D. Paton, 'Income Tax in Relation to Trust and Executry Accounts' (1937-8)

152. J. Kilpatrick, 'Prospectuses of Public Companies - Behind the Scenes' (1937-8)

153. H. Cowan-Douglas, 'Some Thoughts on Giving Professional Advice' (1937-8)

154. A. Wright, 'Our Managed Money' (1937-8)

155. N.W. Duthie, 'Industrial Development in the Distressed Areas' (1937-8)

156. J.C. Millar, 'Surtax and Private Companies' (1937-8)

157. T.D. Laird, 'Motor-Car Agents' Accounts' (1937-8)

158. R.D. Gairdner, 'Stock Exchange Practice - with Particular Reference to Points Which Affect the Client' (1937-8)

159. A.A. Lawrie, 'Stock Exchange Procedure' (1938-9)

160. W.M.S. Cairns, 'Colliery Costs' (1938-9)

161. R. Crawford, 'Costs in the Light Castings Industry' (1938-9)

162. R. Crawford, 'Costs and Statistics - Their Scope and Function' (1938-9)

163. T.F. Whitewright, 'Prospectuses' (1938-9)

164. A.K. Cairncross, 'The Economic Position of Germany' (1938-9)

165. J. Adair, 'Accountancy and Crime' (1938-9)

166. J.J. Cowperthwaite, 'Valuation for Rating' (1938-9)

167. J. Loudon, 'The Effect of Mechanised Accounting on Audit Procedure' (1938-9)

168. W. Annan, 'Mechanised Accounting and its Audit Features' (1938-9)

169. A.J. Fleming, 'Farm Accounts' (1938-9)

170. S.E. Houston, 'Trade Associations' (1938-9)

171. I.W. Macdonald, 'Supervising the Installation of Book-keeping Machines' (1939-40)

172. - Jones, 'Financial Strength as a Factor in War' (1939-40)

173. R.W. Parker, 'The Accountant's Part in Buying a Business' (1939-40)

174. - Jones, 'Spending and Saving' (1939-40)

175. A.G. Murray, 'The Modern Balance Sheet' (1945-7)

176. J.R. Philip, 'The Art and Ethics of Advocacy' (1945-7)

177. A. Stewart, 'Building Society Accounts' (1945-7)

178. H. Watson, 'Litigation in the Parliament House' (1945-7)

179. D.A. Wright, 'A Partnership is Converted into a Private Limited Company with the Assistance of its Solicitors and Accountants' (1945-7)

180. R.L. Gwilt, 'Staff Pension Schemes' (1945-7)

181. R.P. Burnet, 'Lump Sum Payments in Income Tax' (1945-7)

182. C.I.R. Hutton, 'Consolidated Accounts' (1945-7)

183. L.C. Hawkins, 'Accountancy in a Large-Scale Industrial Undertaking' (1947-8)

184. A.H. Bowhill, 'New Issues' (1947-8)

185. R.T. Young, 'Profits Tax' (1947-8)

186. G. Mackenzie, 'A Bank's Balance-Sheet' (1947-8)

187. J.D. Fraser, 'Pension Schemes' (1947-8)

188. L.A. Elgood, 'Management of a Group of Companies' (1947-8)

189. A.G. McBain, 'Fraud in Taxation' (1947-8)

190. J.F. Robertson, 'The Companies Act 1947' (1947-8)

191. I.W. Macdonald, 'The Companies Act 1948 - Accounts' (1948-9)

192. W. Gordon, 'The Town and Country Planning (Scotland) Act 1947' (1948-9)

193. W.L. Walker, 'The Local Government (Scotland) Act 1947, and the Auditor' (1948-9)

194. J.L. Ferguson, 'The Accountant in Shipbuilding' (1948-9)

195. I.W. Macdonald, 'Accounting Procedure in the Provision of Finance for Commerce and Industry' (1948-9)

196. A.M.C. Smith, 'Standard Costing and Cost Control for Manufacturers' (1948-9)

197. R.P. Burnet, 'Some Aspects of the Finance Act 1948' (1948-9)

198. J.D. Stewart, 'The Presentation of Accounts and Supporting Schedules for Taxation Purposes from the Inland Revenue Point of View' (1948-9)

199. J.T. Dowling, 'The Valuation for Death Duty Purposes of Unquoted Shares of Companies' (1949-50)

200. D.J. Bogie, 'Group Accounts' (1949-50)

201. J.S. Heaton, 'Income Tax Deductions in Computing Profits - Cases I and II' (1949-50)

202. W. Walker, 'Voluntary Liquidation in Scotland' (1949-50)

203. A.N.E. McHaffie, 'Rising Price Levels in Relation to Accounts' (1949-50)

204. A.D. Paton, 'Taxation of Farming Profits' (1949-50)

205. H.H. Monteath, 'Some Aspects of Will Making' (1949-50)

206. R.T.M. McPhail, 'Investigations and Reports on Profits' (1949-50)

207. J.B. Wardhaugh, 'Some Problems in Trust Accounting' (1949-50)

208. G.W. Band, 'Standard Cost Accounting' (1949-50)

209. A.G. Young, 'The Companies Act 1948 and Winding Up Rules as They Affect Procedure in Liquidations' (1949-50)

210. J. Fielding, 'Accountancy Problems in Multiple Stores' (1949-50)

211. R. Peddie, 'Factory Value Accountancy: A Development of Standard Costs' (1950-1)

212. W.T. Baxter, 'The Study of Balance Sheets' (1950-1)

213. J.A. Stodart, 'Farming and the Accountant' (1950-1)

214. A. Noel Smith, 'Accounting and Control in a Departmental Store' (1950-1)

215. F.B. Reynolds, 'The Risks of the Accountancy Profession' (1950-1)

216. T. Lister, 'Accounting Statements - A General Formula' (1950-1)

217. R.W. Foad, 'The Audit of a Public Limited Company's Accounts in Practice' (1950-1)

218. J.S. Craig, 'Industrial Accountancy' (1951-2)

219. C.A. Scott, 'Elementary Trust Accountancy' (1951-2)

220. J.G. Glendinning, 'Income Tax - Treatment of Losses' (1951-2)

221. A.K. Cairncross, 'Economic Review' (1951-2)

222. W. Oliver, 'The Accountant and the Business Man' (1951-2)

223. W.S. Risk, 'Job Analysis and Personnel Rating' (1951-2)

224. F.R.M. dePaula, 'The Effects of the Price Level on Accounting' (1952-3)

225. J. Kinross, 'Financing the Small Business' (1952-3)

226. C.J. Baker, 'Excess Profits Levy' (1952-3)

227. C.J. Baker, 'Excess Profits Levy: Groups of Companies, Finance Act 1952, Twelth Schedule' (1952-3)

228. J.G. Glendinning, 'Settlements and Taxation' (1952-3)

229. A.H. Campbell, 'The Diversity of Legal Systems' (1952-3)

230. R. Macdonald, 'Courts and Procedure' (1952-3)

231. G.G. McGregor, 'Some Aspects of Estate Duty' (1952-3)

232. J. Drever, 'Some Recent Studies in Personnel Management' (1952-3)

233. G.B. Esslemont, 'Financial Control in Local Authorities' (1952-3)

234. C.C. Cunningham, 'Public Finance' (1953-4)

235. W.C. Buchanan, 'The Stock Exchange' (1953-4)

236. T.D. Hay, 'The Organisation and Functions of the Internal Audit Branch of a Large Industrial Undertaking' (1953-4)

237. H.E. Wincott, 'Interpretation of Company Accounts' (1953-4)

238. H. Barton, 'Income Tax: The Machinery of Assessments and Appeals' (1953-4)

239. A.G. McBain, 'Income Tax Back Duty - Some General Comments' (1953-4)

240. N.C. Hunt, 'Profit-Sharing and Co-partnership - A Critical Review' (1954-5)

241. F. Sewell Bray, 'Auditing Theory' (1954-5)

242. T.A. Hamilton-Baynes, 'Share Valuations for Estate Duty' (1954-5)

243. J.R. Blyth, 'Some Uses of Cost Accounting' (1954-5)

244. D.G. Moir, 'Double Taxation Relief' (1954-5)

245. R.S. Johnston, 'The Evidence of the Accountant in Litigation' (1954-5)

246. H.N. Hume, 'The Provision of Capital for Industry' (1954-5)

247. A.R. Reid, 'Pension Schemes and Taxation' (1954-5)

248. L. Gale, 'Industrial Relations' (1954-5)

249. R.P. Burnet, 'Recent Legislation on Income Tax Losses' (1954-5)

250. T. Lister, 'An Accountant's Thoughts on Valuation' (1955-6)

251. W.S. Risk, 'The Accountant in Industry' (1955-6)

252. I.W. Macdonald, 'Financing and Accounting Features of Bank Administration' (1955-6)

253. R. Browning, 'The Professional Accountant and the Family Business' (1955-6)

254. I.H. Shearer, 'Presentation of Evidence' (1956-8)

255. H. Barton, 'An Introduction to Estate Duty' (1956-8)

256. J.R. Leitch, 'The Accountant and Inflation: Changing Price Levels' (1956-8)

257. A.D.R. MacPhail, 'Investments for Individuals, Trusts and Companies' (1956-8)

258. A.N.E. McHaffie, 'Amalgamations and Reconstructions' (1956-8)

259. W.Q. Russell, 'The Carry-Over Fraud and Associated Activities' (1956-8)

260. D.J. Bogie, 'Some Controversial Points on Group Accounts' (1956-8)

261. R. Browning, 'The Annual Reports and Accounts of Limited Companies' (1956-8)

262. R.D. Rawson, 'The Taxation of Farm Profits' (1956-8)

The late Mr George Johnston Hutton.—The death took place, on the 6th of January, after a short illness, of Mr G. J. Hutton, in his sixty-fourth year. He was the son of Mr James Hutton who for many years had a school in Nicolson Square. He was educated at the High School, and afterwards entered the Accountants' profession, being trained partly in Edinburgh and partly in London. More than thirty years ago he entered the office of Messrs Lindsay, Jamieson, & Haldane, and remained with them until the time of his death, being for many years chief Assistant in their Audit Department and latterly Cashier. Mr Hutton carried out most efficiently the work entrusted to him, and gained the confidence and respect of all those with whom he came in contact.

Outside the office Mr Hutton was well known, on his own account, as an authority on book-keeping and account-ing, and in 1889 was chosen to read a paper to the Chartered Accountants' Students' Society on "Auditing Commercial and Company Books," which was published among their Transactions. He also had a great reputation as a Coach, and for a number of years very successfully tutored candi-dates for the Chartered Accountants' Examinations, and many members of the Society have reason to be grateful to him for his services in this direction.

He took a keen and active interest in Church work, having been an elder in Nicolson Street United Free Church for a great number of years, and for the last five years was Preses of the Congregation and Chairman of Managers.

Mr Hutton will be remembered by those who knew him not only as a good accountant and a sound man of business, but as a man of integrity and uprightness of character.

George J. Hutton, 'On Auditing Commercial and Company Books' (1888-9)

This lecture was one of the first given to the Edinburgh Students' Society. It was on a subject which was relatively new at the time, and reflects the practices of the day. The subject was auditing, and much of the emphasis was on the detection of fraud as the main audit objective. Little attention was given to the role of financial statements as an aid to decision making. In fact, no mention was made of financial statement users.

Not only was the audit aim different from that of today but the responsibility for the financial statements (particularly the balance sheet) was seen by Hutton as that of the auditor - presumably the latter prepared the statements and, in addition, thereby verified the figures contained in them. The approach to the accounting was seen as a conservative one so far as assets and liabilities were concerned - for example, goodwill was recommended to be written off as quickly as possible; and, in the split between capital and revenue transactions, Hutton did not see anything wrong in erring on the side of 'safety' when the profit statement was charged with expenditure. On the other hand, when depreciation was discussed by Hutton, he stated there were no fixed rules governing its provision, and felt this should be left to the auditor's discretion (again, emphasising the latter's role in the preparation of statements).

So far as auditing was concerned, its implementation was structured around detailed checking. Interestingly, despite the detailed descriptions of how to audit books and records, Hutton did evidence his awareness of the need for the auditor to check the system of internal control (admittedly in the context of a fraud detection audit). Great faith was placed in the lecture on the examination of written records to verify the 'truth' (for example, in relation to the audit of inventory). The approach appeared to be one of an acceptance of recorded figures as sufficient evidence. A similar acceptance was to be seen with regard to the receipt of financial statements and accounts from overseas operations, and asset valuations provided by management and others. By way of contrast, students of auditing were given considerable guidance regarding the examination of hand-written records.

This paper represents a valuable exposition of auditing in its earliest days prior to the large-scale involvement of the accountancy profession in its execution in practice.

PREFACE.

THE aim of the following paper was above all to be practical, but it was impossible in the limits originally prescribed to include therein everything connected with the subject. Some points which some may consider of importance may have been omitted; it is thought, however, that the main points taken up are sufficient to suggest what further work should be done by an Auditor.

G. J. H.

ON AUDITING COMMERCIAL AND COMPANY BOOKS.

BY

GEORGE JOHNSTON HUTTON,

Accountant, Edinburgh.

23rd January 1889.

WHAT a vast place of business the world is now becoming! Every country seems to be tumbling out its wares and its goods to the outside of its windows and its doors that they may be seen, and, by means of the telegraph and the telephone, is shouting to the ends of the earth that its prices are so and so, and indeed a great deal cheaper than any one's else. Moreover, it sits in its back-parlour, and, counting up its wealth, it launches out anew on some fresh startling scheme to the green envy and violent irritation of its neighbour. Every day thousands of ships are ploughing away through the seas, carrying to and fro the produce of toiling millions. Throughout all the earth the din of business and the noise of the toilers are becoming ever more and more heard the more you sit down to listen to them. A few hundred years ago Venice and Amsterdam were commercial centres in their day, and were accounted splendidly rich and influential; but what were they to the London or New York of to-day? What a volume of trade there is throughout the whole world flowing in and out of these and other great cities, the value of which is simply incalculable! The volume is such that it might indeed fitly be likened to an ocean rather than a river. In the midst of so much wealth, so much noise, so much eager buying and selling, is there not a splendid opportunity for fraud and dishonesty? The deed will be done before it can be noticed, and the robber will escape with impunity. What remedy for this? How can we protect ourselves, cries the whole community, against such insidious enemies?

It is only in comparatively late years that the profession of an Auditor has risen in public estimation, but within that time it has risen very rapidly, and now the office of an auditor is one of distinction and desire. An auditor stands as the one reliable man, so to speak, amidst all. *He* is trusted, *he* is believed as no other man in the whole mass of business in the world is trusted and believed.

Thus saith the world unto every auditor, " Is this state of affairs true ?" and he, putting his hand to the document, replies, " It is no sham ; it is no lie ; it is truth." That document is then looked upon by all mankind as irrefragable. It is a fixed fact for all time, and the world frames its actions for ever in accordance therewith.

Woe be to the auditor who knowingly subscribes to a lie ! He of all men will never be forgotten—he chose to pose on his height as a man of virtue and truth ; but he attempted in the sight of all to deceive, and he fell, never to occupy such an honoured height again ; to the end of life he is discredited.

In the days of Diogenes, it seems to have been a wearisome matter to find an honest man, and the grim old philosopher seems to have been bitterly hopeless as to his success. Let us hope that nowadays honesty is not so rare. Indeed, I am strongly of opinion that it is not, seeing the numbers of accountants who now stand forth to the world as men who can be relied upon in telling the truth as to a state of business affairs.

Ye are auditors, or wish to be—how then will you conduct your audit in order to attain to a true statement of affairs ?

What follows is an humble attempt to show a practical method by means of which such a desirable end may be arrived at.

In an audit you have got (first) to see what the accounts before you say, and (second) to consider whether they tell the whole truth.

First, then, how are you to satisfy yourself as to what the accounts say ? This will necessitate a large amount of detail work, portions of which are highly disagreeable to apprentices as being irksome and laborious, but which nevertheless are of the greatest importance—such as summing pay-sheets and long ledger accounts, or posting journals and cash-books. Yet I would impress upon apprentices that such work is very important, for in many cases frauds are only detected by means of checking weary lengths of summations and volumes of postings. I would further remind apprentices that it is *not* because such work is unimportant that they get it to do, but because it is comparatively easy work. Wherefore, comfort one another with these words.

Strictly speaking, every single transaction made during the period under review should be examined, and an experienced auditor always satisfies himself that practically he does examine every transaction. Now, if what I say is to be beneficial, I wish to show how such thorough examination can be made.

We are all aware that the four principal Books kept by a merchant, in which all entries of transactions are made for the first time, are—

1. The Invoice-Book, or Purchase Day-Book, in which all purchases are entered as they occur.
2. The Sales Day-Book, in which all sales are entered as they occur.
3. The Cash-Book.
4. The Bill-Book.

There are a few other subsidiary books, which are of minor importance. If we know how to grasp the larger books, we shall know how to master these smaller ones. I shall therefore confine my attention principally to these four larger books, for through them we may say almost every transaction of the business passes. Almost nothing enters the ledger but from them, except it be transfer-entries from one ledger account to another. If, then, we are satisfied that every entry in these four books is correct, and that such entry has been correctly posted to its last resting-place in the ledger, we may assure ourselves that, so far as the actual transactions have taken place, we are able to make a report, either favourable or unfavourable. How then are we to get at such a desirable standpoint in our audit?

THE PURCHASE DAY-BOOK.

Let us take up first the Purchase Day-Book. Here we enquire at the outset who has the authority to make purchases; are the invoices certified by managers of departments that the goods have been received; who gives authority for accounts being paid; and who pays the accounts? Our enquiries may not always be thrown into such form as I have formulated them, nevertheless we ought always to obtain the information, the more especially if it falls to our lot to audit the books of a large commercial concern. It is quite clear that there are many opportunities for fraud in connection with the purchases made for a business, unless precautions are taken. Has it not often happened that where no supervision was made in regard to purchasing, payments have been made for purchases which never took place ? It has also been the case that goods got and paid for during one month, have been paid for again during some succeeding month, the accounts for the goods having been discharged by the cashier, or other official forging the signature. All this has taken place through there being no proper system in force for sanctioning the payment of accounts. It is not only undesirable, but improper, that in a large establishment the same official should have the power both of authorising payment and of making payment. It is true, in some houses, a partner has this power, and perhaps less can be said against the arrangement in that case. I would, however, remind you that a partner has long ere this defrauded his copartners. It is the duty of an auditor to point out such precautions ; and in cases of the audit of limited companies' books it would be his duty to insist upon such precautions being taken, because the auditor is an officer appointed directly by the shareholders. Unless the invoices are certified by managers of departments, what guarantee is there that the goods were ever received into stock ? Moreover, the invoice being certified by the manager will prevent it being used again by a fraudulent official for a double payment of the account.

Having then satisfied ourselves that what is in the purchase day-book has entered it under some authority, we have the book summed. It should then be compared with the invoices, but this would be in some cases an enormous labour. If such a system, however, in reference to the invoices, is in use, as I have pointed out, it is perhaps only necessary to make a general comparison of invoices so certified, with the invoice book, because it is quite possible to have another check upon the total sum of the purchases. In this way; if some official or partner has the duty of sanctioning payment of the accounts, he no doubt will satisfy himself that the invoice is certified, and he will keep some record of all accounts he authorised to be paid, and then he will hand over the account to be paid to the cashier, whom I presume to be a separate official from the party *authorising* payment. If then the record kept by the party authorising payment agrees with the total in the invoice book, say month by month, we may have some confidence that the invoice book is correct. He will then see that the totals of the book are carried by means of the journal (if such a book be in use) into the proper accounts in the ledger, and our examination of the book is at an end.

THE SALES DAY-BOOK.

Turning now to the Sales Day-Book, we enquire what there is to instruct it ; and if the business is a general one, dealing with many kinds of merchandise, we are met with serious difficulty. Where the business is all of one kind, such as of iron or cotton, where the quantities sold should correspond with the quantities purchased or received, after taking into account the stocks on hand, we have not much difficulty in satisfying ourselves how the whole goods are disposed of. But in a large miscellaneous business, as a store of any kind, or large retail establishment, it is evident such a check cannot be obtained without extremely minute detail. In such businesses, however, it is usual that money is not paid to the shopman or party selling, or if so, only after the note of goods sold has been initialed by the supervisor or by the cash clerk. These notes of sales are filed by the cash clerk and recorded by him, the total of which record should agree with his cash in hand. By such a method, or some such adapted to the require- ments of each business, if efficiently carried out, the cash sales, even of a large miscellaneous business, may be said to be sufficiently instructed. Without some such system there would be great opportunity for robbery, for it is in cash sales more readily than in credit sales that theft will take place. Indeed, with credit sales the auditor should feel confident that if such methods of procedure as he approves of are carried out, there should be no room for theft, and he might suggest something on the lines of the following method :—

All the orders having been entered into the order book, the orders are then made up from that book, and an outvoice prepared and certified by the despatching department, with a number corresponding to the order in the order book. The outvoice is then sent to the counting-house, where it is entered in the sales day-book, and having been copied into a press copy-book, it is finally despatched to the customer. Thus every entry in the sales day-book will be instructed by a copy of the certified outvoice in the press copy-book, and also by the entry in the order book.

If the sales day-book has been correctly kept in some such

fashion as this, all we may find necessary to do will be to test the entries in the book, here and there, with the order book and with the press copy-book, so satisfying ourselves generally that it is correct; and after we have seen the book summed, and that the totals are carried into the ledger, our intercourse with it for the meantime is finished.

If, however, as I have already stated, the sales consist of one species of merchandise, it is most probable you will be able to see whether the total quantities sold account for the whole stocks in hand at the commencement, *plus* the new goods procured during the period. Moreover, as it is most likely that contracts will have been entered into for the larger sales, such contracts should be examined to instruct the sales made and the prices received for them. If we have some such evidence as that laid before us, we may rest assured that the method in use for recording all sales transactions is a reliable one.

THE CASH-BOOK.

We take up next the Cash-Book. Naturally an auditor will look to see if it is closed off in ink. It is not an unheard-of thing that a cashier has handed over his cash-book closed off in pencil. It has also, I believe, been stated as a fact, when the auditor has returned the book after his audit, that the cashier has altered the figures in it to cover certain cunning devices of his own. Don't begin work on the cash-book until it is finally closed off in ink; but that being done, we proceed to examine the vouchers, as it is more than likely they will be arranged according to the dates of the cash-book. As I am speaking to many apprentices, I would impress upon them the importance of care in examining vouchers. It is often thought to be easy work, and in a sense it is; looking to the amount, the signature, the date, and, of course, if stamped where necessary, is not very difficult; but more than this ought to be done. The eye should certainly travel over the voucher to see its general contents. Especially in the audit of a commercial or manufacturing business should the contents of the voucher be scanned so as to see, at least in a general way, that the amount of the payment has been posted to the proper account, for much depends on the decision whether it is a capital or a revenue payment. Serious error might happen from an injudicious allocation of payments to capital account. Thus, though the examination of vouchers may be routine work it is highly important. Apart, however, from questions of capital or revenue the examination of vouchers is important, for an auditor must be careful that a voucher is sufficient, as such, to stand before a Court of Law. I commend, therefore, this portion of the work to the care and attention of senior apprentices who often are entrusted with it.

Of course, for every payment there should be a voucher, and this leads me to say that every entry for a payment into Bank or draft on the Bank account should be checked with the Bank pass-book. In fact, the whole Bank pass-book ought to be posted into the cash-book and into the ledger. It is not sufficient to find that the balance on the Bank account in the ledger agrees with the balance in the Bank pass-book, or Bank certificate. Notwithstanding the apparent correspondence of these balances, it has been found that fraud has been possible by manipulation of the Bank account in the ledger. In this way : A sum of say £10 is received in payment of a debt, it is duly debited in the cash-book, and credited to the debtor's account in the ledger. Thus far all is well. It is then credited in the cash-book as a payment into the Bank, and is posted to the debit of the Bank account in the ledger, but the sum is never actually paid into Bank. Were the ledger to stand without any further entry it would show £10 more in Bank than the Bank pass-book did. An entry is, however, now made in the ledger (and this time not in the cash-book) crediting the Bank account with the £10, as if it was drawn out of Bank, and to balance the amount some expense account or wages account in the ledger is debited. In this way the Bank account in the ledger, having had now both a debit and credit entry made in it, the balance of the account will agree with the balance shown on the Bank pass-book. If the entries in the Bank pass-book should then be checked into the ledger Bank account, it would at once be found that apparently transactions were recorded in the ledger which did not appear in the Bank pass-book. This would suggest inquiry, and the fraud would then be on the point of detection.

The debit side of the cash-book, in addition to the sums drawn out of Bank, consists very largely of debts paid by customers which are instructed by the sales book. But an examination of the whole of the debtor side is always necessary, for it may happen that considerable sums may be received out of the ordinary course of sales. The sales day-book would not instruct such receipts. The auditor will therefore require to be satisfied in

E

regard to them with particular evidence. Thus, supposing sums were received as a loan on mortgage of certain properties, the correspondence relating to the loan should be seen; and finally, the letter forwarding the amount, or some such evidence, could be produced to instruct the actual amount received.

Having then summed the cash-book, and satisfied ourselves that the cashier is duly lodging in Bank the monies received by him, our audit of the book is almost complete, unless we have to take up in connection with it the examination of the bill-book, seeing that in some businesses the whole of the bills, whether discounted or not, are passed through the cash-book.

THE BILL-BOOK.

I am not here to discuss the best system of book-keeping, it is my duty only to consider business books as they are put into our hands for audit. An auditor may think he could put the books on a better system, and do away with certain books as superfluous : but he must just take the books as he finds them ; he cannot compel alterations, though he may point out improvements. I confess, however, that passing bills receivable and payable through the cash-book immediately they are drawn, and again to pass them through on their maturity, or when discounted, seems to me clumsy and unnecessary work. When a bill receivable is drawn, or a bill payable is accepted, the only entries necessary are to pass them to the bills receivable or payable accounts respectively, by means of the journal, if a journal is in use, and on the bills coming to maturity, or being discounted, to pass them through the cash-book. But should any books submitted for audit deal with the bills through the cash-book immediately on their being drawn, every entry in the cask-book in regard to them should be carefully compared with the corresponding entries in the bill-book, and also with the Bank pass-book when they are discounted. It has been known that the entries of the bills in the cash-book towards the close of the period have been so manipulated as to deceive in regard to the real balance in hand; of course, as a necessary consequence, the false entries were either omitted from the ledger accounts, or the ledger had to be falsified also.

Where a business has many bill transactions, an auditor should certainly keep in view to see that the bills are being met regularly. Without doubt a bill that is constantly being renewed will raise suspicions as to the debtor's stability; and, when valuing the debts of the firm, for the preparation of a balance-sheet, your judgment should certainly be influenced by your knowledge of such renewals. I need not say that all accommodation bills should always be particularly noticed. Upon them no profit will accrue to the business, and it will not be surprising if loss rather arises. It is not a true statement of affairs to include them among ordinary trade bills, for to all intents they are simply loans, and should ever be pointed out as such.

I have now gone over the four principal books in which, in a commercial business, all entries are made for the first time. The exigencies of each kind of business always require certain subsidiary books, more or less important; but, practically speaking, we may say that almost nothing enters the ledger unless it has first appeared in one or other of these four books—the Purchase Day-book, the Sales Day-book, the Cash-book, and the Bill-book. I have suggested methods by which these books may be examined without going into the most minute detail—a more minute examination means checking the posting of every item, which is very laborious, and consumes much time. The circumstances of each audit must determine whether the audit requires to be minute or not.

Passing then from these books and taking up the ledger, if the audit of the accounts for the previous year had not been done by you, you would first of all satisfy yourself that the starting balance on each of the accounts at the commencement of the period you have to audit agrees with the entries in the balance-sheet of the previous year. That being done, and having summed the ledger, we check from it the revenue account and balance-sheet, which have been prepared by the book-keeper. We may now say that we have completed to a large extent the detail work of our audit. The revenue account and the balance sheet, as they at this point stand, give the result of the business according to the books, subject to any alterations we may hereafter make upon them.

I have thus endeavoured to fulfil the first part of an auditor's duty, viz., to see what the accounts say.

We now proceed to the second part of our duty, which is—To consider whether the accounts, as they have been made up by the book-keeper or the firm, tell the truth, and the whole truth.

This part of our work demands careful consideration, as under it questions of principle have to be discussed and decided. Especially is this so if the audit be of the accounts of a limited liability company. The Prospectus and Articles of Association often lay down certain lines upon which the business of the Company is to be conducted; and where such is the case it is clearly the duty of an auditor to point out where such lines of conduct have been deviated from, or where the directors have exceeded their powers. Then there are the ever-recurring questions—What is capital? and What is revenue?

In order to give some point to our subsequent observations, I have prepared what may be called a skeleton revenue account and balance-sheet (see Appendix), presumed to be of a large commercial business in existence for several years, and having a house in Edinburgh and in Calcutta. The figures are omitted, as in the present case they are unnecessary, and might be rather distracting. It is to be noted that I have supposed the revenue account and balance-sheet to be applicable to a limited liability company as well as to a commercial company, as I wish to utilise certain headings in them for what I may have to say afterwards in regard to limited companies' books. You will see, however, that only a few entries refer specially to a limited company's accounts; the other entries might apply either to the one or the other. In the meantime I shall not refer to the limited company's entries.

THE GROSS REVENUE ACCOUNT.

The Gross Revenue Account, or, as some would call it, " The Trading Account," should clearly contain only such earnings and such expenditure as are properly applicable to actual trade for the period under review, and the balance thereon should be carried to a nett revenue account, where any payments not properly chargeable against the trade of the period may then be set against it. The revenue account must include *all* the earnings and expenditure for the year—not simply such earnings as have been *received*, or such payments as have been made, but also all earnings and expenditure that have accrued or have been incurred. This distinguishes the revenue account from a mere statement of receipts and disbursements.

With this preliminary remark upon the account, let us proceed to go over the different items contained in it; and, looking at the credit side, we find " gross profit for the year." This is found, as shown in the explanatory note, by adding to the total sales the stock in hand at the close, and deducting therefrom the stock in hand at the commencement and the total purchases. In regard to the total purchases and sales referred to here, we have by our previous examination of the purchase day-book and the sales day-book, by some such method as I have suggested, satisfied ourselves as to their accuracy. We saw that all the purchases and all the sales had been instructed, and that all had been included up to the last day covered by the audit. We were careful to see that the purchases did not include any in respect of machinery or plant, but were altogether for goods for resale. Passing now on to the "stock in hand at the close," we are met with the question, How far is an auditor bound to check a statement of stock? In most cases he will have to accept as correct the quantities stated therein. No doubt he will see that the manager will certify the statement; but, in addition, I think it is an auditor's duty to take an intelligent survey of the whole statement, contrasting it in a general way with last year's statement; and, moreover, satisfying himself that the values put thereon may fairly be held to be cost price. There are conceivable instances where a somewhat higher price than cost price may be permitted, as where large contracts are in force for delivery of goods at a certain price. In such an instance a price higher than cost, but lower than the contract price, might be taken; as a general rule, cost price should be held as the value. Sometimes it may happen that cost price is higher than market price; if that be so, then it is clear that market price, or rather a figure below market price, in order to cover expenses of sale, should be taken. It is evident that the profit of the year will be materially affected, according as you value the stock high or low. It is always safe to value it at a low rate, because if prices rise next year your profits will be so much higher; if, on the other hand, prices are low, then by your low value of stock you will be able to meet the market, and probably escape a loss. You see, then, by our previous examination of the purchase and sales day-books, and by our general survey of the stock-sheets, we are enabled to say at once whether this main item on the credit side of the revenue account is correct or not.

The next head shows a "profit on production of silk at Calcutta." This is the balance on a profit and loss account made up from the books at the branch in India. To support this sum we may have to rely to some extent on the account sent home. As the house in Edinburgh is supposed by us to be the sole purchaser of the goods manufactured in Calcutta, we can see that the gross sums *received* by the India Branch agree with the amounts which the house in Edinburgh states as sums *paid* to the India House for silk. The credits in India agreeing with the debits in Edinburgh, the one thus instructs the other. In regard to the payments made in India for labour and materials, certified statements might be sent home, signed by the manager and head of the firm in Calcutta. It is rare that vouchers ever accompany accounts sent from abroad. An auditor, however, should carefully consider such accounts, especially with a view to capital and revenue payments, and obtain information upon any points that seem to him to call for enquiry. Where the accounts have been examined by an auditor abroad, of course we may accept the balance on the production account he certifies without going into any detail.

Turning now to the expenditure side of our gross revenue account, we remark that most of the items should be instructed by vouchers properly discharged. These we saw when examining the cash-book, and so far that is satisfactory. But that is not enough. In an earlier portion of this paper I referred to the likelihood of many vouchers containing both capital and revenue payments. At this point we come to recognise the importance of great care being bestowed on such vouchers, for it will be evident that the more you put to capital the less will be your revenue expenditure, and, as a necessary consequence, the larger will be your balance of profit for the year. I would, therefore, impress upon you the necessity of examining closely the voucher, where any portion of it is charged to a capital account, and, having been satisfied as to all such payments being proper charges on capital, then check the posting of them to their account in the ledger. When speaking of the day books and cash-book, I pointed out that in many commercial businesses it would be almost impossible to check the posting of every item into the ledger owing to the innumerable entries; but I would insist on checking the posting of every capital item into the ledger. It is true that a revenue charge may be posted to one account in place of another, and as you do not check the whole posting of the ledgers you fail to notice the error. But practically no great harm will be done, as the *balance* on the revenue account will be the same, whether you post the sum to the one account or the other. It is different, however, as I have said, in regard to capital and revenue charges. If an error takes place in posting a revenue charge to a capital account, you will, of course, have a larger balance of revenue apparently in hand than you ought to, and most probably such false balance will be paid away to the partners or shareholders. It is clearly then the duty of an auditor to guard against such errors.

Some controversy may arise as to what may be a capital charge, but, generally speaking, all cost, whether for material, labour, or management in the erection of buildings, machinery, plant, etc., may be considered capital outlay, unless such buildings, etc., are only renewals of old buildings, etc. Extensions of works are capital, but renewals, replacements, repairs are of the nature of revenue charges. Where very extensive repairs have taken place, and it is evident that for the next year or two the ordinary repairs may reasonably be expected to be small, it is doubtless within the discretion of an auditor that he should allow some portion of such extraordinary repairs to stand over to be met out of the future year's profits. A strong business will, however, wipe out all such repairs at once. It is never lost money to do so, for next year the profit will be greater by the charges against revenue being proportionately smaller.

Keeping these points in view, let us take up rapidly each item of expenditure.

Wages.—In a large business this will be a considerable item, and will consist of the pay of many departments. The manager of each department should certify as to the work done by those employees under him, especially should this be so in a manufacturing concern. He alone can tell whether the work is of a permanent nature or otherwise; that is, whether you are to regard it as for capital or revenue. Grievous as the labour may appear, you will not lay aside the pay-sheet without having summed it, for you are bound to take every precaution you can against fraud. There is some room for theft in connection with the wages lists. Where many men are employed, it is quite imaginable that a pay clerk who has no proper supervision over him might insert a name and a wage, and draw the money himself. To guard against that I have pointed out that managers of departments should certify the lists. Again the pay clerk, if he observed that the magnitude of the pay-sheets so appalled the auditor that the summations were left unchecked and accepted as correct, might boldly increase the summations, and pass these false figures through his books. It is an auditor's duty, then, to sum at least the total columns of the pay-

45

sheets if he sees that that is sufficient to guard against fraudulent figures being passed into the ledger.

Salaries.—This account can be examined more minutely, because usually the separate salaries are fixed and known amounts, and an auditor by a scrutiny of the ledger account can see that these amounts have been paid.

Repairs to Machinery, Plant, etc.—As already pointed out, we need not concern ourselves too seriously whether this amount is overcharged to the advantage of some capital account; no principle of right and wrong is violated. By overcharging ordinary repairs' account we err on the side of safety, and to the extent of the overcharge we retain profits in hand which can be divided at some future time, if it is found safe. If the vouchers, then, are all in order, and the outlay has been duly authorised, we can with all safety pass the account.

Discounts and Allowances.—This is the balance of abatements allowed to customers, less allowances received from creditors. Much of this account is as a rule unvouched, and can only be instructed in a general way—such as a fixed rate of discount being allowed. The auditor, however, when he comes to make a scrutiny of the customers' accounts in the ledger can keep in view the amounts of discounts allowed, and get explanations of such as seem extraordinary. The discounts on bills receivable discounted, which may be debited to this account, will be vouched by the discount statement got from the bankers, and the discounts received from creditors is generally noted on the voucher for the payment to them.

Travelling Expenses, Trade Charges, and Rents, Rates, and Taxes, and Office Expenses and Commissions, will be instructed either by agents' accounts or by properly discharged vouchers, and I need not further refer to them.

Bad Debts.—This account should contain not only such debts as have actually turned out bad, but also the allowance which is often made against possible loss in respect of the debts still due. A percentage is taken of the debts outstanding, including the bills receivable current, but that percentage will vary according to the nature of the business and the customers. If there be few customers comparatively, possibly the percentage might be only 1½ or 2; while if there were a multitude of small accounts, even 10 per cent. has been taken as the rate to cover possible loss. Here again it is proper to err on the side of safety than to risk loss.

46

Depreciation.—With regard to this account much difficulty may arise. It is a right principle that all property, whether of a fixed or a semi-fixed character, employed in trade should be held to have deteriorated after a year's use. But how to assess that deterioration has always been the difficulty. Fixed property, such as buildings, will not depreciate so rapidly as semi-fixed property, such as machinery. The life, so to speak, of machinery may be a few years, while that of buildings might be fifty. As the outlay for both of these may be greatly intermingled, it becomes very difficult to fix a rate, and in many cases it will be found that a rate when fixed is an arbitrary one. It might be 5 per cent. or 7 per cent., or more. Sometimes a round sum is taken to cover the depreciation. So far as I am aware, though after all my information does not extend very far, there is no fixed rule how to assess depreciation. In some cases depreciation has not been charged when it can be pointed out that extensive renewals and repairs, much beyond the ordinary outlay, have taken place, and that the whole have been charged to revenue. But, as a general rule, it should be held that a sum should be charged against each year's profits in respect of depreciation. How that sum is to be arrived at must be left greatly to the auditor's discretion, influenced by the circumstances before him.

Difference in Exchange.—This is an account that arises in respect of the difference in exchange on the transactions between the house in India and the house in Edinburgh. It is quite evident that if all transactions could be made in sterling, and that if a sovereign was in India of the same value as it is in Edinburgh, there would be no difference between the balance on the "Home Account" as it stood in the ledger in Calcutta, and the balance on the "India Account" as it stood in the ledger in Edinburgh. But the Calcutta accounts deal with rupees and the home accounts with sterling. The exchange between the two countries may vary often during a year; when, therefore, at the close of the year, you come to make a conjoined balance of the Calcutta and home accounts, you will most probably find, when you turn the balance on the "Home Account" in the Calcutta ledger into sterling that that sterling equivalent will not be of the same amount as the balance on the "India Account" appearing in the home ledger. The reason is that the book-keepers in Edinburgh have entered certain items in the "India Account" in their ledger at a rate of exchange different from the rate of exchange you are using at the close of the year

47

when turning the balance on the "Home Account" on the Calcutta ledger into sterling. This difference is called the difference
in exchange. It may not, however, necessarily be a loss ; there
might be an apparent profit.

NETT REVENUE ACCOUNT.

We now arrive at the close of the Gross Revenue Account, the
balance on which is carried to the credit of the Nett Revenue
Account. As has been already stated, the Nett Revenue Account
contains all charges not of the nature of trade transactions. For a
like reason it will be credited with all extraordinary receipts.

The only sums, beside the balance of the Gross Revenue
Account appearing here at the credit, are the balance brought
forward from last year, and the amount received for transfer fees.
The first of these items is verified from last year's balance-sheet ;
the other item, " transfer fees," is only to be found in the accounts
of limited and corporate companies. This item calls for little
remark farther than that these fees, being a fixed charge, the total
sum got during the year can be checked by the number of transfers
that have taken place during the year.

On the debit side of the account, as has been said, we place such
charges against profits as do not form natural expenses in connection
with the carrying on of the business. And first we have—

Dividend at 5 per cent. to Shareholders.—That this sum was
authorised to be paid it would be found on referring to the minutes
of the company ; and to meet it we have on the credit side of the
account the balance brought forward from last year's account. To
vouch the payment of the dividend you have dividend warrants
returned discharged. But most dividend-paying companies usually
pay the exact amount of the total dividend, less tax, into a special
account with the bankers, against which the bankers place the
amount of the dividend warrants as they are presented. After a
period of a month or two the Bank gives to the company a statement
of the dividends paid, showing any balance yet unpaid. Such a
statement, or something similar, if presented to the auditor, may, I
think, with all safety be accepted by the auditor as sufficient evidence
of the dividends paid, without going over every separate dividend
warrant.

In like manner a separate account with the bankers may be
opened to provide for payment of the *Interest on Debentures.* If

that be so the Bank's statement of the interest coupons paid will instruct the total payment made. But in addition to that, an auditor can certainly satisfy himself whether a whole year's interest has been entered in the accounts. He knows the total amount of debentures in force for the whole year,—in respect of that amount a whole year's interest will be due. He knows the amount of new debenture money got; interest on *that* amount will then be due from the dates when the debentures money was received up to the last date of the accounts under audit. He further knows what debentures have been paid off during the year; interest on *that* amount will be due from the beginning of the year we are auditing up to the date when the debentures were paid off. Adding these three interests together (the interest on the debentures in force for the whole year, the interest on the new debentures, and the interest on the debentures paid off, for the portions of the year they were in force) will give the total debenture interest which should be debited to the nett revenue account. If you find the amount on the statement of interest thus independently made up by yourself corresponds with the amount in the revenue account, and that the payment thereof is instructed by the Bank's pass-book, you may, I think, pass the item.

The "*interest on mortgages and on prepaid calls*" you can of course check by calculation, and instruct by voucher.

The proportion of preliminary expenses written off is a sum that is generally arrived at according to the circumstances of the company. Sometimes these expenses may be written off in the first year's accounts, if profits will permit. Sometimes the amount of the expenses may be spread over five or six years. In a dividend-paying company they will certainly not extend over a longer period.

The proportion of goodwill of the business written off admits of more debate than the previous item. It does not very often appear in accounts, but I have referred to it here for the purpose of keeping it in view. It is a somewhat doubtful asset, and should be written down as rapidly as possible during years of profit. It is only of value whilst there is a profit. If a loss through depression of trade sets in, the value disappears, and yet there will be no profit with which to wipe out of the books the amount at which it stood. Let it be cleared away, then, as speedily as possible, although the firm may uphold that if they were to sell the business they would get its worth. The fact is, however, they are *not* selling the business, and you as auditor have to keep in view that in years following there may be great losses; then, the goodwill being of no value, you will require to add the amount at which it stands in the books to the loss, and so increase the loss.

You will observe that in the nett revenue account I set aside a sum to meet *income-tax*. My reason for this is that income-tax is a purely personal payment, as personal indeed as expenses of housekeeping. It is a tax upon profits, and not upon earnings; it would be wrong, therefore, to place it amongst the charges entered in the gross revenue account. It would be an oversight, however, not to set aside a sum to meet the tax out of the nett revenue account; if you do not do so you will allow the nett revenue account to show a larger balance which may be drawn out of the business than ought to be. The sum which is to be set aside will, of course, be ruled by the amount of profit made, and the rate of the tax.

Having thus carefully charged against revenue every expense which properly should be charged against it, there will be some satisfaction if we find there remains such a balance at the credit as will be available towards payment of dividend; and so our investigation of the revenue account comes happily to an end, and we turn to

THE BALANCE-SHEET.

This final statement of all the affairs the auditor must examine with care under the "light and leading" he has got by means of his previous examination of the revenue account, for it may be that the result of his examination will be to sweep away the balance of profit on the revenue account. There is a natural inclination to state the assets very favourably, and to diminish the weight of the liabilities. You must therefore exercise your own judgment upon every item, and not be influenced by the future prospects, however bright, turning out any better than the past and present state of matters. Every possible information should be exacted until you are able to form a solid opinion. Securities should be examined, valuations procured, documents of debt or certificates produced. The auditor must ever remember that it is *his* statement of the assets and liabilities, and he cannot shift from his shoulders to those of some one else the responsibility for it, unless he publicly states that he has had to accept certain values because he has found it impossible to obtain better evidence in regard to them.

ASSETS.

The first item of the assets, *"value of warehouses,"* etc., forms somewhat of a case in point where no proper valuation can be got. Presuming that our balance-sheet was one of a limited liability company, it is possible that the original purchase price of the warehouses would be mentioned in the prospectus of the company; and we are entitled to hold that when we enter the purchase price as the value of the properties, every shareholder is cognizant that we state the figure correctly. At the same time the real present value of the warehouses may be less than the figure stated, even although sums for depreciation have been written off. But as there has been no formal valuation we cannot give any better figures for the asset in the meantime, and to guard against all misunderstanding on the point we distinctly state, that the asset is stated at the purchase price. For a like reason *the additions* to the price for subsequent capital outlay are distinctly pointed out, and every one interested must just draw his own conclusions whether the asset is worth the sum put upon it.

In regard to *waggons, horses*, etc., no doubt a detailed valuation will be produced, and the auditor will possibly, from a general perusal of it and from its being signed by some responsible party, be more in a position to decide as to its reliability.

On the subject of *depreciation* here deducted from value of warehouses, etc., I have already made remark when dealing with the gross revenue account in detail, and I shall not refer to it here further than to repeat the warning that the auditor must keep it ever in view; and if nothing is charged against profits in respect of it, such a fact should be distinctly stated, either on the face of the balance-sheet or in the auditor's docquet.

The *"value of goodwill"* I have also referred to when speaking of the proportion of it to be charged against the nett revenue account. Of course the sum here stated is the original price paid for it, less the sum written off and charged against revenue. As there is no possibility of valuing such an asset, each year it must be stated at its original price, less what has been written off.

The *value of stocks*, both at Edinburgh and Calcutta, will be instructed by detailed valuations certified by the several managers. As I have already stated, it seems to me an auditor's duty to look over these valuations, and form an opinion whether the values are fair. My reason for this is, an auditor is put exactly in the position of a partner of the firm. Now I cannot conceive a partner being so indifferent as never to look over the valuations made of his stocks. No doubt a partner is better able to judge of values than an auditor, yet an auditor is not so helpless as that he cannot test values by invoices of purchases, or statements showing cost of production, if the goods happen to be manufactured on the premises. I merely contend for a general survey of the valuations, without going into any minute details.

Debts due by Customers.—Without fail detailed lists of all the open accounts should be produced and checked from the ledger. I understand that instances of fraud have been undetected for some time where such lists, though forthcoming, were left unchecked. It is quite a common thing in very large businesses, where hundreds, even thousands, of small accounts are open at a time, to have a single account in the general ledger for these accounts, and at the same time a separate ledger where all these accounts were individually recorded; the balance of that separate ledger would, if properly kept, always agree with the balance on the general account in the general ledger. If any cashier or collector, who had the charge of that separate ledger, should collect some of these accounts and pocket the money, he could, if he saw that the auditor did not go over the balances of the separate ledger, produce to him a detailed list as usual, with these sums he had collected still standing as open accounts due, although he had marked the amounts off in the separate ledger as paid properly enough. The auditor having a detailed list of accounts apparently all due, the total of which corresponded with the account in the general ledger, and being contented with it without further examination, would, of course, fail to find out the embezzlement. The auditor should further go over the lists of balances in the ledger for the purpose of judging whether the accounts may be considered good. Generally speaking, all accounts are paid within some recognised time—such as a month, two months, or three months. The auditor, knowing the recognised time, ought to see that no customer falls beyond it to any serious extent; and if there are any in such a position, some enquiry should be made in regard to them, and the amounts written off, if found to be bad.

The debts due on bills receivable should be vouched by the production of the bills themselves; and here again care should be taken to see that the parties granting the bills are accustomed to pay regularly, as bills that are renewed should ever be viewed with suspicion. In the balance-sheet before us I have made no special reference to bills discounted and yet current. Should there be any such, it is clearly our duty to keep the amount of these in view as a possible liability, through some of them becoming dishonoured when presented to the customer. Among the liabilities we would therefore state the amount under discount as a contingent liability, without extending the sum into the outer column. In calculating the sum to be set aside to cover bad debts, the amount of bills receivable current should be considered in order to influence you in your provision against bad debts.

Balances in Bank and in hand.—The balance in Bank will, of course, be instructed by the Bank certificate, and the balance on hand by the cash-book. When referring to the examination of the cash-book in a former part of this paper, I pointed out the necessity of comparing the drafts on the Bank account, and the payments into Bank as recorded in the cash-book and ledger, with the entries in the Bank pass-book. If that has been done, and found to correspond, we may rest assured that the balance in the ledger is arrived at in the same manner as the balance on the Bank pass-book and certificate.

Preliminary Expenses.—This, in the present instance, we presume to be the balance on last year's preliminary expenses account, as appearing in the previous year's balance-sheet, less the proportion of preliminary expenses written off, as shown in the nett revenue account which we have examined. It must ever be borne in mind that preliminary expenses account, however, is no real asset of a business. It is only an account of expenses held in suspense in order to be written off against profits of future years. Such expenses are those unavoidable in the formation of a company, as preparation of the memorandum and articles of association, printing, stationery, books, advertising, plans, and generally all expenses incurred up to the date of the allotment of shares; there is, however, no hard and fast rule as to these expenses. If the business was to fail, both the preliminary expenses account and the value of goodwill would be struck out of the assets. No division of profits therefore ought ever to be made unless something is written off these accounts. Such accounts ought indeed to be made to disappear as rapidly as possible.

Having thus gone over the assets of the business, and having observed that some of the assets are only estimates or approximations, that some are of doubtful value, and that some are of no real value, we pass over to the

LIABILITIES.

Here we first observe that one or two of these items are such as are found more particularly in the balance-sheets of limited liability companies, such as share capital, debentures, and reserve fund.

As I have already said, I have supposed the balance-sheet before us to be one of a company which has been in existence for a year or two, and that being so, the liabilities in respect of *share capital* are not very difficult to verify, seeing that in all likelihood the amount will be the same as in last year's balance-sheet, unless indeed a further call had been paid during the past year. But in the meantime I shall assume that no call was paid, and that the share capital remains therefore at the same amount as last year, any transactions which have taken place with the shares having been by transfer from one holder to another. As this is sufficient to instruct the money liability, I shall reserve what I have to say in regard to the share registers to later on. It is to be observed, however, that the balance-sheet of a company should always distinctly state the amount of the authorised capital, how much is subscribed, how much is paid up, how much of the calls are in arrears, and what calls have been paid in advance. These are all points which ought to be made known in order to give the shareholders a proper knowledge as to their own stake in the company. Moreover, the public may be said to require to know this information, because if, on the one hand, the public allows a number of people to trade with only a limited liability, it certainly, on the other hand, is entitled to demand that the whole of that liability should be made known.

In regard to the *debenture* liability, this will be instructed by the Register of Debentures which the Companies' Act enacts must be kept. I shall refer to the Register of Debentures further on.

The liability under *mortgages* we were careful to see instructed when examining the debtor side of the cash-book; and we would at the same time, no doubt, find further evidence in the interest which was subsequently paid.

You will observe I have entered *reserve fund* as a liability, but

I wish to point out that this is, as the balance-sheet presently stands, quite an anomaly. Whoever heard of there being a reserve fund whilst there was an account for preliminary expenses entered as an asset on the other side. The thing is absurd; no such reserve fund should be begun unless such useless assets as preliminary expenses accounts are first wiped out. I have merely stated the account here, because it is so often an item in balance-sheets. The sums put to the credit are usually specially authorised, and, if that be so, the auditor must see that the particular sum authorised is set aside.

In regard to the remaining liabilities, those due to *sundry creditors* on open account, etc., will be instructed by detailed lists, which we compare with the ledger accounts; those on bills payable will be found in the bills payable book, and the liability in respect of interest accrued on debentures and mortgages is the portion unpaid of the year's interest on debentures and mortgages which is charged against nett revenue account, and which when examining that account we checked.

Drafts in transit from Calcutta.—This is a merely temporary account which is opened at the end of the year in respect of drafts which the house in Calcutta has drawn on the house in Edinburgh, but at the date of the balance-sheet the bills had not been presented for acceptance in Edinburgh. As the amounts appear, however, in the statement of accounts sent home from India, and as the balance-sheet before us is supposed to be a conjoined balance of the home and Indian books, we must make provision for the amounts as drafts in transit. As soon as these drafts are presented in Edinburgh and accepted, this temporary account will be debited (thus squaring the account) and bills payable will be credited.

The only other item of the balance-sheet is the balance brought from the nett revenue account, of which we satisfied ourselves when examining that account, and our audit is at an end, excepting some short reference as to the manner of dealing with certain special books kept by limited companies. We thus have endeavoured to sketch out a method by which a revenue account and balance-sheet may be examined, and how to deal with the books of the business so as to make them, in as reasonably short time as possible, tell what they have got to say. We took up first the four primary books—purchase day-book, sales day-book, cash-book, and bill-book, and having satisfied ourselves as to what they contained, we next took up the ledger, which is principally an analysis of these four books, and we compared it (1*st*) with the revenue account to see that the latter contained a full year's revenue transactions, and every kind of transaction which properly should belong to it; and (2*nd*) with the balance-sheet, where we saw what the assets were worth as near as possible, and whether the whole liabilities were fully and correctly stated. It is impossible not to have omitted important points, and I can only regret now the omissions, as my time is already, I fear, much too far exceeded.

COMPANY BOOKS.

Will you permit me a few words in reference to Company Books, and an auditor's duty in regard to them? The principal books I need refer to are the Share Register, the Transfer Register, the Debenture Register, the Mortgage Register, the Loan Ledger, and the Minute Book.

1. *The Share Register.*—As this book contains the names of the shareholders, it is clearly the duty of an auditor, in auditing the first year's account of a company, to see that each shareholder has been recorded therein, so as to carry his due burden of liability. For this purpose the auditor calls for production of all letters of application, and sees that these instruct the deposits made on shares applied for. Following upon that, the directors' certified list of allotments will be examined, and if the applicant for shares has made no valid objections, the applicant will then be held to be a shareholder of the company, and the auditor will see that his name is entered on the register. When certificates of shares are issued, the auditor will take such means as he finds within his power to see that none but shareholders obtain certificates; such means adopted might be the examination of the certificate counterfoils, to see that the shares' certificate issued corresponds with the register and with the allotment letter returned; and as a final test of the share register, he will have a statement made up showing the whole balances of shares held by the shareholders, the total of which should agree with the Directors' certified List of Allotments.

2. *Transfer Register.*—This register, containing as it does the names of both the transferror and the transferree of shares, should be examined with the transfer agreement, the cancelled certificates returned by the transferror, and with the counterfoils of new certificates given to the transferree. Without doubt the directors of

a company should see that no new certificates are given out unless the old certificates are cancelled, and the auditor should endeavour to see that this duty is fulfilled. The minute-book should be examined also to see that such transfers were duly recognised by the directors.

3. *Debenture Register.*—This book will record all money got on debenture and the debenture bonds issued. The usual information will also be found here as to the debenture holder, the period for which the debenture is to run, and the rate of interest. It should further contain the directors' certificate that the bonds have been issued with their authority; and the total amount recorded, as received, will agree with the liability on debentures shown in the cash ledger. Of course, when the company repays a debenture bond, the auditor should see that the bond is produced and cancelled.

4. *Mortgage Register.*—This is a register that many companies will not require, as it is only in use where money is borrowed on mortgage. Some companies, however, are in that position, and as the book is a statutory requirement, the auditor must see, where it is necessary, that it is kept up.

5. *Loan Ledger.*—This is a book of great importance to a company which lends out its money. Each borrower's account should have prefixed to it a short statement of the loan, its security, its period, the rate of interest, and the dates when instalments of principal fall due. Columns should be set aside separately to show the amount of principal and interest due, in order that it may be seen at once whether the borrower is in arrear for interest, or for instalment of principal due. The total of the balances of principal shown in this ledger should agree with the amount of "loans account" which would be found in the *General* Ledger.

6. *The Minute-Book* is the only other book to which I need call attention, but no auditor will fail to consult it, and to see that its resolutions in regard to financial matters are carried out. In it will be found the authority for particular outlay and for particular expenses of management, and in it will be recorded the transactions regarding the shares and the debentures or loans to or by the company.

Most of the other books kept by a company are such as any commercial firm might also keep, and so need not be referred to by me. But I must not omit to call your special attention to the Memorandum and Articles of Association. These documents must be carefully considered, and if at any point the directors appear to have gone beyond their powers as laid down in them, it is within the auditor's province to acquaint the directors with his opinion. In the Articles the auditor moreover finds his *own* position and powers laid down, which are, generally speaking, wide enough to give him full control of every book belonging to the company ; and which, standing as he does between directors and shareholders, lay upon him a responsibility often both heavy and delicate.

I trust now from this necessarily fragmentary and incomplete review of auditing, that this much at least will have been gathered : That in the audit of any considerable business, the labour to be undertaken is not small ; that if the audit is to be efficient, it must be methodic ; that the position of the auditor is one of independence; that he is expected to be confidential, and, above all, that his aim is to report truthfully.

The wider an auditor's experience is the more effective will his audit become—the more ready will he be to grasp results—the more able will he be to point out improvements where such are necessary and can be introduced. Need I say that a great deal more help and information is gained by tact than by the want of it, and that courtesy and uprightness gives more moral influence than will sharpness and trickiness. A man of honour, who values his own self-esteem, and the respect both of heaven and earth, will refuse to subscribe his name to any certificate that conceals a doubtful or untrue state of affairs, for an auditor's chief end is to find out the truth, the whole truth, and to tell the truth.

APPENDIX.

APPENDIX.

BALANCE-SHEET.

LIABILITIES.

Share Capital
Authorised, 10,000 Shares of £10 each . £100,000 0 0
Whereof £2 per Share have been called up . £
Less in Arrear . £

Calls on Shares paid in advance . £
Debentures, amount authorised . £
Whereof Subscribed and paid up
Mortgages over Warehouses, etc.
Reserve Fund
Sundry Creditors . £
  On Open Account
  On Bills Payable
Interest accrued on Debentures and Mortgages . £

Drafts in transit from Calcutta
Balance of Nett Revenue Account .

£

ASSETS.

Value of Warehouses, Machinery, etc. . £
Purchase price of Warehouses, Machinery, etc. . £
Additions during the past year . £

Waggons, Horses, etc. . £
Less Written off for Depreciation . £

Value of Goodwill of Business . £
Value of Stocks
  At Edinburgh . £
  At Calcutta . £

Debts due by Customers . £
  On Open Account
  On Bills Receivable . £

Balances in Bank and in hand
Preliminary Expenses at formation of Company

£

GROSS REVENUE ACCOUNT.

EXPENDITURE.	£	RECEIPTS.	£	£
Wages		Gross Profit for the year	.	
Salaries		Stock at commencement	.	
Repairs to Machinery, Plant, etc.		Purchases during the year, less Returns	.	
Discount and Allowances				
Travelling Expenses		Sales during the year, less Returns £		
Trade Charges		Stock at close of year	.	
Rents, Rates, Taxes, Office Expenses, etc.				
Commissions				
Bad Debts		Profit on production of Silk at Calcutta	.	
Sum written off for Depreciation				
Difference in Exchange				
Balance carried to Nett Revenue Account				
	£			£

NETT REVENUE ACCOUNT.

	£		£
Dividend at 5 per cent. on paid-up Capital, as authorised at Meeting of Shareholders		Balance brought from last year	.
Interest at 4 per cent. on Debentures paid up	.	Amount brought from Gross Revenue Account	.
Interest at 5 per cent. on Mortgages over property		Transfer Fees	.
Interest on Prepaid Calls	.		
Proportion of Preliminary Expenses written off	.		
Do. of Value of Goodwill of Business written off			
Income-Tax set aside in respect of Profits	.		
Balance of Nett Revenue	.		
	£		£

61

FRANCIS MORE, C.A.

(With Portrait.)

IN our last number we noted the death of Mr Francis More, C.A., which took place on 16th October last.

Francis More was born in Dundee on 31st March 1838. Educated at the High School there, he passed at the age of nineteen into the office of Messrs Reid, Herron, & M'Lauchlan, writers, remaining there for five years. In 1862 he, like so many others of Forfar county, migrated to Edinburgh. He continued his legal training in the office of Messrs Duncan & Black, but his leaning towards accounting asserted itself, and he soon changed to the office of Messrs Lindsay, Jamieson, & Haldane, C.A., where, first as assistant and afterwards as partner, he was destined to accomplish his main life-work. He qualified as a member of the Edinburgh Society in 1875, and in 1879 (soon after the liquidation of the City of Glasgow Bank had thrown a stress of work on "No. 24"— Mr George Auldjo Jamieson and Mr James Haldane having been appointed two of the liquidators) he was assumed a partner in that leading firm, and this he remained until his death.

First with that colossal accounting performance, the liquidation of the City Bank, and afterwards with many other duties of less financial moment but of equal responsibility and intricacy committed to his firm, he became identified as an exponent of the special qualities which such affairs demand. Mr More's forte was Chamber practice. He did not seek the contests of the profession—whether it was a fight for a large sequestration or liquidation, or the battlefield where accountants as skilled witnesses prove that figures can be made to prove anything. But in the administration of a sequestration or a liquidation, or in the adjustment of those questions where such skill was exercised, he was eminent. His work was thorough: as with all true accountants, no detail was too insignificant to consider; and when the facts were acquired, he had in an eminent degree that gift which so many lack, a sense of proportion, enabling him to select the leading factors in any situation, and, having focussed them, to shape the policy or develop the scheme best suited to the circumstances. And the result he was sure to state clearly and precisely, bearing the impress of his own conviction, and almost always carrying a like conviction to others. Even when he differed from others, he did so modestly, and he was not readily led into the heat of controversy. He was typical of those of his profession whose care, thoughtfulness, and judgment make them the trusted advisers of men in all ranks and callings.

Mr More's appointments were numerous, but his unobtrusiveness and devotion to his profession ensured that these were mostly of a professional character. Among others, he was a director of the Mersey Railway and the Scarborough and Whitby Railway, a manager of the Edinburgh Savings Bank, and an auditor of the Cardiff Railway, the Royal Bank of Scotland, and the Union Bank of Scotland, and also one of the first auditors of Parish Councils under the Local Government Act, 1894, in virtue of which, until his retirement under the age limit, he held a large number of appointments.

To those of his own profession he did more than his share. A member of Council of the Edinburgh Society for some years, he was a member of the General Examining Board for Scotland from its inauguration in 1893 till 1903. All along he took a great interest in the C.A. Students' Society, and in 1900, on the death of his partner, Mr George Auldjo Jamieson, succeeded him as President. Previously he had contributed to that Society an interesting and instructive paper on "Goodwill," which having gone out of print was, on request, revised and reprinted a few years ago. These are, however, merely the external signs. To everyone, whether qualified brother or budding student, or outside the pale, he made available with uniform courtesy that professional knowledge and judgment which a busy life, full of special opportunities, had enabled him to gather.

He carried the same geniality and unobtrusiveness into private life. Always pleasant in his home circle, he avoided those positions which are thrust upon successful professional men through the Church or politics.

Although a member of Augustine Congregational Church for over thirty years—attracted there by the preaching of Dr Lindsay Alexander—he repeatedly declined office in the church, contenting himself with discharging gratuitously the duties of Treasurer of the Edinburgh Auxiliary of the London Missionary Society.

Again, in politics, though he was a Conservative, many must have known him for years without ascertaining this.

He is survived by a widow, four sons, and two daughters: his eldest son is a partner in his father's firm, and his second son was recently called to the Scottish Bar.

The portrait which prefaces this number is taken from one painted in 1904 by W. Onslow Ford, son of the well-known sculptor.

Francis More, 'Goodwill' (1900-1)

This paper was given originally in 1890 and, because of its popularity, was revised and reissued in 1900. More commenced his discussion of a complex topic by defining goodwill as the patronage of the public and linking it with profit returns. A considerable part of the paper was devoted to this relationship in terms of the problem of valuing goodwill. More was concerned to demonstrate the determination of such values by separating normal from excess returns on capital. In his view, the latter constituted the basis for the production of goodwill valuations - the excess profits being suitably discounted over a number of years at the excess rate of return.

More's contribution represents a scholarly paper, well ahead of its time - the usual practice for valuing goodwill being a multiple of total profits minus the valuation of tangible assets (a practice which More did not favour). The paper also discussed other related and important matters - the need to create reserves out of profits to replace purchased goodwill as it reduces in value over its useful life; and the existence of goodwill in a variety of forms such as monopolies, patents, leases, founders' shares and public house licences.

GOODWILL.

By FRANCIS MORE, C.A., Edinburgh,

Honorary President of the Society.

Reprint from Volume IV., revised by the Author.

GENTLEMEN,—As you know, my subject is "Goodwill"—not the goodwill we read about in good books, but the goodwill which can be bought and sold, and which, in these days of Company-making, is an item of great importance to sellers of going businesses. I propose to consider the subject under four heads :—

I. What Goodwill is, where it is to be found, and at what stage in its growth it becomes a marketable commodity.

II. What the law on the subject of Goodwill is.

III. How the Goodwill of a trading concern may be valued, as between a willing seller and a willing buyer ; and

IV. What provision ought to be made out of revenue, for the replacement of the capital sum which may be paid for Goodwill.

We all know—in a general way at least—what goodwill is. It is, I take it, just another name to designate the patronage of the public. Goodwill can have no existence apart from some particular going trade or business ; without some measure of it, no trade or business can live, far less thrive, and the larger the measure, the more does the trade or business prosper. But although we may all have a pretty correct idea of what

67

goodwill is, it may not be unprofitable to consider the subject in some detail.

The goodwill attaching to Professions, as distinguished from Trades, is seldom of any great value, the reason being that there is so much of the individual element bound up with it—that, for sale purposes, it is practically valueless. For instance, there can never be any saleable goodwill attached to the profession of an artist or a play-actor, nor can there ever be much marketable goodwill attached to the practice of a Lawyer or a Chartered Accountant. The really valuable goodwill is almost always found attached to trading concerns which exist for the manufacture, or the distribution, of the necessaries or the luxuries of life.

It may, I think, be taken for granted that a valuable goodwill is rarely acquired except by men of energy and ability, and only after a great deal of patient hard work. If we look around and ask ourselves what is the secret of the success of this and that concern, we are generally forced to the conclusion that it is the man, even more than the superiority of the commodity dealt in, that has brought the success. And although the goodwill of a trading concern, after it has been fairly established, is not generally dependent, to any great extent at least, on the man, still there must always be more or less risk of the goodwill going down on its being transferred to a new man, even although he should be in every way equal in energy and ability to the founder of the goodwill.

As I have already said, it is essential that there should be attached to every trade or business a certain measure of goodwill. In some cases it may be so small as not to be sufficient to secure to its possessor any adequate return for his services and capital ; in that case the capital itself becomes depreciated. In other cases, the goodwill may just be large enough to secure to its possessor a fair return for services and capital. In other cases, it may be so large and valuable as to secure to its possessor far more than an ordinary return for his services and capital, and it is only in these cases that there can be said to be any marketable goodwill—I mean goodwill which a buyer may fairly be asked to pay for in addition to paying the full value of the tangible assets given over.

The goodwill which I am mainly to deal with is the ordinary goodwill attaching to trading concerns. There are, however, exceptional kinds of goodwill, to a few of which I will briefly refer at this stage.

1. MONOPOLIES.—The value attaching to a monopoly is practically just goodwill. Monopolies may either be complete or partial. When the city of Edinburgh, in 1888, purchased the Edinburgh Gas undertakings, the Gas Companies held a complete monopoly, so far as the supply of gas to the city was concerned; but had the Gas Companies been allowed to get the Bills which they promoted in Parliament, the monopoly would have become a partial one, because, in that case, the price of gas would, to a certain extent, have been regulated by the dividends paid to the shareholders of the Gas Companies.

The goodwill attached to a monopoly is generally regarded as being more stable, and therefore more valuable, than the ordinary kind of goodwill, which is at all times liable to be filched by able competitors. Monopolies are always considered, and I think rightly so, to be more or less of an evil; and in these democratic times and in this age of discovery, most people would be inclined to call the man a rash buyer who purchased a monopoly on the footing that the revenue derived from it was equal, or something like equal, to a perpetuity.

2. PATENTS.—The value attaching to Patent Rights is another kind of goodwill. As you know, these rights run out in fourteen years, unless the holder can satisfy the patent authorities that, owing to exceptional causes, he has been unable to take full advantage of the rights, in which case he may probably get an extension of time.

Owing to the long start the patentee gets of all other competitors, he is generally able—provided the public take to the article patented—to rear up a valuable goodwill, which continues after the patent has become common property. It is always, however, risky to pay a large price for patent rights unless their value has been clearly demonstrated.

3. LEASES.—The value attaching to Leases may also be

said to be goodwill. In the case of mineral leases large prices are often obtained, notwithstanding the exceptional risks which attend the purchase of such rights.

4. PUBLIC COMPANIES.—There is another kind of goodwill, or something akin to it, which has come to the front in recent years, viz., the right which promoters or originators of companies—principally trust and finance companies—claim as their own, and in lieu of which they accept what are known as "Founders' Shares." These shares, although representing a mere fraction of the capital, usually carry something like fifty per cent. of the profits remaining over after the ordinary shareholders are paid a fair trading return of, say, seven or eight per cent.

When we speak of promoters or originators of a company, we usually refer to the two or three clever men who devised the scheme. These men ought, I think, to be liberally dealt with, especially if they allow their remuneration to be dependent on the success of the venture, as they do when they accept founders' shares. I have therefore nothing to say against *bona fide* promoters being paid in founders' shares, although I think fifty per cent. of the surplus profits is far too high a price to pay.

But while I do not see any objection to the two or three clever men I have referred to being paid, and well paid, in founders' shares, I see great objection to founders' shares being used, as they are now to a large extent used, to remunerate those who undertake to subscribe for shares. The company in this way is made to pay not only promotion money, but also underwriting charges. This, it humbly appears to me, is an evil. It encourages undue multiplication of companies, and diverts from those who provide almost all the capital, and run all the risk, profits which they ought to get.*

5. PUBLIC-HOUSES.—The value attaching to public-houses is another kind of goodwill. But for the fact that the traders'

---

* Founders' Shares have now (1901) gone almost entirely out of fashion.

license requires to be renewed once a year, the goodwill would just be of the ordinary kind, with this difference, that the goodwill cannot be detached from the premises in which the business is carried on. As it is, the trade is somewhat of a monopoly, terminable, however, at the will of the licensing authorities. Notwithstanding the risk of the license being withdrawn, the value of the goodwill attaching to public-houses is generally large, compared with the amount of capital embarked in the business. In acquiring this kind of goodwill, very little of the ability and patient waiting and working required in other trades are needed; all that is required in order to secure a valuable goodwill is a licensed house favourably situated.

I will not trouble you with any more examples of what I have called special kinds of goodwill; and as I shall be able to say all that I am going to say about the goodwill of ordinary trading companies under the third and fourth heads of this paper, I will proceed to consider the second head, viz. :—

II. *What the law on the subject of Goodwill is.*

As I am not a lawyer, but only one of a profession whose members ought at least to know something of law, I will not attempt to deal with nice questions. I propose merely to refer to a few leading points, which even laymen may grasp and remember without difficulty.

Goodwill, or, at all events, a certain kind of it, is, in the eye of the law, property, which may be transferred from one man to another. There is often a valuable goodwill attached to business premises, a firm-name, trade marks, and patent rights; and it is this kind of goodwill, or what is called "legal" goodwill, which the law regards as property. The law, however, does not regard as property goodwill which rests on the personal influence or recommendation of its possessor. It is true this kind of goodwill is often sold; but should the seller refuse to give the buyer the benefit of the personal influence he promised to give, the law will not force the seller to give it, but will leave the buyer to recover in name of damages what he had paid for as goodwill. These are, I think, the *two* different meanings which the law attaches to what goes under the common name of goodwill.

A seller of goodwill is entitled, unless there is a special bargain to the contrary, to start business in the same line, and in his own name, and even to solicit the customers of the old business for orders. The law will not, however, allow him to deceive the public and defraud the buyer of the goodwill, by doing anything which would lead the public to think that he still represented the business, the goodwill of which he had sold. It is important, therefore, that a purchaser of the goodwill of a business should see that as stringent a provision as the law will sanction is made against the seller competing with the buyer. It is also very important that a buyer should acquire any rights which the seller may hold against his employés becoming competitors ; indeed, if I mistake not, these rights are held to be included in the sale, even in the absence of any express bargain.*

A sale by a trustee in bankruptcy of the bankrupt's business, and of its goodwill, carries only what I have referred to as legal goodwill, and the bankrupt is free to enter into competition with the buyer of the old business, only he must not represent that he is carrying on the old business, nor must the buyer of the old business do anything to make the public believe that the bankrupt is in any way interested in the old business; in short, there must be no deceit on either side, otherwise a claim of damages will arise against the offending party.

The law also provides that where the premises of a trader are compulsorily taken from him, the trader is entitled to compensation, even although it should be proved that the

---

* This must now (1901) be regarded as modified by the decision of the House of Lords (reversing the Court of Appeal in Trego *v.* Hunt (1896), A.C. p. 7). As Lord Macnaghten there puts it, you cannot sell the custom and then steal the customers. But a seller of goodwill, unless he contracts otherwise, can start a rival business, and a bankrupt whose trustee has sold the goodwill of his business may solicit his old customers.

goodwill had no saleable value, in respect that, while the goodwill to a third party may be worthless, it might nevertheless have been of considerable value to its possessor.

In the case of a doctor's or a lawyer's practice sold by executors, I do not suppose the duties reach the price paid for goodwill, because it is really paid, not for anything *in bonis* of the deceased, but for the personal recommendation of the purchaser by the executors to the patients or clients.

I will not trouble you with any further remarks under this head.

III. *How the Goodwill attaching to a trading concern may be valued as between a willing seller and a willing buyer.*

A cautious buyer will at the outset consider carefully (1) Whether the retiral of the seller is likely to weaken the goodwill; (2) whether the transfer of the business is likely to induce any of the principal employés of the seller to become competitors, in that case some of the goodwill is almost sure to disappear; and (3) whether, taking all the circumstances of the case into account, it is likely that the goodwill will remain as stable, and be as likely to grow, under the new management, as it would had it remained with the seller.

In the old days, a seller was usually paid for goodwill by being allowed a share of the profits, or a fixed annuity for a longer or a shorter period. After this custom had gone out of fashion, the plan adopted was to pay cash for the goodwill as well as for the tangible assets, and the way by which the *cumulo* price was reached, was by adding to the value of the tangible assets so many years' purchase of the profits to represent the value of the goodwill; this made the tangible assets the basis of the valuation, and the profits the adjunct of the property to be transferred. The plan, however, which is at present (1891) in favour is to regard the profits as the real basis of the valuation, the tangible assets being regarded merely as one of the means whereby the profits are earned.

I much prefer the old plan of giving a share of the profits. Were it reverted to, it would, I think, add greatly to the stability of Limited Liability Companies that take over going

73

businesses; the payment for this thing we call goodwill would be regulated, as, I think, it ought to be regulated, by *results;* and besides, a great danger would thereby be avoided, viz., the danger of the capital sum paid for goodwill being—unconsciously perhaps—eaten up by the shareholders in the guise of profits. Were that course adopted, not only would the danger I have referred to be avoided, but a much smaller capital would in every case suffice; indeed, in many cases, one-half of the capital usually raised would be sufficient.

We must, however, just accept things as they are; and as sellers generally believe that a bird in the hand is worth two or three in the bush, and as buyers nowadays are content to run the risk of catching the bird in the bush, all we can do is to try and instruct buyers as to how they may, before they buy, gauge the value of the birds in the bush.

Of the two later plans I have referred to, I prefer the one which makes the tangible assets the basis of the valuation. It has this important advantage over the other—the buyer is able to see what he gets for his money—he knows what he is asked to pay for the tangible assets, and all he has to do to ascertain how much he is asked to pay for the goodwill is to deduct from the *cumulo* price the value of the tangible assets—the balance must always represent the value of the goodwill. Under the other plan, viz., the plan of making the profits the basis of the valuation, the buyer very often has no idea of the amount, in some cases, the enormous amount, which he is asked to pay for goodwill.*

I know I will be met with the remark that it matters little whether the tangible assets, or the profits, be taken as the basis of the valuation, because on a collapse the tangible assets will become nearly as valueless as the goodwill. It will, of course, depend very much on the nature of the tangible assets whether or not they are likely to disappear on a collapse; they must always retain at least some value, whereas goodwill loses all marketable value so soon as there

---

* In the case of Limited Companies the amount paid for goodwill now requires to be stated in the prospectus (Companies Act 1900, sect. 10). It is a pity, I think, that the Act did not provide for its being shown separately in the yearly balance-sheet.

is a shrinkage of the business sufficient to reduce the profits to the level of ordinary trade profits. The tangible assets may therefore retain their full, or almost their full value, while the marketable goodwill, which alone ought to have been paid for, may have entirely vanished.

I do not think we need concern ourselves about the seller's interests—a seller as a rule is always able to protect himself; nor need we trouble ourselves about the interests of the private buyer—if he is a sensible man, he will consult those who are capable of advising him, and will look all round the thing offered for sale before he makes up his mind as to the price he should pay. It is, however, a different matter with Limited Liability Companies. Of all buyers, there is probably no one so helpless as a newly incorporated Limited Liability Company. In the majority of cases the seller fixes his own price, and there is rarely any one who has the opportunity or the inclination to criticise it. The large majority of allottees of shares have no intention of remaining partners longer than they can net a premium on their shares, and if the premium does not come quickly, they sell out; it is not surprising, therefore, that they should think, if they think at all, that the question of price concerns them very little, although it may concern their successors in the partnership a very great deal.

If, therefore, there is any truth in what I have said, you will agree with me that it would be well if there were some recognised general rules for valuing going concerns. The valuation of the tangible assets is a simple matter; the difficulty is to fix a fair price for the goodwill. I hope it may not appear presumptuous if I state, with all humility, my views on the subject.

In a previous part of this paper I have stated that there can be no marketable goodwill—I mean, goodwill which a buyer ought to pay for, over and above paying for the tangible assets, except in those cases where the return on capital is *in excess* of an ordinary return, and I hold that it is only this excess which ought to be paid for as goodwill.

An investor in consols expects a return of, say, three per cent. on his investment; an investor in second-class heritable securities expects, say, four-and-a-half per cent.; and a person who embarks in a trading venture expects, and I think is entitled to expect, a return on capital of from six to ten per cent., according to the nature of the business—probably eight per cent. may be taken as a fair average return. Should the return from an investment in consols, or in heritable securities, or in a trading concern, fall short of the above rates, or something like the above rates, the capital invested falls below par. I repeat, therefore, that it is only the excess beyond, say, eight per cent. which a buyer of a trading concern ought to pay for in respect of goodwill. Of course, I can only deal with ordinary cases. I can quite conceive that the goodwill of a young growing business may be worth paying for, although at the time it is not earning eight per cent., just as I can conceive that the goodwill of an old failing business earning more than eight per cent. may not be worth even so much as the full going value of the tangible assets.

But although the whole return from a trading venture, in excess of, say, eight per cent., may fittingly be paid for by a buyer under the name of goodwill, I would strongly recommend buyers, before deciding as to the *cumulo* price to be offered, to split up the excess profits into two or three parts, and to assign a value to each part. An excess of five per cent. over the ordinary rate is more likely to be maintained than an excess of ten per cent., and an excess of ten per cent. is more likely to be maintained than an excess of fifteen per cent., and so on. I would therefore put a higher value on the first five per cent. (over the ordinary rate), than I would on the second five; and, in like manner, I would put a higher value on the second than I would on the third five per cent. In these days of keen competition and labour questions, it is very hazardous to reckon on a continuance of abnormally high profits; and as it is for the most part concerns yielding exceptionally high profits which are floated on the public, great care should be taken by buyers before making up their minds as to what they ought to pay for goodwill.

I will best explain my views as to how the goodwill of such concerns may be valued by supposing a case.

Take, for example, a trading concern with tangible assets, the full going value of which is ascertained to be £100,000, and suppose it is earning, and is likely to earn, eight per cent., or £8,000 a year, I would say that the total price should not exceed the value of the tangible assets, viz., £100,000, because no more than an ordinary return is being got.

But suppose the concern is earning, and is likely to earn, thirteen per cent., or £13,000 a year, then I think a fair price might be 'seven annual payments of the extra £5,000, or a present payment of £26,030, being the amount of seven annual payments of £5,000, less eight per cent. discount. In this case the price would be the above £100,000 *plus* £26,030, or together £126,030.

Suppose, again, it is earning eighteen per cent., or £18,000 a year, then I think a fair price might be the above £126,030 *plus* five annual payments of £5,000, or a present payment of £19,963; in this case the price would be £145,993.

Suppose, again, that the business is earning twenty-three per cent., or £23,000 a year, then I think a fair price would be the above £145,993 *plus* three annual payments of £5,000, or a present payment of £12,885; in this case the price would be £158,878.

Of course, in every case the seller's statement of the profits earned would have to be carefully verified.

I do not for a moment presume to say that the above "Table of Prices" ought to be adopted; the average ordinary trading return, and the number of years' purchase of the marketable goodwill I have quoted, may be too high or too low; each buyer must judge for himself, after considering all the circumstances of the particular case he is dealing with. What I wish more particularly to say is, that, in my humble opinion, the plan of giving a present payment equal to so many years' purchase of the *total* profits is a haphazard plan, and that a buyer is much less likely to make a mistake if, before he fixes on the price he is prepared to offer, he first of all procures a careful valuation of the tangible assets, and then breaks up and values the marketable goodwill in some such way as I have indicated. I do not forget that in some cases it may be worth while to pay a small bonus for a ready-made business earning only ordinary trade profits; it is, however, only the excess profits which ought to be paid for under the name of goodwill.

Some of you may be thinking that a concern with tangible assets worth £100,000, and earning £23,000 a year, would be very cheap at £158,878, as the profits would yield a return on the price of about 14½ per cent. Before, however, forming your opinion, I would ask you to wait till you have considered what I have to say under the next head of my paper.

IV. *What provision ought to be made out of revenue to replace the capital sum paid for Goodwill?*

I think it may be taken for granted that sound private firms rarely regard goodwill as an item which can safely be reduced to figures, and seldom have a sum for goodwill in their books. It may be said that this is because private traders when they do pay cash for goodwill, generally treat it as a personal payment by the partners, who accordingly pay it out of their own private funds; this, no doubt, may so far explain the matter, but I think the real explanation is, that prudent traders feel that goodwill is not an item which ought to appear in a balance-sheet. Be that as it may, the point which I more particularly wish to call your attention to is, that in the balance-sheets of private traders there is very rarely any item corresponding to the one which must necessarily appear (either by itself or in conjunction with other items) in the balance-sheets of all Limited Liability Companies that purchase going concerns at a price in excess of the value of the tangible assets acquired.

Where the consideration is a cash payment, there is great danger of the payment being treated as if it were a permanent investment of capital, in place of its being regarded, as I think in such cases it ought to be regarded, merely as an advance by capital, which falls to be replaced out of revenue at the earliest possible date.

The reply which many will be inclined to give to this view is that there can be no good reason for setting aside year by year out of revenue a sum towards replacing the cash paid for goodwill, unless there is reason to believe that the goodwill is shrinking, and that it is not likely to get back to where it was when purchased. I need hardly say that I do not concur in that view. Goodwill, and especially that portion of it which I have styled marketable goodwill, is an item which may disappear any day; and therefore it is highly injudicious and unsafe for any Company to allow a large sum to stand in its balance-sheet against this intangible thing called goodwill; unless there be on the other side of the balance-sheet a reserve to fall back upon in case of the profits falling to the level of ordinary trade profits, and thereby causing the goodwill, which alone should have been paid for, to disappear. The reserve cannot, of course, be reared up all at once, but I think shareholders and directors of public companies ought to make a point of not allowing a year to pass without setting aside out of revenue a suitable sum to form a reserve. This is a matter which not only concerns ordinary shareholders, but also holders of Debentures and Preference Stocks; for it must be apparent to all that every penny that is paid away in the shape of dividends to the ordinary shareholders, which ought in prudence to have been applied, either in replacing capital, or in securing capital, lessens the security which by right belongs to the holders of Debentures and Preference Stocks. At present these holders, as such, are rarely represented at the boards of our public companies; I cannot but think that it would add to the stability of our companies if Debenture holders and Preference shareholders had always some voice in the management; I am sure, they, at least, would not regard with complacency a large sum standing opposite the item of goodwill, which an eminent American writer says is nothing more than "a hope grounded on a probability."

What may be a suitable provision to make out of revenue to meet depreciation and replacement of capital, must always be a matter of opinion, and there is probably no subject as to which more diversity of opinion exists. Provided shareholders do not violate their own articles of association, they may in this matter practically do as they like. That has been clearly laid down in a recent case. The case I refer to is that of *Lee* v. *The Neuchatel Asphalte Company*, decided in the Appeal

Court of the Chancery Division in February 1889. This Company acquired a concession to work bituminous rock, in a specified area, during a specified time. The action was at the instance of a shareholder to prevent the Company paying away in dividends the whole sums received for the rock sold, remaining over after paying for the working expenses, in respect that each ton of rock removed represented a part of the capital sum paid for the concession, and that therefore that part ought to be replaced to capital before arriving at the amount of profits which could legally be divided among the shareholders. The Court however decided that, in the absence of any direction to that effect in the Articles of Association of the Company, the Company was not bound to replace capital realised in that way. From this decision I would infer that shareholders have a free hand in the matter of providing for the writing down of goodwill, provided, of course, that the Articles of Association are not violated.

But although there may be no *legal* obligation on share-holders to make what prudent business men would consider suitable provision for the replacement and security of capital, it is none the less important that sound views on the subject should prevail, and that auditors should still point out any failures in that respect which they may have to deal with. I have already taken it upon me to state my views as to how the goodwill of trading concerns should be valued. I will now venture to state my views as to what provision ought in prudence to be made to replace the price paid for goodwill, and this I will do in a single sentence.

It appears to me that the period within which the price paid for goodwill should be replaced out of revenue, ought, to a large extent at least, to be regulated by the number of years' purchase of the profits which the price represents. For instance, in the case which I have assumed in order to illustrate my views as to how the price should be ascertained, I assume that £26,030 would be a suitable present payment to make for a goodwill which produced £5,000 a year in excess of the ordinary return. This present payment of £26,030 represents *seven* yearly payments of £5,000 (less discount at eight per cent.), and I am disposed to think that in such a case one-seventh of the present payment of £26,030 should be set aside yearly out of revenue until a reserve of £26,030 was reared up. If this plan were adopted, the result would be, so far as the payment of dividends is concerned, that the ordinary shareholders would only get during the first seven years eight per cent. on their money, *plus* any increase on the profits beyond the amount dealt with in fixing the price, and *plus* also any saving which might be effected by raising money either on debenture or on preference stock at a lower rate than eight per cent. Of course, the profits might fall below the amount reckoned on when the purchase was made, and in that case the shareholders would have to judge whether they would continue to set aside yearly the amount I have indicated, and be satisfied with smaller dividends. The shrinkage of the profits would, however, only emphasise the risk which had been run in purchasing the goodwill. I need not go further in the way of illustration; I merely wish to point out what would, in my opinion, be a sound principle to go upon.

I have now dealt with the subject under the four heads into which I said at the commencement I would divide it. Perhaps you will allow me to say a word in conclusion.

Every business man knows that a great many, perhaps the majority, of the liquidations of public Companies which occur, are brought about either by the purchase price having been too high, or by money having been paid away in dividends which should have been set aside as a reserve to meet possible shrinkage of assets, tangible and intangible. If, unfortunately, there should happen to be a combination of these two evils (and this is not unlikely to happen in those cases where a large sum has been paid for goodwill), disaster is almost sure to follow, and that within a comparatively short period. I have said that in my opinion there is no more helpless buyer than a newly incorporated Limited Liability Company; and I am quite sure that, apart from the inherent risk which must always attend the purchase of goodwill, there is no kind of asset in the purchase of which a Limited Liability Company buyer is more apt to make a mistake than in the purchase of goodwill. It would therefore, I humbly think, go a long way

F

to prevent disaster if there were some recognised general rules in the matter of the purchase of goodwill. It is wonderful how goodwill grows in importance in the eye of its possessor the moment he resolves to sell, especially if he is going to sell to a newly incorporated Limited Liability Company. I do not mean to insinuate that sellers make up their minds to cheat simple buyers; but every one knows who has any experience in such matters, that provided a scheme is likely to take with the public, a big price is just as easily got as a small one, and, of course, sellers naturally prefer to ask the big price. Hence arises the handicapping of so many concerns. I have endeavoured to the best of my ability to indicate how I think buyers should proceed before determining what they should pay for goodwill; but, of course, I do not pretend to say that my formula should be adopted; but I do say that the plan usually adopted is, at the best, a haphazard one.

As regards the rearing up of a reserve to set against what may have been paid for goodwill, all I can say is, that I cannot see how Limited Liability Trading Companies are ever to equal in stability our best private trading companies, so long as any considerable portion of their capital is represented by nothing more tangible than goodwill. If in their balance-sheets companies would show under separate heads the value of the tangible and of the intangible assets, it would not, I think, require much argument to convince all concerned that the wise course would be to rear up as fast as possible a reserve to set against the amount standing against the intangible assets. It is, I am persuaded, the bad practice of slumping the items which, to a large extent, makes shareholders and debenture holders oblivious of the danger they run, when they regard the sum paid for such an item as goodwill as a permanent investment of capital.

Now, gentlemen, I have finished. I know that from beginning to end my paper is open to criticism, but I do not think that that is a serious objection. Young men, if they are to grow strong in mind as well as in body, must get food for criticism as well as food for digestion. Goodwill at the present time is a subject well worth discussing.

Obituary.

The late CHARLES KER, D.L., LL.D., M.A., C.A.

Charles Ker, one of the oldest members of the Institute of Accountants and Actuaries in Glasgow, passed away very suddenly on Monday, 8th July, while at work in the Glasgow office of the London Midland and Scottish Railway, of which he was a Director; he was also Chairman of the Scottish Committee of the Railway.

At the time of his death Mr Ker was in his eightieth year and had almost reached his eightieth birthday, as he was born in August 1860. He came of a well-known and highly respected Glasgow family, his father being a partner of Messrs Ker, Bolton & Co., East India merchants. He was educated at Glasgow Academy and Glasgow University. His father was a Director of the Academy, and in his later years Charles Ker was an Honorary Governor of the school and took a keen interest in its welfare.

Mr Ker was the fourth of five brothers. His eldest brother, Mr William Paton Ker, was Professor of Poetry at Oxford University : a man of the highest distinction in the world of scholarship and letters. As a young man Charles Ker found recreation in walking and hill climbing. He played Rugby with some distinction as a quarter-back in the Glasgow University XV. His brother Hugh was also well known in Rugby circles as a Glasgow Academical and International forward in the days of J. B. Brown and John A. Walls.

He left school in 1877 and entered the office of Messrs M'Clelland, MacKinnon & Blyth in 1878 while his M.A. course was still incomplete. He did not graduate till 1880. He was assumed as a partner of the firm ten years later, and as the result of his industry and ability soon made his mark. On the death of Mr Andrew S. M'Clelland in 1909 he became senior partner of the firm which since 1901 had been known as Messrs M'Clelland, Ker & Co. Under his guidance the business continued to make steady progress and to consolidate its position as one of the leading firms of Chartered Accountants in Glasgow. In later years his services were in much request as adviser and administrator, and at the time of his death, in addition to his railway connections mentioned above, he was Chairman of the Clyde Valley Electrical Power Co., Ltd., and a Director of Lloyds Bank, Ltd., the National Bank of Scotland, Ltd., Bairds & Dalmellington, Ltd., and the North British & Mercantile Insurance Company.

Mr Ker was admitted a member of the Institute of Accountants and Actuaries in Glasgow in 1883. He served on the Council of the Institute from 1896 to 1899 and from 1910 to 1913, and was President from 1924 to 1926. In the years 1898 and 1899 he was a member of the General Examining Board, and from 1924 to 1928 he represented the Glasgow Institute on the Joint Committee of Councils, and for part of that time he acted as Chairman of that Committee. He was a generous donor to the funds of the Glasgow Chartered Accountants' Benevolent Association, and served for several years on the Executive Committee of the Association. During all those terms of office he devoted much time to the interests of his profession.

He was a man of modest and retiring disposition, but he

gave generously of his services where he thought he could be useful. During the last war he served on a Commission appointed by the Government to investigate the question of the Control of the Liquor Traffic, and when the Church of Scotland Act, 1925, became law he was nominated as one of the Scottish Ecclesiastical Commissioners, a body appointed to adjudicate on many important matters arising under that Act. In 1926 the Merchants' House of Glasgow called him to the Chair, an appointment carrying with it the office of Lord Dean of Guild of the City of Glasgow, with a seat in the Town Council. In a quieter sphere of service he took a deep interest in several of the charitable institutions of his native city. In 1928 the University of Glasgow conferred on him the honorary degree of Doctor of Laws, and later he was appointed a Deputy Lieutenant of the County of the City of Glasgow.

For many years he had occupied a foremost place in his profession. A man of the strictest integrity, he was held in the highest esteem by his professional brethren and throughout the community. He belonged to a generation in the history of Glasgow which produced many fine men of business, and of these he was one of the best. The writer had the privilege of being trained in the office of Messrs M'Clelland, MacKinnon & Blyth, and he has nothing but the happiest memories of Charles Ker, who had a kind and generous heart and was a gentleman in the best sense of the word.

Charles Ker was always a lover of the hills. In April 1879, along with a small coterie of intimate friends, most of whom had been class mates in the Glasgow Academy, he paid a short visit to Arran, when the party climbed Goatfell. This proved to be the first of a series of expeditions made annually without a break for fifty-nine years. At first their headquarters were at Brodick, but from 1894 onwards Corrie Hotel was the rendezvous. Like other members of the little party, Charles Ker was not present on every occasion, but there are only five blanks in the rough diary of these visits which he kept. From this diary it appears that he was on the top of Goatfell at least fifty times, in addition to many other climbs on the surrounding hills. In 1936 he alone was equal to the climb. He was then in his seventy-sixth year, and when the party paid its last visit to Corrie in 1937 the summit of Goatfell was left untrod. In his later years Mr Ker was tenant of a small house on the Braes of Balquhidder, close by the Kingshouse platform on the Callander and Oban Railway, which he visited at all times of the year. There, amidst the quiet of the hills he loved, he found rest of body and refreshment of spirit.

Charles Ker, 'Depreciation' (1899-1900)

Ker's paper represents a major contribution to the late Nineteenth Century debate on depreciation. He commenced by defining profit as that surplus which remains after replacing capital. He believed the problems associated with the latter centred on fixed rather than circulating capital, particularly with regard to the inter-relationship between various fixed assets. (In a sense, this is a problem rarely considered by modern theorists except in relation to goodwill accounting.)

Ker, whilst recognising the purely voluntary nature of depreciation accounting at that time, dismissed the idea of total and immediate write offs of fixed assets, and considered revaluation (presumably on a sale value basis) to be impracticable. He described historic cost depreciation, and recognised its problems; particularly the difficulty of associating depreciation with the physical use made of fixed assets.

However, the major contribution of the paper to accounting thought is the distinction which Ker made between the renewal of fixed assets (which he regarded as depreciation), and 'depreciation' or the 'carrying' of profits to reserve (which he regarded as a necessary part of the profit distribution function - such 'depreciation' preventing over-distribution). In this respect, Ker appeared to be describing replacement accounting. He approved of the German approach to this form of accounting, and criticised the influence in the United Kingdom of the Income Tax Act 1878 which allowed depreciation provisions as well as repairs and renewals.

Depreciation accounting has remained a vexed issue, and Ker's paper is important for its views and approach at a time when the accountancy profession, Parliament and industry were most undecided as to its benefits and disbenefits in financial reporting.

DEPRECIATION.

By CHARLES KER, C.A., Glasgow.

*Read to the Chartered Accountants' Students' Society of Edinburgh,
22nd February 1900.*

WE accountants are constantly dealing with profits — and losses. We have to make up or verify balance-sheets of all sorts of concerns, in every state of prosperity or the reverse. We have in the same concern, from year to year, varying conditions and problems arising from those conditions, and we require not only knowledge of different industries and of the difficulties that may arise in considering each of them, but also certain general principles which can be applied all round.

This paper is an attempt to discover principles underlying professional practice, and the decisions of the Courts in regard to deductions from profits for depreciation.

I shall ask you to consider what profits are: (1) in the ordinary sense, (2) under company law, (3) under the Income Tax Acts. At the close I shall endeavour to make some practical suggestions. The little political economy I ever knew has become somewhat musty from want of use, but we used to be told that profit is the reward of capital, the fruit or product of capital, or something like that. The idea being that the capitalist puts his capital to some use, and gets it back and something more, which is his profit. That may not be political economy, but it seems sense, so let us assume that it is true.

Profit, then, is what remains after replacing capital. If

capital be replaced and no more, there is no profit. If it be not replaced, there is a loss. It is very simple so far. It is when one tries to discover whether capital has been replaced or not that the trouble begins. To take a homely illustration. A small boy invests his capital of 5d. in the purchase of one dozen 'Evening Dispatches,' and sells them for 6d. His profit—he has no doubt about it—is 1d. He knows he can spend the 1d. of profit and continue his trading career with his capital intact. His business is one of quick returns, and any eccentricity of view on the question of capital and profits is soon corrected by hard experience.

As you rise in the scale, the question becomes more complicated. The middleman, buying goods for re-sale and turning over his stock many times in the year, has not the certain test of realised cash as the newspaper boy has. He has to value stock and book - debts and to deduct liabilities, and also—you will note—the capital he started with, before he arrives at the year's profit. Still it cannot be said that here there is any difficulty, provided the stock is turned over sufficiently often to correct, at short intervals, any errors that may arise in the stock valuations.

Of course there has been trouble over stocks and book-debts—stocks being overstated, bad debts not written off, and so on. But these are minor worries, and do not concern us now. The real difficulty appears when you leave the domain of circulating capital and enter that of fixed capital —*i.e.*, capital not invested in articles for re-sale at a profit, but in fixtures to be used in production.

Well, our newspaper boy, we shall suppose, has developed into a newspaper proprietor, with a building and boilers, engines, machinery and plant, utensils, type, floating stock, book-debts, and, we will hope, a reasonable balance at his banker's. If profit in this case also is the product of capital, and if the capital employed must be replaced before the profit is arrived at, questions begin to be put which it is easier to ask than to answer.

The stocks do not present much difficulty; as in the case of the middleman, errors in stocks soon correct themselves. Tools and utensils are constantly being renewed, and the value put on them can be checked by re-valuations—the market value is easily ascertainable. It is the fixed capital that gives difficulty. How is our friend to know whether his year's work has returned him the capital with which he began the year plus a profit? That depends on the value of his possessions at the end of the year. How is he to arrive at this?

Now, when the elements named ground, buildings, machinery have been combined, they undergo a radical change. They are combined into a "Work," a producing unit, a complicated tool, the value of which cannot be got at by appraising the cost of the component parts. One can tell what it cost, but what it is worth depends on different considerations altogether. An article bought for re-sale may pass through many hands at progressive increases in price. An article bought for use tends to· drop in value as soon as delivered. The term "second-hand" carries a sort of stigma.

When many articles are put together to form the unit called a factory, the parts lose their individuality and become atoms in a whole, whose value is determined not by its cost but by its profit-earning power. If there be no demand for the whole because its profit-earning power is nil, its value is the aggregate of the values of the component parts—the break-up value, as it is called. How, then, is profit to be determined? What test must be applied to ascertain that the fixed capital is intact? Is our friend, the newspaper proprietor, to consider that he has made no profit until he has written down his works to break-up value? Or is he to estimate the life of his works as a whole and write the value down by instalments over that period? Or is he to take the probable lives of the separate items and write them down by instalments? Or is he to re-value his works each year, as he does his stock, and, if so, what is to be the basis of valuation? And how are repairs, renewals, and outlay on extensions to be treated?

The problem is to find out if the original capital is represented by assets of equal value when it is not possible to bring that value to an accurate test. The usual practice is to estimate the lives of the different assets and to write off yearly instalments from their book value for the estimated depreciation for the year. If the estimate of the life and of the ultimate break-up value of the subject be accurate, this method may be as good as any; but there are no "mortality tables" or statistics on which to base them which can be applied with certainty to things.

In the first place, it is not enough to say that there has been use, therefore there is depreciation. There is a tendency to depreciation, that is all. Land used as a works site may steadily improve in value. There was a case the other day where improvement in the value of surplus lands was used as some condonation for showing a fictitious balance of profit on the working of a dock.

Buildings deteriorate in time, but the period is so long that annual depreciation of buildings kept in repair is practically *nil*.

Machinery in theory wears out, but, if well looked after, the rate in most cases is very slow. Witness the old blowing engines at many iron-works going as well as ever after fifty years of service.

A great deal has been heard of depreciation in ships, but how much of the loss from this source is due to use, to tear and wear, and how much to bad times in shipping?

Considering all these different kinds of property, it appears that the physical life of the subject is not of much practical use in determining a rate of depreciation.

Secondly, even if one could fix the life of the asset, how long it will take to use it up—that is only one factor in the question. Buildings, machinery, &c., may appreciate or depreciate according to outside conditions. Buildings in use for many years may become more valuable, owing to advances in material or wages making them more costly to replace. Old machinery, plant, and tools, when times are good in the engineering trade, may fetch more than new. Ships have sold lately at more than their cost five years ago. In a recent "going" valuation of buildings, machinery, and plant, which was to be on a low basis to avoid over-capitalisation, buildings came out 18 per cent and machinery 85 per cent over their book value, after deducting 3 per cent depreciation on buildings and 6 per cent on machinery, calculated in each case on the values as reduced from year to year.

Examples might be multiplied, but I think it is clear that depreciation is not necessarily to be inferred from the fact that a subject has been in use for some time. Property in patents and copyrights and in leaseholds does, of course, depreciate from efflux of time, and mines and quarries are gradually worked out. But even in such cases the statement that the use of an article tends to lessen its value must be qualified by the consideration that at any given time the age or condition is only one element of value, and that the market value—what the thing will realise—is regulated by supply and demand.

There are thus disadvantages in attempting to provide out of profits for capital used in earning them by estimating the life of the different assets and writing their value down by instalments.

Is our friend then to attempt a yearly valuation of his whole business and assets? Is he, when times are bad and his profits *nil*, to write down his works to break-up value? I have seen it maintained by a well-known man, a man looked upon by some as an authority on financial matters, that the directors and auditors of a company should give effect in the balance-sheet to what may be called market depreciation, depreciation due to outside causes, and that the balance-sheet in question was incorrect because it did not show the depreciation in the market value of the assets due to outside causes. I do not think that view deserves serious consideration. Even if the principle of revaluation were adopted, the appreciation and depreciation in the value of the assets would have to be dealt with in capital account, not in revenue account. The capital would be written up or down according to the result of the revaluation. Otherwise you would have companies paying in one year dividends of 100 per cent, and going into liquidation the year after.

We see then, on the one hand, that depreciation, according to a fixed scale based on the life of the subjects, is unreliable from causes (factors of value) that cannot be foreseen: on the other hand that periodic revaluation to determine profits is impracticable. Let us consider now what company law requires on the subject.

A distinction is made between "fixed" and "circulating" capital, and all that authorities seem to require is that floating assets, such as stocks and book-debts, have to be valued in order to arrive at profit or loss. These represent circulating capital, and any increase or decrease in value belongs to revenue. The assets representing fixed capital on the other hand, which is retained and employed for the making of profit, need not be valued but may be retained at cost.

There is no provision in the Companies Acts that depreciation shall be provided for — the Acts do not seem to recognise it in any way. There is Art. 73, Table A, in the Act of 1862, which states that no dividend shall be payable except out of profits. That does not help one to decide what profits are. All that the Courts seem to require is that floating assets should be valued. There does not seem to be any obligation to provide for depreciation of fixed assets. Lindley, L.J., in *Lee* v. *Neuchatel Asphalte Company, Limited*, stated that in the absence of provision in the articles as to how accounts are to be kept, shareholders in limited companies "may do what they like so long as they do not misapply their capital and cheat their creditors." The articles do not, as a rule, define how accounts are to be kept, and the articles may always be altered by special resolution. The partners in a limited company therefore are in most cases left to decide, as a question of internal management, what are profits.

There are many decisions bearing on the subject quoted in the text-books, though I do not think there is any House of Lords deliverance on it. All point to this, that so long as there is a surplus of earnings over disbursements, it may be divided as profit without making any provision for lost capital. In the recent case in the Court of Appeal, *National Bank of Wales* v. *Cory*, the Court went so far as to say that the surplus of earnings over disbursements might be divided without providing for bad debts. This seems to me to go beyond all previous decisions, and to be as indefensible on the grounds of law as it is on the grounds of common sense; because lawyers have hitherto held that losses of circulating capital must be made good out of revenue, and if a bank's advances to customers are not part of its circulating capital, what are they?

It is not unusual to find the balance-sheet of a limited company docquetted as correct, "subject to provision for depreciation." This I take to mean that the auditor, having satisfied himself that the balance-sheet is correct, does not consider that an allowance, or at all events a sufficient allowance, has been made out of revenue for fixed capital that may have been exhausted during the year. If this is the meaning of the phrase, it is somewhat difficult to defend on grounds of law. It implies that the auditor considers it his duty not merely to see that the balance-sheet which he docquets is correct—that it honestly sets forth the position of the company—but to point to a line of policy in framing the accounts which the Companies Acts do not prescribe. German mercantile law lays down definite rules to be adhered to in preparing balance-sheets, and *inter alia* prescribes: That "plant and such articles as are not intended for sale, but, on the other hand, are intended for carrying on the trade of the company, may be put down at purchase price or cost of producing the same without deduction for deterioration in value, provided that an equivalent amount for wear and tear has been deducted, or that a relative renewal fund has been opened."

This is a good working rule to go on in balancing. It is one which most companies here adopt. But in our country it is not statutory. The Courts leave a great deal to the discretion of shareholders, and an auditor who qualifies his docquet in a way that implies censure or even hints at a line of policy, assumes a position and responsibility which he must be prepared to defend on grounds of common-sense. He lays himself open to the remark that he is going beyond his province, and he must look outside Acts of Parliament to justify his docquet, for all that he is required to do is to certify facts; the shareholders are to draw their own conclusions.

But while providing for depreciation is a matter within the shareholders' discretion, and while there is no duty on directors or shareholders to set aside annually a sum to replace capital so that in a winding-up the shareholders may receive the face value of their shares, the auditor is within his province in pointing out to shareholders that, in the absence of such provision for redeeming the capital through writing off for depreciation, they cannot expect to get their capital back on a winding-up—that they cannot eat their cake and have it. Capital, it has been said, is not a debt of a company, and dividends are constantly being paid which include part of the capital, not only in companies formed to work the so-called wasting subjects, but also in shipping companies and others. The auditor in such cases should see that the shareholders are not misled. If the interests of creditors were at all imperilled, the auditor would probably be legally responsible if he approved of accounts where no proper provision was made for exhaustion or waste in assets. But whatever opinions may be as to this, probably all will agree that, if an auditor be of opinion that the balance-sheet either does not clearly show the facts as regards depreciation, or that prudence requires that more should be provided than has been set aside, he should point the facts out in his docquet.

This is not a paper on auditing, and I apologise for the digression. I said first that depreciation was, in practice, very difficult to fix ; and, second, that the Companies Acts do not recognise it, profits in limited companies being the excess of earnings over disbursements, without any deduction for loss of capital. Turning to the Income Tax Acts, we find that in the 1842 Act deductions for repairs alone were allowed, but that in the Act of 1878 the Commissioners were directed to "allow such deduction as they may think just and reasonable as representing the diminished value by reason of tear and wear during the year of any machinery or plant" belonging to the person carrying on the concern, or held by him on lease with an obligation to maintain it.

Before the 1878 Act was passed, deductions for depreciation of buildings, plant, and machinery were disallowed in respect that such deduction represented a loss of capital. The 1878 Act modified the law to the extent of allowing the capital lost by depreciation of machinery and plant to be deducted. But the whole tenor of the decisions is that it is only physical deterioration by tear and wear of machinery and plant that is to be allowed. It makes no difference to the Courts that an allowance for depreciation has been charged to profit and loss account. The Acts tax all sorts of incomes, whether from permanent investments, terminable annuities, professional fees, or from wasting subjects, without any deduction for the capital sum included.

Some of the decisions are interesting, and, as accountants are often asked questions about income tax returns, I propose to go over a few of the leading cases. The results are embodied in a letter from the Treasury to the Associated Chambers of Commerce, which I shall read to you, but the cases are of interest not only from the decisions but from the remarks of the judges.

I shall refer first of all to cases dealing with depreciation of fixed plant and machinery, some decided before, and others after, the passing of the 1878 Act.

I. *Hall* v. *King's Lynn Harbour Moorings Commissioners*, 9th June 1875, 1 T.C. 23.—In this case, decided before the 1878 Act, the Harbour Commissioners were found entitled to a deduction for revenue applied under Act of Parliament to renewal of works.

They stated that they had put down screw moorings instead of mooring chains, and had raised money on bonds to pay the cost, and contended that the surplus shown in the accounts was not profit, as it had, under their Act, to be applied to the bond debt.

The Exchequer Division were of opinion that the £400 appearing in the accounts for 1873 as a payment to bond-holders in reduction of debt was a proper deduction to be made, as it had been applied in repayment of money expended in the renewal of works.

II. *Forder* v. *Handyside*, 29th January 1876, 2 T.C. 65.—

This case also was decided before the passing of the 1878 Act. The Company carried on business as ironfounders, and in returning their profits assessable to income tax in respect of their trading for the first year, they deducted a sum of £1509, 7s. 6d. (the allowance for depreciation), on the ground that that sum should be added to the actual expenditure in order to arrive at the "average expenses on account of repairs."

The claim of a deduction for depreciation as averaging expenses for repairs was unsuccessful. The Crown was supported in its view that the deduction represented capital, not revenue.

III. In the *Caledonian Railway Company* v. *Special Commissioners of Income Tax*, 18th November 1880, 8 R. 89, the Commissioners, in assessing the Company under the Income Tax Act, 1842, Schedule D, allowed deduction of sums expended or set aside for renewals and repairs of plant during the year. The Company demanded a further deduction, under the Act of 1878, of a sum representing the "diminished value, by reason of tear and wear," of new additional plant purchased within five years, which had hitherto required no repairs.

The Commissioners refused the additional deduction, holding that the deduction allowed to the Railway Company from year to year for actual renewal and repairs to the plant was all they were entitled to. The Court confirmed this view; but it is curious to note that the Company was allowed not only the actual outlay on renewals and repairs of locomotives, carriages, and waggons ("of better quality and more expensive") for the year, but also a sum of £20,837 set aside under the same heading in the accounts for future renewals.

The Company claimed an allowance, in addition to repairs and renewals, of $4\frac{1}{2}$ per cent of the cost of additional new plant added during the last five and a half years, stating that the average life of the plant was twenty-two years, equal to depreciation at the rate of $4\frac{1}{2}$ per cent per annum, whereas the sum allowed showed only $2\frac{1}{2}$ per cent of the cost. That this arose from the fact that a large amount of new plant had been added (not replaced), which required little or no repair during the first five and a half years, though depreciating at 4½ per cent per annum. The cost of additional new plant during the five and a half years prior to 31st January 1879 was £1,096,534, on which 4½ per cent equals £49,344.

The Commissioners' finding was that renewals, repairs, and sums carried to renewal fund had been already allowed; that this allowance kept up the value of the plant; that this being so, diminished value by tear and wear did not exist; and that to allow depreciation, and also repairs and renewals, would be to allow twice deduction for the same thing. This finding was confirmed.

Lord Gifford said that, instead of "the Commissioners attempting to fix diminishing value by reason of 'tear and wear during the year,' they have allowed the Company deduction of the actual sums expended by them for repairs and renewals amounting to £253,389, and as it certified that the plant has been kept in good order, this may be taken as making up the whole deterioration for the year. This, over a series of years, will be perfectly equitable."

IV. In *Smith* v. *Westinghouse Brake Co. (Ltd.)*, 29th June 1888, 2 T.C. 357, a company had fitted up machinery to extend its business, and had afterwards closed the manufactory and removed a portion of the machinery. Thereafter it had opened the manufactory on a smaller scale, and thereby lost a portion of the original expenditure. It was held that this was a loss of capital, and that no deduction could be allowed.

V. *Highland Railway Company* v. *Balderston*, 10th July 1889, 2 T.C. 485, is an interesting case. The Company had made certain alleged improvements on the permanent way, which they had charged in their own books to capital, but in spite of that they claimed the outlay as a deduction from the amount of their profits assessable to income tax. The claim was disallowed.

The Company had charged to capital account for outlay on steel rails, &c., ...   £13,574

Less for old iron flange rails taken up,   .   1,266

£12,308

This sum they wished to deduct in their income tax return. The Court disallowed the claim. Would the Court have allowed the loss on the old rails, &c., which were removed— *i.e.*, the difference between their cost and the sum received for them? It is probable that they would, on the ground that up to the cost of the old rails, the new were merely a replacement, not an improvement. One cannot help feeling that the Railway Company were facing both ways—showing to the Government that their expenditure was a charge to revenue, and to their shareholders that it was a charge to capital.

VI. In *Clayton* v. *Newcastle-under-Lyme Corporation*, 29th June 1888, 2 T.C. 416, it was held that a corporation purchasing gas-works in a defective structural condition is not entitled to deduct sums set aside annually to be expended in future years on restoring the plant and apparatus.

In the assessment deduction of £707, 2s. 11d. had been allowed for the actual cost of renewals, repairs, and maintenance, such as new retorts, annual repair to plant and apparatus, &c., for the year, but it was sought to deduct in addition £500 appropriated yearly out of the profits as annual depreciation of the retort benches, engines, boilers, and purifying plant.

The surveyor contended that the annual £500 was capitalised for the specific purpose of reconstructing the works or a portion of them, and that it was not a legal deduction.

The Court supported this view, there being no appearance for the Corporation; and there is no getting even depreciation for tear and wear on plant in gas-works to this day.

The six cases above quoted all deal with claims for an allowance for depreciation of machinery or plant.

100

In four of the cases the Courts do not recognise depreciation or its equivalent as a revenue charge under the Income
Tax Acts, in addition to cost of repairs and renewals.

In the Caledonian Railway Company's case, however, provision for future renewals is allowed, and that although the
ordinary repairs and renewals for the year have been already
deducted; and in the first case, decided under the Act of
1842, the Exchequer Division (under somewhat special circumstances, it is true) seem to allow as a deduction a sum
paid to creditors on bonds in respect that the bonds represented cost of renewals.

The next five cases relate to " wasting subjects " of different
kinds.

VII. *Addie* v. *Solicitor of Inland Revenue,* 16th February
1875, 1 T.C. 1.—In this case, decided prior to 1878, a claim
was made for deduction of sums necessary to replace capital
expended in sinking pits or lost by depreciation of buildings
and machinery. The claim was disallowed in respect that
no deduction is allowed by the 1842 Act on account of sums
employed as capital.

VIII. *Coltness Iron Company* v.´ *Black,* 7th April 1881,
1 T.C. 287, is a leading case, and it is interesting to note not
only the result, but the judges' remarks.

The decision was that the company, which wrote off by a
tonnage rate the average amount of capital expended on pit-
sinking exhausted by the year's working, was not allowed to
deduct the amount from the profits assessable.

The case was taken to the House of Lords, who confirmed
the judgment of the Court of Session.

In the lower Court, Lord President Inglis said: " The
statute requires the full balance of profit without any deduction except for working expenses, and without regard to
the state--of the capital account or to the amount of the
capital employed in the concern, or sunk, or exhausted, or
withdrawn." And again: " It makes no difference on the
incidence of the tax that the income has been created by
the sinking of capital, as in the case of purchased annuities,

instead of being the natural annual product of an invested sum."

In the House of Lords, Lord Cairns said: "It may be proper for a trader to perform in his books an operation of this kind" (making a tonnage charge for depreciation) "every year in order to judge of the sum that can in that year be safely taken out of the trade and spent as trade profits."

This sentence I shall refer to again. It seems to me to go to the root of the matter.·

Lord Blackburn said: "The same annual charge is imposed upon a terminable annuity and on one in perpetuity, and what seems harder, the same annual charge is imposed on a professional income earned by hard labour often extending many years before any return is got, and when earned, precarious, as depending on the health of the earner."

One might imagine that Lord Blackburn had our profession in his mind when he said this, were it not that the words are even more applicable to barristers. One can imagine his lordship thinking out the analogy between the Coltness pits and himself as a mine of legal learning.

Years of outlay in boring and putting down mines and driving levels followed, when coal is won, by the rapid exhaustion of the field, suggested apparently a parallel to the case of the professional man whose outlay for years in fitting himself for his work has to be made good in a brief spell of full activity if he achieves success. If income tax is exacted on the gross receipts in the latter case, why not in the former?

IX. In *Gillatt & Watts* v. *Colquhoun*, 17th and 18th December 1884, 2 T.C. 76, it was held that when leasehold premises are purchased and used for trade purposes, the deduction from the assessment for trade profits in respect of such premises must be limited to the existing annual value thereof, whatever the premium originally paid for the lease may have been.

X. In *Edinburgh Southern Cemetery Company* v. *Surveyor of Taxes*, 29th November 1889, 17 R. 154, 2 T.C. 516, it was held that proceeds of lairs sold during the year are assessable without deduction of any part thereof in respect of its being a realisation or conversion of capital.

The Lord President (Inglis) held that this case was governed by the decision in the Coltness case.

XI. In *Paisley Cemetery Company (Ltd.)* v. *Reith*, 5th July 1898, 25 R. 1080, 4 T.C. 1, the Court went a stage further, and held that lump sums received in lieu of annual payments by purchasers of lairs for keeping them in order in perpetuity are assessable, and this though the sums received were not treated as profit in the accounts.

One feels that this decision goes too far. If it is sound, it would justify the charging of income tax on all sums received by insurance companies in respect of an undertaking to pay annuities.

The Lord President (Robertson) said that the case resolved itself into the question—"Is income tax chargeable where money is received and a perpetual obligation undertaken?" and answered the question (if properly reported) by saying that it would be going against the theory of decided cases to countenance it. I cannot reconcile the remark with the decision, and one may be allowed respectfully to have doubts both as to the decision and as to the theory on which it was founded.

I shall now touch briefly on one or two shipping cases.

XII. In *Burnley Steamship Company (Ltd.)* v. *Surveyor of Taxes*, 10th July 1894, 21 R. 965, 3 T.C. 275, it was held that the owners of a ship engaged in trade were not entitled, under section 12 of the 1878 Act, to a deduction for depreciation in the value of their ship caused by ships of a better construction being built.

The surveyor allowed 5 per cent per annum on the reducing value. It was held that it is only physical deterioration that is covered by the Act of 1878, not loss of earning power through obsolescence.

XIII. In *Leith, Hull, and Hamburg Company* v. *Bain*,

B

1st, 2nd, and 16th June 1897, 3 T.C. 560, the Commissioners allowed 5½ per cent on the reducing value. The Company asked for a reduction in the assessment on the ground of insufficient allowance for depreciation.

The Company owned thirty-seven ships: eleven from twenty-nine to thirty-six years old, of which three were from thirty-four to thirty-six years old.

The average age was fifteen and a half years. They claimed a deduction of £28,208, being 7½ per cent on £376,110, the reduced value of the fleet, and were allowed by the Commissioners £20,686, being 5½ per cent on that value.

The case was badly stated to the Court, and the Company's appeal was refused.

This case is interesting, because the Crown for the first time puts forward a claim that sums allowed for depreciation shall be treated as carried to a sinking fund, and separately invested with compound interest at 3 per cent.

XIV. In *Leith, Hull, and Hamburg Steam Packet Company* v. *General Commissioners of Income Tax*, 16th June 1899, 36 S.L.R. 745, it was decided that in estimating the deduction to be allowed for wear and tear under the Act of 1878, section 12, the Commissioners are not allowed to make any deduction upon the sum representing the wear and tear during the year in question on account of any interest which may be earned on the sums allowed.

XV. In *Peninsular and Oriental Steam Navigation Company* v. *Lee*, 1898, 7A L.T.R. 118, the Company claimed a deduction of 5 per cent on the original cost of their fleet.

The Commissioners found that 6 per cent on the reducing value was a sufficient allowance to cover wear and tear.

It was held that the Commissioners had dealt with all that was properly before them, and that the questions were substantially questions of fact.

It appeared in the case that all repairs and renewals had been allowed, that the average duration of service of the Company's ships (as distinguished from the average duration of life) was about seventeen years, and that the average duration of life was twenty-eight years.

Mr Buckley, for the Company, argued that the word "value" ("diminished value by reason of wear and tear") means value to the person assessed, and that as the average life to the P. and O. Company was seventeen years, they should be allowed one-seventeenth of the total depreciation at the end of seventeen years, as depreciation for the year.

It was, however, pointed out that it is only physical deterioration that is contemplated. The Court took this view.

The following is the letter from the Treasury to which I referred above:—

TREASURY CHAMBERS,
WHITEHALL, S.W., *May* 28, 1897.

DEAR SIR,—The Chancellor of the Exchequer has had under his consideration the Memorial of the Association of the Chambers of Commerce of the United Kingdom, which you sent him in the beginning of April.

The chief points raised in the Memorial are as follows:—

1. That the allowances in respect of repairs and depreciation of machinery are insufficient, and the methods of calculating such depreciation are unsatisfactory.
2. That no allowance is made for the cost of replacing machinery which has become obsolete.

As to the first point, I am to say that, as the law now stands, deductions are allowed both in respect of expenditure incurred in repairs and alterations of machinery according to an average of three years preceding the year of assessment, and also in respect of diminished value of machinery by reason of wear and tear during the year. The allowance of these deductions is in the hands of the District or Special Commissioners, as the case may be, and they have to decide in each case as it arises the adequacy of the deductions allowed.

As to the second point, I am to say that the Board of Inland Revenue have given instructions to their surveyor at Leicester, which is particularly referred to in the Memorial, that where a claim is made in respect of the introduction of more modern machinery in a factory, no objection is to be taken to the allowance, as a deduction from the assessable profits of the year, of so much of the cost of replacement as is represented by the existing value of the machinery replaced. Any excess in the cost of the new machinery over the actual purchase value of the old is an addition to the capital of the business, and cannot properly be regarded as a charge upon revenue for the purposes of income tax assessment.

I am to add that similar instructions will be given to surveyors in other districts when the question arises there.—I am, sir, your obedient servant,

A. A. MOUNT.

THE SECRETARY,
    Association of the Chambers of Commerce.

I have gone into the income tax cases in detail, as they have not, so far as I know, been much referred to in papers dealing with depreciation. The decisions of the Courts are, of course, limited by the Income Tax Acts, and the chief interest of the cases is found in the remarks of the judges. By the Act of 1842, assessable profit, like profit divisible among shareholders under the Companies Acts, is the surplus of earnings over receipts without deduction for capital lost or exhausted. Under the 1878 Act, capital lost through wear and tear of machinery and plant may be deducted, and that apparently in addition to repairs and renewals—the amount of wear and tear for the year being a question of fact to be determined by the Commissioners. Apart from this exceptional treatment of machinery and plant in income tax law, the theory in both company and income tax law seems to be that fixed capital has not to be replaced before profits are arrived at.

I have tried to show the difficulty of arriving, in practice, at a principle to guide one in providing for depreciation, and that neither company law nor income tax law gives much assistance. I begin to fear that at this point you feel inclined to say of principles of depreciation as Betsy Prig said of Mrs Harris, "I don't believe there's no sich a person."

Well, the principle that I suggest is no principle at all, but for all that it may be a good enough working guide for accountants. It is this: that such provision should be made for depreciation as will keep intact the working capital of the concern, so that, in the words of Lord Cairns in the

Coltness case, "the trader may judge of the sum that may safely be taken out of the trade and spent as trade profits."

Repairs are, of course, a working charge on profits. Renewals are a charge to profits of the nature of a depreciation allowance. A direct charge for depreciation, while, in theory, a provision for exhausted capital, or for future renewals, is, in practice, only an expedient—though an excellent one—for keeping in hand a portion of the earnings which might without it be withdrawn and spent; or, in other words, an expedient for keeping intact the working capital. . This is specially true of limited companies. The working capital is the life-blood of a company, and it is in this essential that limited companies are limited. They cannot draw on their partners beyond a certain amount. Private partnerships, where each partner is liable for the whole debts, need not, and do not, as a rule, concern themselves much with depreciation, and many a successful business is carried on without any attention being paid to it. But where success is attained in such private concerns one finds due regard paid to keeping up the efficiency of the business by spending money in replacing assets which have served their turn, and are for one reason or another out of date. I have known a prosperous concern in which the books were kept by single entry, with no ledger accounts but those of debtors, creditors, and bank. The test there of the year's profit was the rough and ready one of the increase for the year of money on deposit receipt. That concern prospered, one might almost say, because of its rudimentary book-keeping, which showed this fixed idea—that it is only free money not required for the business that is truly divisible profit. So when the concern had to spend £5000 on extensions, that sum came out of the bank account and out of the "profits" for the year. Such accounting is too heroic for most public companies.

We see the other side of the question in private partnerships in which the personal drawings of partners have led them to scrimp repairs and renewals in order that they may spend the last penny of profits which have been arrived at without any attempt being made to retain in their businesses, by depreciation or reserves, the cash required to keep the businesses alive. This latter case is one which auditors should keep in mind. Money paid to shareholders, like money drawn by extravagant partners, is gone so far as the business is concerned. As in private partnerships personal extravagance is one of the most common causes of bankruptcy, so in limited companies one of the most serious risks run is that shareholders may not realise the importance of keeping working capital intact, or may elect to ignore it. It is, unfortunately, too much the rule to assess the value of shares in a company by what that company pays away in dividends instead of by what it does not pay away, and it requires some self-denial for a shareholder to vote for a 5 per cent dividend when he knows that a 10 per cent dividend will not only give him more money in his purse but will add to the value realisable for his shares.

It would be going too far to say that the only true profit is the free divisible sum that may be paid away without encroaching on working capital. But, if there has been such encroachment, it suggests a line of inquiry which the auditor should follow up in order to find out where the money has gone. In the case of a company showing a profit where working capital has been diminished, the profit may be represented by an increase in the fixed assets, and there should be little difficulty in ascertaining that the additions are genuine capital additions, and not merely repairs and renewals. The simplest cases are those in which the company keeps a detailed inventory and valuation of its fixed assets, the total corresponding with the total of the respective ledger accounts. This inventory should show the cost of each asset, the amount written off in each year for the share of depreciation allocated against each asset, and the balance remaining. When the asset is realised, the proceeds are credited to the relative ledger account, any shortage is written off to profit and loss account, and the asset disappears from the inventory. The replacement of an asset disposed of in this way is not, of course, a charge to profit and loss account, but is a proper capital addition, because the "defunct" asset replaced has been written off. It may be that the circumstances of a company require a further provision for depreciation than is afforded by the mere writing off of defunct assets, but such writing off will so far prevent the depletion of working capital, the danger indicated above. It may not be sufficient allowance for depreciation, but it is an allowance, and the auditor will note it as this, and, if necessary, will inform the shareholders that it has been made.

If there is no inventory, the auditor's task is more difficult. Plant may have been sold, and the proceeds credited to plant account, or even to profit and loss account. There may be no data to show at what figure the asset stood in the books, or if it appeared there at all. It is not uncommon to find proceeds of old plant credited to plant account or to profit and loss account, and the price of new plant added at cost to the value of the fixed assets—a system which inflates profits and tends to disaster unless adequate provision be made in other ways for depreciation.

To take simple examples of the two methods :—

1. A. Limited buys an additional machine, costing £1000, and that sum is added to machinery account and to the inventory and valuation. At the end of ten years the share of annual depreciation allocated to the machine has brought the book and inventory value down to £600. The company then replace the machine by a new one of the same capacity, and sell the old machine for £200. This sum is debited to the purchaser and credited to machinery account, and the £400 difference between the price realised and the book value is written off to profit and loss account. The old machine is taken out of the inventory. The new machine is added to machinery account and to the inventory.

2. B. Limited keeps no inventory of plant, and cannot tell at what figure the machine stands in the books. The £200 received for the machine is credited to machinery account, and the price of the new machine is added to machinery account. No charge is made to profit and loss account. The result is that the profit for the year is increased on paper by £400—the amount standing in machinery account not represented by any asset. The company may not know

that they should write off the cost of defunct plant in this way, but the result is to inflate profits.

I do not say that the course followed in the second case is illegal, only that it should be noted, so that the auditor may be able to inform the shareholders that, if they divide profits ascertained in the way supposed, they are withdrawing capital from the business. Of course, the test of profits by reference to the working capital is not a final one. In the second example given, had the machine not been renewed, the working capital would have been increased by £200. And genuine profits may have been earned though the working capital is largely reduced—a common enough case where a go-ahead business has been under-capitalised. So that working capital may show an increase even where the profit is not a true profit, and a decrease where it is. It comes to this, I think, that auditors should scrutinise the capital expenditure accounts, verify all sums treated as capital additions, see that proceeds of fixed assets sold are credited, not to profit and loss account, but to the proper capital account, and that any loss on realisation is duly debited to profit and loss account. Finally, that they should see that the docqueted accounts give the information necessary to guide shareholders in deciding as to how much of the profits shall be retained, and how much can safely be paid away in dividend.

The exact form in which capital necessary for assuring continuity in a business by maintaining the working capital should be reserved out of profits, is not of much moment. Providing for depreciation is favoured, because by this method the profits set aside are put out of reach and cannot be brought back into account as sums in reserve account can. I have seen on the credit side of a company's balance-sheet a sum placed opposite what was called " Depreciation Fund." The sums allowed for depreciation were carried to it, and against them were placed not only outlay on repairs and renewals, but also odds and ends that would not have looked well in the balance-sheet or profit and loss account. The name of the thing is enough to condemn it. But, as I said, the form in which profits are reserved is not of much consequence. The main thing is to adhere to a policy of laying by. I compared the other day the balance-sheets of three companies, one British, the other two foreign. They were all alike in this—they were all manufacturing companies, all earning large profits, all short of working capital, and each with about £500,000 sunk in works. The profits reserved by provision for depreciation and otherwise in the last year of each company amounted, in the case of the British company, to about 17 per cent of the sunk cápital, and, in the two foreign companies, to about 15 per cent and 16 per cent of the sunk capital respectively. These percentages are largely in excess of the usual allowances for depreciation and reserves, and are explained by the want of working capital in each case. They illustrate what I wish to emphasise—the prudence of writing down for depreciation and of carrying profits to reserve. You may be told that the conserving policy is hard on shareholders who have bought shares on the basis of previous dividends. But the investor (I do not speak of speculators) is shrewd enough to see that he is not benefited by receiving an increased dividend when the working capital is impaired to meet it, when it involves either borrowing money or raising additional capital, or going without some useful outlay on improvements. The investor, even when dependent on his dividend, will not grumble if he is satisfied that the decrease in his dividend is for the good of the company in the long-run.

I need not labour the subject further. It comes to this, that provision for depreciation is necessary, not specifically to meet anything that is accurate and scientific and definable, but to prevent the dispersion among the shareholders of funds which may be required to meet the varying contingencies and perils of trade, so that the company may keep abreast of the times, vigorous and well equipped for the struggle with competitors at home and abroad. I do not say that sums voted for depreciation should not be applied to the assets in a discriminating way, according to a plan based on the estimated life of each asset, so as to provide for its future renewal. I say that the main point is that such sums should be voted, and that the allowance, if it err at all, should err on the side of fulness. Our German competitors

C

realise this.   I have referred to their Government's paternal guard over the preparation of accounts.   German law does not, I understand, allow goodwill or promotion expenses to appear as assets, and lays down rules for building up reserves. There are State auditors in Germany to see that the law is kept.   We in Scotland consider that State auditors are quite unnecessary.   Have we not three Chartered Societies ? Scottish investors do not require State protection.   They are able to judge for themselves, and can appreciate honest and independent work done for them by our profession.

Let us see, then, that our work is honest and independent. We are going through a period of prosperity at present, but there are signs that lean years are not far off.   It is in the fat years that depreciation should be written off and reserves built up, so that when the periodic depression sets in and there are no profits being earned, our companies may enter on the struggle for existence with well-filled purses.   So that we accountants should do what we can to preach the policy of thrift, and testify, when necessary, against such neglect of it as seems dangerous.

Since this paper was written I have seen the proofs of a paper on Depreciation of Machinery by Professor Robert H. Smith, which is to appear in 'Fielden's Magazine' in March, and can commend it to those of you who wish to go into the scientific side of the question.   I have tried to set out some aspects of it from the point of view of the accountant. There are many points on which I have not touched — *e.g.*, sinking funds, the statutory requirements of gas and electric lighting Acts, depreciation allowance as an item in cost of production, claims for deduction for depreciation from income-tax assessment, and the relation of such claims to the assessed value of the subjects.   Perhaps some of my audience will take up these matters and deal with them now or on some future date.

RICHARD BROWN,

*President of the Society of Accountants
in Edinburgh.*

BORN 17th August 1856.
DIED 24th May 1918.

WITHIN these two dates an ever-growing life was maturing
for the end, on this earth, that came all too soon.

Richard Brown's life began at Kirkhouse, Dolphinton, in
the Upper Ward of Lanarkshire, where his forebears were
farmers in the parish for more than 200 years, and where
his father was farmer at Kirkhouse for two tacks of nineteen
years each.

He received a useful, sound, and thorough education at
the parish school of Dolphinton.   His subsequent education,
in addition to attendance at private classes and at the Law
classes of the University of Edinburgh, consisted of continuous self-culture and extensive travel during holiday
times, extending over a period of about twenty years, in
France, Spain, Algiers, Italy, Germany, United States, of
America, Canada, and other countries.

He entered into an indenture on 17th August 1872—the
day when he was sixteen years of age—with Messrs Kenneth
Mackenzie & John Turnbull Smith, C.A.   After the usual
apprenticeship, he was admitted a Member of the Society of
Accountants in Edinburgh on 5th February 1879.   Until
the death of Mr Mackenzie in September 1880, and thereafter until Dr Turnbull Smith became Manager of the Life
Association of Scotland in February 1885, he was a most
capable and valued member of the staff of his old apprentice
masters.

Having succeeded to part of Dr Turnbull Smith's business when he retired from accounting work, Mr Brown began on his own account in 1885; and in 1893 he assumed as partners Mr Harry Lawrence Usher, C.A., and Mr Kenneth Mackenzie Gourlay, C.A., and then founded the firm of Messrs Richard Brown & Co., which has attained a position well known in the profession.

Mr Brown was elected a Member of the Council of the Society of Accountants on 4th February 1891, and was appointed Secretary and Treasurer on 3rd February 1892, an office which he retained, with the greatest acceptance, until there was unanimously conferred upon him, on 2nd February 1916, the highest honour the Society could bestow, that of being their President, which he held at the time of his death.

No honour ever came more fittingly and deservedly to any man. Mr Brown's high character, his professional ability, his position in the profession, and his services to the Society and to the Accounting profession generally, amply justify this statement.

Apart from his long and wholly admirable work as Secretary of the Society, perhaps the most important service he rendered to the profession was in connection with the formation of what is known as "The General Examining Board." One who is not a Member of the Edinburgh Society, but occupies a high position in a sister Society, says: "Mr Richard Brown held the profession of Chartered Accountant in very high esteem, and exerted himself in no ordinary degree to maintain and promote the ideals at which he aimed. He was one of the first to foresee the great advantages which would accrue to the profession by the closer union of the three Chartered bodies, and he took a leading part in furthering the adoption of the Agreement which was come to in 1893 for the purpose of regulating the training and examination of candidates for membership, under which a joint Board, composed of Members of the three Societies, was provided for supervising and carrying out the terms of the Agreement. As Secretary of the General Examining Board from the beginning until 1916, when he was elected President of the Edinburgh Society, Mr Brown carried out all the arrangements for the examinations, including supervision of the preparation and assessment of papers, &c., with very marked ability and to the entire satisfaction of the Members of the Board. The skill and accuracy which he displayed in submitting to the Board the examination results were very marked, and showed a complete mastery of the innumerable and intricate details involved."

Many other benefits which Mr Brown's foresight and wisdom conferred upon the profession might be alluded to, but only two may be mentioned. The first is the Evening Classes for Apprentices and Clerks which were started practically on his suggestion, and which were a great success, being, up to the outbreak of war, always well attended. The second is 'The Accountants' Magazine,' which, when it was started, he worked hard to make a success. He then wrote many of the editorial articles, as well as articles on specific subjects. Two of these appear in the first volume of the Magazine. One is on the "Bibliography of Book-keeping," which probably suggested to him the profound and interesting 'History of Accounting,' published in 1905, and of which he was editor and part author.

In 1908 the American Association of Public Accountants commemorated their "majority," and the various Accountant Associations all over the world were invited to send Delegates to Atlantic City, New Jersey. Mr Brown was one of the representatives from Scotland, and spoke on two occasions. On the authority of one of the other Delegates who was present, it may be mentioned that he most worthily maintained the reputation of those he represented, and that he made a great impression upon the American Association.

It may not be without interest to mention, as indicative of the bent of his mind, that when Mr Brown was in Dr Turnbull Smith's office he secured his and the members of the staff's cordial support in the formation of "The Office Debating Club," which was instituted on 29th November 1880, and which had a useful existence for five years, until a motion was passed on 23rd March 1885 to the effect that,

"As the Office of Mackenzie & Smith is now broken up, the Club be dissolved at the close of the Session." Mr Brown subsequently compiled "Memoirs of the Office Debating Club," but as these are somewhat private in their nature and have not now the interest they originally had, they need not be further referred to, beyond mentioning that they record the fact that Mr Brown, who was President of the Club in 1882-83, was during its existence present at fifty-one out of fifty-seven meetings, and that he read essays on (1) The Accountant, (2) National Revenue and Expenditure, (3) Thomas Carlyle, (4) The Duties of an Auditor, and (5) Some Characteristics of the Age.

It may be permissible to refer specially to Mr Brown's connection with "The Church of Scotland," of which he was an attached member and a devoted elder. He was appointed Auditor of the Church in 1910, and soon made his initiative and organising power evident. One who came much into contact with him at the Offices of the Church says: "I speedily recognised his many good qualities and his outstanding ability. Few men have impressed me more than he did with his power to grasp and deal effectively with difficult questions and problems of finance. I found him a friend who could be trusted to do the right thing without sacrificing the interests of the Church to personal feeling or interest. He was of a calm and equable temperament, and I never heard him speak ungenerously of any one, even although he might differ from him. He never failed to impress a meeting with his complete grasp and understanding of any question he had to explain or discuss. I felt I could always depend upon him for help and wise counsel in any difficulty which might arise."

Not only in his official position as Auditor of the Church, but in much work undertaken cheerfully and ungrudgingly, Mr Brown was looked upon as one who could be confidently relied upon. For example, as Joint Vice-Convener of the Endowment Committee, he gave an amount of time and thought and exercised a sound judgment which were highly appreciated and valued. In like manner, he took a deep interest in the work of the Committee on the Religious

Instruction of Youth, and acted as Convener of the Sub-Committee on Publications and Finance. In that capacity his knowledge and experience were very valuable; but in truth in every branch of the Committee's work he took a deep practical interest, and, in particular, he had a prominent share in carrying out the arrangements between the Committee and the Youth Committee of the United Free Church for the introduction of a joint Teachers' Magazine. The General Committee of the Church, the Aged and Infirm Ministers' Fund, and the Committee on Small Livings, all shared in the benefit of his wide knowledge, his prudent counsel, and his disinterested zeal.

Mr Brown served in the Eldership of the Church for nearly a quarter of a century, first at Midcalder, and afterwards for twenty-two years in St Andrew's, Edinburgh, where he took a keen and practical interest in the Religious Instruction of the Young, and in the Psalmody, as well as in the financial affairs of the congregation, having been Treasurer to the Kirk-session for over ten years. The Minister aptly says: "I shall never forget one so loyal, so wise, so kindly, and so true."

For seven years Mr Brown was representative Elder from the Burgh of Selkirk to the General Assembly, and received the gratitude and appreciation of the Town Council for his services.

It is not to be wondered at, in view of what has been said, that in a touching tribute paid to Mr Brown at the close of the General Assembly of 1918, immediately after his sudden death, it is recorded that "he was a man fervent in spirit, not slothful in business, and carefully employed innumerable opportunities of serving the Lord"; and further, that "the General Assembly gratefully pay this tribute to his high personal character, his beautiful Christian walk, and his eminent services to the Church he loved."

Although Mr Brown spent the greater part of his life in the city of Edinburgh, he never forgot his boyhood days in the country, and a country life was ever dear to him. The Upper Ward of Lanarkshire had a strong claim upon him, and he joined the Edinburgh Upper Ward Association in

1877, when he was twenty-one years of age. He became Secretary of the Association in 1885, and continued to discharge the duties with whole-hearted zeal until 1902. He presided at the Annual Meeting and Dinner in 1913, and those who were then present will not readily forget the speech he made on that occasion, which showed wide research and warm interest in all the localities embraced in the district of the Upper Ward.

Without losing this interest, the charm of Yarrow took possession of him, and after spending some time at Broadmeadows Cottage, he became the tenant of " The Hangingshaw," the ancient seat of "the outlaw Murray," which was his country home for thirteen years, up to the time of his death. The following account of his life there, written by one who knew and loved him, will be of great interest. " He used to spend the summer and autumn months there, travelling almost daily into Edinburgh for business. A more perfect retreat from the rush and worry of affairs cannot be imagined. But Mr Brown's overflowing physical and mental energy never permitted him to rest. To country pursuits he brought the same intensity of zeal which animated all his occupations. Shooting, in its season, occupied much of his leisure; and he enjoyed long tramps over the surrounding moors and hills. He was keenly interested in the history, traditions, and antiquities of the neighbourhood, and especially in the antiquities of the Hangingshaw—the remains of the original castle, the drove road over the Minch, Wallace's Trench, the Catrail, &c. His passion for accuracy displayed itself in the information on these subjects with which his mind was stored. The beautiful terraced garden of his house, the long rows of ancient yews, the traditional hollies, the famous avenues of beech trees, were objects which he exhibited with pride; and his extensive and faultless familiarity with horticultural nomenclature surprised the many visitors whom his hospitality entertained. From his " wild " garden and his rock garden—the creation of his own hands—he derived perhaps even more pleasure than from any other feature of the grounds. He possessed minute knowledge of the wild flora of the neighbourhood. His interest in local affairs in the parish of Yarrow, in the village of Yarrowford, in the people round about, in the little school and Sunday-school of the district, was genuine and deep. He could not endure to see anything go wrong. Upon every trifling problem his advice was given with as much careful consideration as though the matter were one of first importance. His help was always ready, and never waited to be asked for. The Church of Scotland held the foremost place among his many interests. His fertile brain was continually occupied revolving new schemes for its advantage, and the means by which these schemes might be realised. He remained dissatisfied until he had pursued every project into all the minutiæ of its practical details. When in residence, he attended Yarrow Kirk every Sunday. His place was never vacant, however bad the weather; and on Communion Sunday he officiated as an elder. One of the silver patens—one presented by him —remains as a memorial of his association with the services. It bears the following inscription with reference to his mother—' In affectionate Memory of one who loved the House of God.' A stauncher friend Yarrow Kirk never had. Throughout the parish he was held in great and universal respect. The whole valley mourns his loss."

Before closing this all too inadequate account of Richard Brown's life, suffer one of his old office companions and a lifelong friend to speak out of his knowledge: "Even at the commencement of his apprenticeship he showed that he had already laid by a store of information from his reading. He often interested and amused those at his desk by long quotations from Burns, Dickens, Tom Hood, and others. He was full of humour, and a most amusing and intelligent companion. He had a great taste for good music, especially Scotch music; he had early learned to play the violin, and in 1884 became a member of the Edinburgh Amateur Orchestral Society, at whose concerts he played the viola for many years. He was deeply interested in and acquired a great knowledge of Scotch lore, especially of that connected with the Scott country. He was a keen sportsman and a walker who never tired. From being only a moderate one, with his usual perseverance, he became a very useful and reliable shot. With the prospect of more leisure as he advanced in years he cultivated hobbies. The principal of these was books, but gardening also appealed strongly to him, and he acquired a great knowledge of flowers and trees."

After a long day spent in the General Assembly of the Church of Scotland, Richard Brown fell gently asleep in his own home in Edinburgh, on 24th May 1918. He was laid to rest in the Dean Cemetery on Tuesday, 28th May 1918. In very truth it can be said of him that he was a man, great in ability, great in loving friendship, great in service, great in character, great in the simple faith of a true Christian.

J. T. S.

R. Brown, 'The Form of Revenue Accounts and Balance Sheets, and
the Use of Percentages in Connection Therewith' (1903-4)

Richard Brown was one of the most distinguished practitioners of his time,
and he wrote on a subject in which standards in practice were very low.
Brown's theme has an obvious modern-day sound to it - make maximum
disclosure with conciseness; aim for simplicity rather than complexity;
and put the financial statements in a form that avoids diversity and aids
comparability.

The approach is implicitly one of aiding user comprehension, a matter
which has even today failed to appear in the list of reporting priorities
of the accounting policy-makers. For example, Brown suggested that the
Revenue Account (income statement) should not be a transcript of the
relevant ledger account; he prescribed different forms of Revenue Accounts
for different types of business; and he suggested the use of percentaged
data in both the Revenue Account and Balance Sheet.

THE FORM OF REVENUE ACCOUNTS AND BALANCE-SHEETS, AND THE USE OF PERCENTAGES IN CONNECTION THEREWITH.

By RICHARD BROWN, C.A.

Read to the Chartered Accountants Students' Society of Edinburgh on 21st January 1904.

THE consideration of forms is, of course, not a study of the highest importance,—the substance being of more importance than the form,—nevertheless, it is one of some utility. Form in accounts may be said to resemble style in literature, seeing that the form chosen, like the words used, should, to quote Robert Louis Stevenson, a master of style, be " apt, explicit, and communicative." The more perfect the form the better the subject-matter is understood. An investigation of the evolution and development of the various forms of accounts now in use would be an interesting inquiry; but it is with the forms as we now find them, and not with their origin, that I propose to deal in the first part of this paper. In the second part I shall endeavour to show by practical examples the value of percentages when applied both to profit and loss accounts and balance-sheets, and the various ways in which they can most usefully be applied.

I find that both of these subjects are discussed with some fulness in Mr George Lisle's valuable work, entitled 'Accounting in Theory and Practice,' many of the observations in which are repeated in the new 'Encylopædia of Accounting.' No separate paper, however, has, so far as I am aware, been written on these subjects; and although they are by no means new, and may be dealt with in other books besides Mr Lisle's, I hope I may be able to add some fresh interest to them.

I. Revenue Accounts and Balance-sheets.

Dealing then, in the first place, with forms of revenue accounts and balance-sheets, I may say at once that the forms I shall discuss are not necessarily those which the directors of a company should publish for the information of its shareholders. The extent of the information which directors make public is regulated in the first place by the articles of association of the company, and in the second place by the judgment of the directors as to what is best published in the interests of the company. The forms which I shall discuss are those which an intelligent accountant would choose for conveying the maximum amount of information to his clients as to the affairs of a concern in which they are interested, while at the same time preserving that conciseness which is necessary in statements designed to show at a glance how matters stand.

A revenue account and balance-sheet are, in my opinion, the only general divisions in which the normal accounts of an ordinary business concern are capable of being scientifically stated. I am aware that it has become a fashion of many modern theorists to suggest several different statements, which they say are necessary to give a complete and accurate view of the accounts of a business, some even proposing as many as five or six; but personally I do not favour such a high development of the theory of accounts. It seems to me to be travelling in the wrong direction—that is to say, towards complexity instead of towards simplicity. The aim of all statements of accounts should be clearness and simplicity, so that he who runs may read; and when you have five or six different statements to grasp before you can get a complete idea of the position of matters, a much greater intellectual effort is necessary than when you have only to look at a simple profit and loss account and balance-sheet.

Where fuller particulars are desired than can conveniently be shown in one account, it is better to add supplementary statements giving such details and referable to the main account. The two general divisions should first of all be presented in their simplicity. But in the great majority of cases there need be no difficulty in including in the revenue account and balance-sheet all the detail which is likely to be wanted outside of the books themselves.

I must therefore regard all trading accounts, profit and loss accounts, and appropriation accounts as mere subdivisions of the revenue account, and all capital accounts, reserve accounts, and general balance accounts as mere subdivisions of the balance-sheet. The term trading account I consider a peculiarly inappropriate one, and I have not found the authorities agreeing as to its precise meaning. In a great many cases it is not really a trading account but a manu-facturing account, and in some cases it is both combined. Apart, however, from the ambiguous nature of the term, I do not find the account itself very satisfactory; here again authorities differ as to what should go into a trading account and what should not. Some put depreciation in the trading account, others in the net revenue account, and others, again, in the appropriation account. Discount is another item as regards which the practice varies. Personally I have never found any difficulty in drawing out a revenue account in which all the information which can be derived from a trading account is quite clearly given, and where one is not called upon to settle disputed points such as I have indicated or to look through several accounts before you get all the information you want.

In connection with this, I may here state that I see no necessity for the revenue account or the accounts composing it being merely transcripts of the corresponding accounts in the ledger. I have always made it my aim to put a revenue account in as clear and intelligible a form as possible, and if the ledger accounts are not in such a form, why, then, so much the worse for the ledger accounts. The books of a concern should, of course, be closed in such a way as that the annual statements can be readily confirmed from them; but I certainly see no reason why, if the accounts have not been kept or cannot well be kept in a way that the revenue account when posted shall exhibit clearly the transactions of the year, the character of the annual statement should thereby suffer.

Statutory Forms.

Having made these general observations, I shall now take up and examine the various forms of revenue accounts and balance-sheets which have the force of statutory authority. Perhaps we do not all realise how many different forms of such accounts have been prescribed by or through statutes, and how many and remarkable are the differences between them. We have the form given in Schedule A of the Companies Act, 1862; the forms prescribed in the Regulation of Railways Act, 1868; the forms prescribed by the Life Assurance Companies Act, 1870; the forms prescribed by the Gas Works Clauses Act, 1871; the forms prescribed by the Chief Registrar of Friendly Societies under the powers of the Buildings Society Act, 1874, and the forms of the same official under the Industrial and Provident Societies Act, 1893, and the Friendly Societies Act, 1896; the Board of Trade forms under the Electric Lighting Acts; and the forms prescribed by the Secretary for Scotland under the Town Councils (Scotland) Act, 1900. Forms prescribed for county and parish councils I do not propose to refer to, as they do not relate to concerns for which a revenue account and balance-sheet are necessary. There may be other statutory forms which I have overlooked, and there are, I daresay, forms prescribed in private Acts of Parliament, but I do not think it necessary to go into them.

It must not be lost sight of that these statutory forms are drawn up for the most part with the view of providing information required by Government officials for statistical purposes, or with the view of showing that the accounts of the concern comply with certain special statutory provisions, such as those relating to borrowing. Still, even after making every allowance for this, one would like to see greater regard paid to some of the leading general principles applicable to the stating of accounts, and that not merely on theoretical grounds, but because it would make the intelligent comprehension of published accounts easier for the general public. It would seem that there has been a little too much display of individuality and too little consideration given to the general convenience and advantage in drawing up these statutory forms.

The form given in Table A of the Companies Act, 1862, is peculiar in respect that under the head of liabilities the first item is the shareholders' capital, the second the debts and liabilities of the company, the third the reserve fund, and the fourth the balance of profit and loss account. The liabilities to the public and the liabilities to the shareholders are thus mixed up. The liabilities are placed on the left-hand side of the account and the assets on the right-hand side, thus reversing what appears to have been the usual practice up to that time. This point I shall discuss later. No form of revenue account is given in connection with the Companies Acts.

The accounts attached to the Regulation of Railways Act, 1868, are very elaborate, comprising separate statements of capital raised and capital expended. The revenue is shown in two accounts—viz., a revenue account and a net revenue account, to which is added a statement of the proposed appropriation of the balance. The so-called general balance-sheet merely shows the unexpended amount of capital. To obtain a complete view of assets and liabilities there must be combined with this account the account headed receipts and expenditure on capital account. In this account both share capital and loan capital are included.

The forms attached to the Life Assurance Act, 1870, are peculiar in this, that in the revenue account the income appears on the left-hand side of the account and the expenditure on the right-hand side; the account also begins with the amount of funds at the beginning of the year, and ends with the amount of funds at the end of the year, so that it is not a true revenue account for the year. As is of course well understood, the real revenue of a life assurance company can only be ascertained when a valuation is made; at the same time, there is no reason why the annual revenue account, which requires to be published, should not be stated in proper form so far as it goes. Moreover, the form prescribed for use when a valuation is made is open to the same criticism. The form of balance-sheet given, although the divisions are headed liabilities and assets, does not give a true statement of liabilities, and this cannot be correctly done except at a valuation. The amount of the assurance and annuity funds, &c., is what is entered under liabilities as representing the value of the company's obligations contingent on mortality. In this form also the shareholders' capital, reserve fund, and profit and loss balances are not clearly separated from the liabilities to the public. The form of revenue account for a company doing both fire and life business is divided into three parts—viz., a life account, a fire account, and a profit and loss account; each of these accounts commences with a balance brought forward from the previous year, and the income is again on the left-hand side and the expenditure on the right.

The forms prescribed under the Gas Works Clauses Act, 1871, divide the revenue account into two—viz., a revenue account, and a profit and loss or net revenue account. The general balance-sheet, as in the railway form, includes only the unexpended capital, and for a view of assets and liabilities the capital account must be combined with the balance-sheet. In this capital account, loan and share capital are not in any way treated as different in character; and in the balance-sheet the liabilities to the public are not treated as if they were in any way different from the balance of a profit and loss account or the reserve and depreciation funds. A separate account of the reserved fund requires to be published according to a form given.

The forms of account prescribed by the Chief Registrar of Friendly Societies under the Building Societies Acts consist of a receipts and payment account, a statement showing the operations of the year, and a liabilities and assets account.

The account of the operations of the year is decidedly peculiar in form. It is in two parts, the first relating to revenue, and the other to capital. The income is on the left side and the expenditure on the right, columns being added on each side to show the balances at the beginning and end of the year on each account. The liabilities and assets account is like an ordinary balance-sheet, and the form of it appears to me to be all that could be desired, except that liabilities to depositors and others would be better placed before liabilities to holders of shares, so that the latter might be found next to the item undivided profit. There is another form issued by the Registrar for unincorporated benefit building societies, which follows the same lines as the one to which I have just referred.

The Chief Registrar also issues three forms under the Industrial and Provident Societies Act, 1893—one for a society carrying on industries and trades under the above Act, another for a society carrying on business, and a third for a land society under the above Act. They are all three of the same nature, and consist of a cash account; a general account (in reality a revenue account), which is divided into three parts—viz., (a) trade of the year, (b) profit and loss, (c) application of profit. In all these the expenditure is properly placed on the left-hand or debtor side, and the income is on the creditor side. Depreciation is brought into the (a) or trading account, and in other respects these accounts seem to follow correct lines. The balance-sheet, which completes the statements, is also well drawn out, with the exception that the order of the entries might be slightly improved, particularly in the way of keeping together all the money due to the shareholders.

The Registrar also issues four forms under the Friendly Societies Act, 1896: the first for a registered friendly society; the second for a registered working men's club; the third for a specially authorised society other than a loan society, and for a benevolent or medical society; and the fourth for a registered collecting society. The first has an income and expenditure account, with the income on the left and the expenditure on the right, and a balance-sheet, which is some-

what similar in form to the balance-sheet under the Life
Assurance Act. The second has a cash account, a general
account—divided into an income and expenditure account—
and a profit and loss account; here again the income is on
the left and the expenditure on the right-hand side. There
is also a balance-sheet, the form of which is good. The form
for benevolent societies has an income and expenditure account headed general account, with the income on the left
and the expenditure on the right, and a balance-sheet like
that for a friendly society. The form for a registered collecting society has its income and expenditure separated into
two accounts, one called general account and the other management fund; again the income is on the debtor and the
expenditure on the creditor side. The balance-sheet is like
that under the Life Assurance Act.

The forms prescribed by the Board of Trade under the
Electric Lighting Acts are somewhat similar to the forms
under the Gas Works Clauses Act, and include a revenue
account and a net revenue account. In the first, depreciation
is entered, and in the second, besides interest on loans, the
appropriation of the net profit is shown. There is also a
capital account showing the capital raised and expended, a
reserved fund account, a depreciation fund account, and a
general balance-sheet. In the case of the last-mentioned,
the total capital raised is shown as a liability, and the total
capital expended as an asset, so that it is not necessary, as in
the case of the railway and gas works accounts, to bring in
another statement in order to get a full view of the assets
and liabilities. There is one form prescribed for a company
and another for a local authority, but the only noteworthy
difference between the two is that a sinking fund account
is substituted for the depreciation fund account in the case
of the local authority, and that no mention in the latter
case is made of depreciation at all—an omission which is
significant. The form of both these accounts is, in my
opinion, good.

As regards the forms prescribed by the Secretary for Scotland under the Town Councils Act, most of them being
merely cash accounts, I shall only refer to the forms of

revenue-producing undertakings; and as those given have been modelled on the forms prescribed by the Board of Trade with the view of saving double returns, it is not necessary to go into them in detail. Statements of assets and liabilities are required in connection with the common good accounts, the assessment accounts, and any other miscellaneous accounts, and these are in the ordinary form.

To recapitulate—of eight distinct classes of revenue accounts examined, three have the income on one side of the account and five on the other, four have the statement divided up, and four have it in one account; of nine balance-sheets examined, two are divided into two parts, while four have the liabilities to the public and to the shareholders more or less mixed up.

I think you will agree with me that as regards the form of accounts the ideas of the Government of this country and its responsible officials are not lacking in variety. There is no real reason for so much diversity of form. Greater or less detail one can understand, or additional accounts for some special purpose, but in all the essentials there might be something like uniformity. However, there they are, duly authorised and imposed, and we must just make the best we can of them. Fortunately they are each of comparatively limited application, and as regards the great majority of business concerns we are left with a free hand.

Suggested Forms of Revenue Accounts.

Let me now put before you my own views as to the form of the revenue account of an ordinary trading concern. In the first place, the account being essentially a ledger account, though not, as I have said, necessarily a mere copy of such an account, should be in Dr. and Cr. form, with the income on the right or Cr. side and the expenditure on the left or Dr. side. The first item on the Cr. side is the sales, from which I deduct returns, and also, in those trades where there is a recognised trade discount allowed, the amount of such discounts. From the balance, being the net sales, I then deduct the purchases, adjusted by the addition and deduction of the stocks at the beginning and the end of the year, so as to bring out the cost to the business of the articles sold. If separate general ledger accounts are kept for goods purchased and goods sold, as is, for several reasons, desirable, they will each show the proper balance to carry to the revenue account. The difference between the two is the gross profit. Next come any items of miscellaneous revenue, such as commissions.

On the Dr. side I take the items in the following general order : wages, warehouse charges including packing, carriages, travellers' salaries and expenses, rent, taxes, repairs, &c. ; office salaries and expenses, any bad debts, the balance of the cash discounts received and paid ; and lastly, any balance of interest paid, exclusive, however, of interest on partners' capital. At this point I make a summation to show the total expenditure of the concern.

As regards income tax, in private partnerships the best plan is to debit the net amount paid, including any sum assessed under schedule A., direct to the accounts of the partners in the proper proportions. By entering the amount in the revenue account the burden of it will fall on the partners in erroneous proportions, unless their shares of interest on capital are in the same proportion to one another as their shares of profit, or unless such interest is only credited to their accounts after deduction of tax. In companies where the net amount of income tax must appear in the revenue account, it should be stated separately as the last item. The balance of the account, being the net earnings of the business during the period, may now be extended. In private concerns it may require to be shown in two or even three portions—viz., salaries to partners, interest on partners' capital, and surplus profit divisible. A balance of profit brought forward from the previous year should not be shown here, but in the balance-sheet.

In manufacturing concerns no advantage is gained by deducting the purchases of material from the sales. They are better entered on the expenditure side, the stocks being of course debited and credited to each account in the usual way. In such businesses I arrange all the manufacturing expenses together, and make a summation distinct from the selling and other expenses, so as to show the net cost of manufacture. In manufacturing charges I include rent and upkeep of works and depreciation of plant. The stock of the finished product I add to the net sales, deducting the stock with which the year commenced, and thus bringing out the value of the out-turn for the year.

It is important in all manufacturing concerns to have a ready means of ascertaining the cost of manufacture, as where the stock of the finished product fluctuates in quantity to any great extent, and is valued either over or under cost, misleading results may be shown in one year as compared with another. Thus, where stock is systematically undervalued, a year which started with a large stock and finished with a small one would show a higher profit than had been truly earned in that year, while a year which started with a small stock and finished with a large one would show a lower profit than had actually been earned on the goods sold. Where it is desired to provide against the possibility of stock having to be sold at less than manufacturing cost, it is better to do so by means of a sum placed to a special reserve account.

In breweries and other businesses having a number of agencies it is advantageous to show the net sales of each agency separately, and the expenses of each agency in separate sections of the division for selling expenses.

I submit examples of revenue accounts of a merchant's, a paper manufacturer's, and a brewer's business, illustrating the views I have expressed. I think one or other of them will be found adaptable to the great majority of the business concerns with which we are likely to have to deal in our professional experience.

A & B, Merchants, Edinburgh.

Revenue Account for year ending 31st December 1903.

Dr. EXPENDITURE.	Per cent.	£	INCOME.	Per cent.	Cr.
To Wages	2	£800	By Sales—net	100	£40,000
,, Warehouse charges	·5	200	*Less* Purchases account	85·6	34,250
,, Carriages	1·25	500		14·4	£5,750
,, Travellers' salaries and expenses	3·75	1,500			
,, Rent, taxes, and insurance	1	400	,, Commissions	·6	250
,, Office salaries	1·25	500			
,, Stationery and other office expenses	·25	100			
,, Bad debts	·1	50			
,, Cash discounts—balance	·1	50			
,, Interest—balance	·4	150			
Total expenditure	10·6	£4,250			
,, Balance, being— p.c. £ Salaries to partners 1·5 600 Interest on capital ·6 250 Profit divisible— A, £500; B, £400 2·3 900	4·4	1,750			
	15	£6,000	Total income	15	£6,000

C, D, & Co., LIMITED, Papermakers, Edinburgh.

Revenue Account for year ending 31st December 1903.

Dr. EXPENDITURE.	d. per lb.	£	INCOME.	d. per lb.	Cr.
To Materials	·96	£16,000	By Paper account	3	£50,000
,, Chemicals	·24	4,000			
,, Wages	·42	7,000			
,, Coal, oil, and light	·15	2,500			
,, Rent, taxes, and insurance	·09	1,500			
,, Mill furnishings	·04	600			
,, Upkeep of plant	·08	1,400			
,, Depreciation of plant	·06	1,000			
	2·04	£34,000			
	d. per lb.				
,, Carriages	·09 £1,500				
,, Packing	·06 1,000				
,, Salaries	·07 1,200				
,, Office expenses	·02 300				
,, Bad debts	·015 250				
,, Cash discounts	·03 500				
,, Interest	·03 500				
	·315	5,250			
,, Income tax	·03	500			
,, Balance, being divisible profit for year	·615	10,250			
	3	£50,000		3	£50,000

THE E F BREWERY CO., LIMITED.

Revenue Account for year ending 31st December 1903.

Dr.	EXPENDITURE.	Per Excise Barrel.		INCOME.			Cr.
To Malt		£·371	£13,000	By Edinburgh sales	. . .	£48,000	
,, Hops		·086	3,000	*Less* discounts, 33·3 %	. . .	16,000	
,, Manufacturing charges		·241	8,438				£32,000
,, Depreciation of plant		·057	2,000	,, Glasgow sales	. . £28,570		
,, Duty		·387	13,562	*Less* discounts, 30 % .	8,570		
		£1·142	£40,000				20,000
,, Selling charges and bad debts, viz. :—				,, Dundee sales . . £12,000			
	% to Sales.			*Less* discounts, 25 % .	3,000		
Edinburgh	10·4 £5,000						9,000
Glasgow .	10·5 3,000			,, Beer stock—Increase	. .		1,000
Dundee .	12·5 1,500					Per Excise Barrel.	
	10·75					£1·771	£62,000
		·271	9,500	,, Yeast . . .		·029	1,000
,, General management, including directors and auditors		·029	1,000	,, Draff . . .		·014	500
,, Interest		·058	2,000				
		£1·5	£52,500				
,, Income tax		·014	500				
,, Balance being divisible profit for year		·3	10,500				
		£1·814	£63,500			£1·814	£63,500

Suggested Form of Balance-sheets.

Proceeding to consider the form of a balance-sheet, the first question we meet with is the one so frequently discussed, On which side should we place the assets and on which the liabilities? It may perhaps be said that the statement need not be regarded as one into which the elements of Dr. and Cr. enter at all, and that so long as the divisions are distinctly headed by their proper titles it does not much matter on which side they are placed. It is, however, desirable for many reasons that there should be uniformity in this as in other practices of accounting. It must be admitted that the rule in this country now is to place liabilities on the left side and assets on the right, contrary to the general practice abroad and to what was in earlier days the rule here. If the balance-sheet be regarded as a mere statement of the ledger balances, then our present practice is no doubt wrong, as of course assets are Dr.

balances appearing on the left side in the ledger and liabilities Cr. balances appearing on the right side. But we must consider the heading placed upon each account. The bank account, for instance, is headed in the ledger with the name of the bank, and the bank is *debtor* for the balance at the debit of the account. The owner of the business is, however, *creditor* for that balance, and a balance-sheet is usually and properly headed with the name of the owner of the business. In taking up a balance-sheet, we read the E F Brewery Co., Ltd., Dr. for its liabilities, Cr. for its assets. To make the matter clearer, one may head the statement of liabilities "The Company Dr." and the statement of assets "The Company Cr." It seems to me that the course now generally followed in this country of placing the liabilities on the left and the assets on the right is correct in theory as well as expedient in practice.

Another question of very considerable difficulty is how to treat liabilities in security of which some asset has been specially assigned, such as a bond over heritable property. To include the amount under the heading of liabilities seems natural and proper; but this carries with it the necessity of including the assigned asset along with the free assets, which is slightly misleading even in solvent concerns and entirely so in concerns which show a deficiency. In the latter case you must, as a matter of necessity, deduct the secured debt from the value of the assigned asset before you can show correctly the real position of the business in relation to its general creditors. There are disadvantages both ways; but you must either adopt the first course, and put a note under the asset that it has been assigned in security, or the second, and put a note under the liabilities that there is a sum due under a bond which is deducted *per contra* from the asset on which it is secured. In my own opinion the balance of advantage lies with the latter alternative. Contingent debts, such as the amount of current bills receivable discounted, must also appear under liabilities in the shape of a note.

Coming now to the order of the entries under liabilities, I think it is essential that in a company balance-sheet a clear distinction should be made between liabilities to the public and liabilities to shareholders. I begin with the former, and put first the debts which are payable on demand, such as bank overdrafts or loans at call, next sundry creditors, then bills payable, then interest and other charges accrued but not yet payable, then any fixed loans or debentures. I make a summation at the end of liabilities to the public.

Under the heading of liabilities to the shareholders the paid-up capital comes first, then any reserve accounts, and lastly the balance of revenue account. It is here that any balance of profit brought forward from the preceding year is shown. The amount of liabilities to the shareholders is separately extended.

In the case of private firms the partners' capital and current accounts come in place of this section. Their shares of interest and profit are carried to their credit, so that the balances may represent exactly what is due to them at the date of the balance-sheet.

Turning to the assets side, the items composing it are sometimes arranged in priority of order according to their fixed and sometimes according to their liquid character. The latter I think the better plan on the whole. Accordingly the order I suggest is cash in bank and on hand, investments, bills receivable, book debts, unfinished contracts (if any), stock-in-trade and stores, utensils and furniture, plant, buildings, goodwill (if any), and balance of preliminary expenses (if any). I have already mentioned the necessity of showing clearly when any assets are assigned in security of debt. The form which follows illustrates the way in which I suggest that balance-sheets should be stated.

B

THE E F BREWERY CO., LIMITED.

Balance-sheet as at 31st December 1903.

The Company Dr. LIABILITIES.	Per cent.			ASSETS. *The Company Cr.*	Per cent.	
Bank balances . . .	1·6	£2,000		Cash in hand . . .	·08	£100
Current accounts . . .	3·2	4,000		Investments . . .	4	5,000
Bills payable . ; .	3	3,750		Bills receivable on hand .	·4	500
Accrued interest, &c. . .	·2	250		Accounts due by customers		
Debentures	12	15,000		—net value . . .	40	50,000
Mortgages deducted				Stocks	8·32	10,400
per contra . £5,000				Utensils and furniture .	·8	1,000
				Plant	8	10,000
Contingent liability				Buildings . . £30,000		
on bills discounted £2,000				*Less* mortgages		
				thereon . 5,000		
Total liabilities .	20	£25,000			20	25,000
Share capital 7500				Goodwill	18·4	23,000
shares fully p.c.						
paid . . 60 £75,000						
Reserve account 11·6 14,500						
Revenue account 8·4 10,500						
	80	100,000				
	100	£125,000			100	£125,000

II. PERCENTAGES.

I think this completes what I have to say on the first part of my subject, and I shall now take up the second part—viz., the use of percentages in connection with revenue accounts and balance-sheets. I promise that I shall not occupy any great length of time in dealing with it, as I shall make the accounts which I have already submitted the foundation of my remarks.

By the use of percentages in this connection I mean the system of reducing the figures in the accounts dealt with to a common standard, so that they may be capable of ready comparison one with another. The great practical value of such a comparison scarcely requires to be pointed out. Not only may the causes which have made the results of one year differ from those of previous years be readily seen, but the figures of one department or agency can be easily contrasted with those of another, and their individual influence on the whole business shown. Reliable and convenient data for the purpose of costing or valuing goods are also furnished. It is a comparatively simple matter to calculate these percentages after the revenue account and balance-sheet are prepared, and they are conveniently shown in red-ink figures in a column alongside the money column.

In Revenue Accounts.

The denominator that must be chosen for the percentages of the revenue account is a matter requiring some consideration with regard to the particular trade or manufacture. In an ordinary merchant's business the net sales, or what is generally called the turn-over, is usually taken as the basis. Indeed, where a variety of commodities is dealt in there is hardly any choice. If you refer to the form of revenue account of a merchant which I have produced, you will see how, by taking the net sales as representing 100, the percentage of the cost of goods and of gross profit is shown, and on the other side the percentages of the various expenses and, lastly, of net profit. You will also realise how much easier it is to compare the figures of one year with those of another when you have them thus reduced to percentages.

In the revenue account of a paper-mill, the best denominator is the pound weight of paper, and the figures I have shown on the form produced are the proportions per pound of paper made in pence or decimals of a penny. By making a separate summation of the manufacturing charges you get a useful average figure for checking the valuations of stock of paper.

The brewery revenue account shows the proportions per excise barrel of beer brewed. The excise barrel is the measure of the duty charged, and the number of such barrels is ascertained by reducing the actual quantity brewed to a standard specific gravity. The proportions per barrel are given in decimals of a pound sterling.

As already mentioned, it is desirable in a brewery to show the sales and selling expenses of each agency separately, and as the average rate of discount allowed at each agency is an important factor in comparing results, the amount of discounts allowed at each is also separately shown. Where this is done the percentage of discounts and selling expenses to the turn-over at each agency should also be calculated and noted on the revenue account, as I have shown in the form produced, as these furnish a most valuable means of comparison of one agency with another and one year with another.

In Balance-sheets.

The application of percentages to balance-sheets is not, perhaps, so generally serviceable as with revenue accounts, nevertheless it is valuable as enabling one readily to judge of the financial position of a concern. I have added percentages to the form of a brewery company's balance-sheet which I submitted. You will notice that its outside liabilities amount only to 20 per cent, while its liquid assets amount to 52·8 per cent; that goodwill represents 18·4 per cent of its assets, and that the shareholders provide 80 per cent of the money involved in the business, apart from secured mortgages and bills receivable discounted.

It is, however, in financial concerns that comparative percentages of the balance-sheets are most useful. In fact, they are almost necessary to enable one to make a just comparison of the financial position of such institutions. To illustrate this I have taken the recently issued balance-sheets of the Commercial Bank of Scotland and the National Bank of Scotland, two concerns very much resembling one another, the chief difference being that the National has about £2,000,000 more money on deposit than the Commercial. I have calculated in each case the percentage that each item in the balance-sheet bears to the total, and have made up a statement showing these percentages in parallel columns.

COMPARATIVE STATEMENT of the relation of each item to the total in the 1903 Balance-sheets of the National Bank and the Commercial Bank.

LIABILITIES.	Per cent. National.	Per cent. Commercial.	ASSETS.	Per cent. National.	Per cent. Commercial.
To the public—			Cash	8·1	9·8
Notes	4·6	5·9	British Government securities	5·3	6·3
Deposits . . .	80·1	78·9	Other investments . .	11·7	12·1
Drafts	·4	1·3	Loans in London in short		
Acceptances . .	3·5	1·4	notice . . .	15·9	13·7
	88·6	87·5		41	41·9
			Short loans on securities .	15·7	14·6
To the shareholders—			Bills discounted . . .	9	17·7
Capital paid up . .	5	5·7	Advances on accounts .	28·4	21·5
Reserves . . .	5·2	6	Liability for acceptances .	3·5	1·4
Undivided profit . .	1·2	·8	Heritable property . .	2·4	2·9
	100	100		100	100

An examination of this statement will show you how closely the proportions of the different heads of the balance-sheets of sound banking concerns approximate to each other, and with what precision the business of banking is carried on. You will notice that the National has 41 per cent of its assets in cash and investments, and the Commercial 41·9 per cent. The details composing this are also very much the same. In fact, the only material difference in the whole statement is that the National has 8·7 per cent less of its assets in bills discounted, and 6·9 per cent more in advances on accounts than the Commercial. The shareholders' money represents 11·4 per cent of the liabilities in the one case and 12·5 per cent in the other. It will be seen that both banks are in the eminently satisfactory position of having readily available resources equal to nearly one half of their liabilities to the public. They have also each an uncalled capital of £4,000,000.

Very interesting results are also obtained when the percentages of one year are compared with those of another, but I hope what I have shown is enough to convince you how valuable and convenient this method of calculating and contrasting percentages is, whether with reference to revenue accounts or balance-sheets.

Where it is desired to use the graphic method of presentation, diagrams can readily be drawn after the percentages have been calculated. To exhibit the features of a revenue account of any particular year, a straight line might represent the normal or average percentage of each heading in the account, and a line rising above or falling below this the percentages for the year in question. Thus one would see at a glance in which items and to what extent there had been an increase or a decrease during the year over the figures with which it is being compared.

Conclusion.

In concluding this paper let me say that I am not so vain as to suppose that the views I have expressed and the forms I have submitted are not open to much criticism. From the nature of the subject it is inevitable that some of the ideas I have advanced will not coincide with views and practices adopted in many cases after careful consideration, and followed, perhaps, for a long period of years. It is good that there should be independent thought on these matters, and I would be the last to advocate stereotyped forms or the reduction of the stating of mercantile accounts to a mechanical operation. But I think that enlightened thought applied to the subject is bound to produce less diversity of form and more frequent adherence to certain well understood and generally accepted principles of good accounting, a result which cannot but be beneficial both to the profession and the public.

Obituary.

THE LATE PETER RINTOUL, C.A.

IT is with deep regret that we announce the death of Mr Peter Rintoul, C.A., which occurred on 21st September 1933.

The death of Mr Rintoul removes one who, in addition to occupying a distinguished position within the profession, was widely recognised as one of the foremost figures in financial circles in the country. He was a Director of a large number of industrial and financial companies, and at the time of his death he was Chairman of several of these, including the Coltness Iron Company, Ltd.; R. & J. Dick, Ltd.; Shanks & Co., Ltd.; and what is known as the Scottish National Group of Investment Trust Companies. Since 1915 he had been a Director of the Union Bank of Scotland, Ltd., and he was Deputy Chairman of Stewarts and Lloyds, Ltd.

Mr Rintoul, who was born at Bothwell in 1870, came of

a family which was, through the grain merchants' business long carried on by his family, one of the best known in commercial circles in Glasgow. Educated at Glasgow Academy and Merchiston Castle School, Edinburgh, he began his accountancy apprenticeship in 1887 with the firm of J. & W. Graham and Maccall, C.A., which eventually, through changes in partnership, became the present firm of Grahams, Rintoul, Hay, Bell & Co. The firm was already an old one when Mr Rintoul entered it, having originally practised under the name of Lang & Graham about 1825.

In 1892 Mr Rintoul became a member of the Institute of Accountants and Actuaries in Glasgow, and three years later he became a partner in his firm. At the time of his death he had been senior partner for thirty years.

Throughout his life he took a particularly keen and active interest in the education of young members of the accountancy profession. He conducted the first tutorial class in book-keeping and accounting inaugurated by the Institute of Accountants and Actuaries in Glasgow, and he had served on the General Examining Board. He delivered several lectures to the Glasgow C.A. Students' Society, of which he had been Hon. President and over whose meetings he often presided. During 1928-29 and 1929-30 Mr Rintoul was President of the Institute, having previously served three terms of office on the Council, and had served for a number of years on the Tutorial Classes Committee, and at the time of his death he was Chairman of the Joint-Committee of Councils.

In recent years Mr Rintoul had devoted his time very largely to the direction of joint stock companies. His outstanding professional ability and his personal integrity led the Boards of many concerns to invite his co-operation. Only the day before his death Mr Rintoul attended meetings of the Directors of the Union Bank and of the Scottish Amicable Life Assurance Society in Glasgow. In other directions also Mr Rintoul's abilities were widely recognised, and in November of last year he was appointed by the Secretary of State for Scotland to conduct the official inquiry into objections lodged against the Milk Marketing Scheme for Scotland drafted in accordance with the compulsory provisions of the Agricultural Marketing Act of 1931.

Outwith the various activities of his professional life, Mr Rintoul took little part in public affairs. He was a member of Glasgow Chamber of Commerce and a Director of the Merchants' House, and he was also an elder in Glasgow Cathedral. From 1908 until 1915 he acted as Secretary of Glasgow Royal Infirmary, and at the time of his death he was connected with the governing bodies of both his old schools, Glasgow Academy and Merchiston Castle School. He was also a former Chairman of the Western Club, Glasgow. As a young man Mr Rintoul played Rugby for Glasgow Academicals, and in later years he found recreation in golf.

Mr Rintoul, whose home was at Kildowan, Dowanhill, Glasgow, died at Kilbryde Castle, Dunblane, which he had taken for part of the summer. About a month previously he underwent an operation, but he was thought to have made a good recovery, and he had been attending his office on one or two days each week preparatory to resuming his normal business activities. Mr Rintoul is survived by his wife and a family of three sons and two daughters.

A large congregation was present at the memorial service which was held in Glasgow Cathedral.

Peter Rintoul, 'The Treatment in the Accounts of Joint-Stock Companies
of Depreciation in Value of Assets Arising from Their Employment, and
the Duties of an Auditor Relating Thereto' (1907-8)

The subject of depreciation accounting was considered by Rintoul some years after Ker, this time also considering the duties of the auditor in relation to it. Rintoul defined depreciation more broadly than Ker, believing it to be either a decrease in value due to wear and tear or a fall in market value. He concentrated on the former as he felt there was too much variability in the latter. Later on in the paper, he widened the topic to include obsolescence as well as wear and tear (thus introducing the problem of technological change which is increasingly a problem for accountants today). Rintoul's view of depreciation was conceived within terms of historic cost accounting. Although he mentioned sale values at various times, he swept aside their use without much explanation (a habit of present-day accountants).

Much of the paper is taken up with descriptions and discussions of the factors to be considered when depreciating, and how to account for the provision. This is done, however, within the remarkably modern context of the objectives of financial statements (particularly the balance sheet; the revenue account was not defined), and definitions of wealth (capital as a stock and income as a flow) and profit (those assets which can be withdrawn leaving the 'old' wealth untouched). Rintoul was against the idea of putting current values in the balance sheet because they do not measure the utility of the assets concerned to their owner (value was defined in terms of the present value of future profits). However, although using historic cost, he would disclose the fall in market value of certain assets by way of note.

The final point to be made about this paper concerns the role of the auditor. Rintoul stated it was no duty of the auditor to see that company directors had provided for depreciation. The audit at the time was limited legally to the balance sheet, and this was not considered to be a report

147

affected by depreciation. The paper therefore is a fascinating mixture of descriptions of the then practices and attitudes, and of issues of today.

THE TREATMENT IN THE ACCOUNTS OF JOINT-STOCK COMPANIES OF DEPRECIATION IN VALUE OF ASSETS ARISING FROM THEIR EMPLOYMENT, AND THE DUTIES OF AN AUDITOR RELATING THERETO.

By PETER RINTOUL, C.A.

A PAPER read at a meeting of the Society on Thursday, 9th January 1908.

When I was asked to read a paper before your Society the subject suggested to me by your Committee was "Repairs and Renewals." A short consideration of that subject convinced me that the greater part of anything I could say upon repairs and renewals would be more suitably said in connection with a consideration of part of the much larger subject of "depreciation," and I therefore asked for and obtained permission to adopt as my subject "The Treatment of Depreciation in the Accounts of Joint-Stock Companies." The expression "joint-stock companies" is intended to include limited companies incorporated under the Companies Acts and statutory companies incorporated by special Acts of Parliament, and in dealing with this subject I do not think any distinction need be drawn between these two classes of company.

It may be necessary to make an apology for selecting a subject upon all the aspects of which so much has now been written, and upon which I cannot hope to say anything that has not been already said. Most of those to whom I speak to-night have, I suppose, the Final Examination of the Institute still before them, and belong to this

Society at least partly for the purpose of adding to the facilities for study preparatory to this examination, and my excuse for the selection of my subject is that it is one the study of which is necessary in the preparation for this examination.

The proper treatment in accounts of wear and tear and obsolescence is, moreover, forcing itself upon the attention of all accountants, and it is well that those of us who, though we may have no examinations to pass, are still students in the wider sense of the word, should consider these phases of depreciation and endeavour to formulate the laws which regulate them.

The word "depreciation" signifies the decrease in value arising from many causes, but is often loosely used as referring to decrease in value arising solely from certain of these causes. Let me start this evening by giving you a definition which covers all its meanings. It is that given by Mr. F. W. Densham in a prize essay published in *The Accountant* of 28th May 1898. I used it several years ago when I had charge of one of the tutorial classes here, and I am still unable to find a better.

"Depreciation, or decrease in value, includes not only "wear and tear, &c., of such property as plant and "machinery, but also shrinkage or falling off in market "value of such property as stock and freehold land. It "may therefore be divided into two classes, (a) of property "whose value is subject to decrease through wear and "tear, exhaustion of minerals or materials of manufacture, "effluxion of time, antiquation, supersession by improve- "ments, reduction in cost of labour and materials, &c.; "(b) of property whose value is subject to fluctuation."

The two classes into which this definition divides depreciation may be described as being—

(1) That due to exhaustion, effluxion, or expiration of value.

(2) That due to shrinkage of value.

In one of Professor Smart's essays I found the following passage, which I think will help you to understand
the depreciation which belongs to the first class. He is
speaking of accumulated wealth in its two forms ot consumption—goods and capital—and he says this wealth
has certain characteristic features.

"First it is a human creation. It is matter and force
"put into what one may call non-natural forms—that is,
"into forms which Nature is always trying to break up
"and put together in other shapes. Thus it can be kept in
"existence only by the continuous labour of man. But
"second, it is kept in existence, not as we keep sovereigns
"in a safe, but as we keep grain in the ground, by con-
"tinuous remaking. It is a sum of value, embodied in
"concrete products that preserve and transmit this value
"by continuously passing out of old into new shapes. Its
"type is the tool which wears out with use, but during its
"lifetime makes other tools and perpetuates its value in
"the new tools."

It is the class of depreciation due to this opposition by
natural forces with which my paper to-night has to deal;
but, before passing on, let me say a word or two on the
second class, that due to shrinkage in value.

I do not propose to inflict on you any theory of value,
and you must all know that the value of any thing, be it
material, labour, or money, fluctuates so that it changes
almost daily, and where a decrease in value due to this
fluctuation takes place we get this second class of depreciation. A concrete instance may best make this clear to
you, and perhaps the instance most appropriate at the
present time is the fall in the value of what are known as
"gilt-edged securities." Financial papers for some years
back have chronicled the continual depreciation in the
value of these, and have endeavoured to ascertain the
cause. Whatever has been the cause it is a fact that to-day
securities such as Consols, although they yield the same
annual income to the investor, have seriously depreciated

151

in value, and this depreciation is not due to exhaustion, effluxion, or expiry of value.

Turning now from the definition of depreciation, it may be well to dwell for a little upon the latter part of the title of this essay, "The Accounts of Joint-Stock Companies," and to get a clear idea of the aims of these accounts.

The bookkeeping of joint-stock companies aims *inter alia* at the production of two abstract statements—first, the Balance Sheet, accurately setting forth the position of the company's affairs, which the law provides must be submitted at least once a year to the shareholders; and, second, the Revenue Account, which a company is often under no statutory obligation to submit to the share-holders, although such an account must be prepared before the sums available for dividend can be arrived at with accuracy. We are taught by political economy that wealth takes two forms, viewed from the aspect of time—capital, which is a stock or fund of wealth at a given moment; and income, which is a flow of wealth during a given time. If we follow this definition closely, then the corresponding operations in bookkeeping would be, first, as regards capital, the making of an inventory of wealth at a given moment of time; and, second, as regards income, the registration of outgoing and incoming items of wealth during an interval of time.

What would the making of an inventory of wealth at a given moment of time mean in the accounts of a joint-stock company? Surely it would amount to the preparation of a sort of statement of affairs. If so, could such a statement proceed upon any sound basis, if it were expressed in terms of money values? In the case of a going concern I think we shall find it could not. Somewhere in a paper upon the "Correlation of Accountancy and Economics" Mr. Victor Branford makes the following remarks:—"Where goods are destined for consump-"tion" (which word must be given its full meaning as understood by writers on political economy) "by the

"owner, without the possibility of exchange, then their
"assessment in money value does not in any case directly
"measure, and only accidentally measures indirectly
"their utility to the user, and consequently the only valid
"and legitimate account of them as 'wealth,' from his
"point of view, must be a quantitive statement in
"physical terms" (such as ten acres of land, one ship of
certain dimensions, &c.). Let me now give a quotation
from a paper on "Depreciation" read to the Edinburgh
Students' Society in 1900 by Mr. Charles Ker, C A., of
this city.

"When the elements named ground, buildings,
"machinery have been combined they undergo a radical
"change. They are combined into a 'work,' a producing
"unit, a complicated tool, the value of which cannot be
"got at by appraising the cost of the component parts. One
"can tell what it cost, but what it is worth depends on
"different considerations altogether. When many articles
"are put together to form the unit called a factory, the
"parts lose their individuality and become atoms in a
"whole, whose value is determined not by its cost, but by
"its profit-earning power. If there be no demand for the
"whole because its profit-earning power is *nil*, its value
"is the aggregate of the value of the component parts—the
"break-up value, as it is called."

I have made these quotations and dealt somewhat fully
with this matter so as to indicate to you the questions
which would arise, and the difficulties which would have
to be overcome, if the bookkeeping of joint-stock companies were to aim at the production of any inventory of
their "wealth," in so far at least as that wealth is represented by "fixed assets."

Whether such an inventory or statement of affairs would
be of any practical value I leave to you to judge, but,
were it made, "shrinkage in value," or the depreciation
belonging to the second of our two classes, would require
to be taken into account. As a matter of fact, no such
statement in regard to "capital" wealth is required or

153

attempted by joint-stock companies, and this class of depreciation does not, therefore, fall to be considered by us to-night, except perhaps in so far as it affects the statement in a Balance Sheet of the investments representing a Reserved Fund intended to be available for meeting payments requiring to be made in cash—such as, for example, for the redemption of debt, the renewal of assets, the payment of dividends in unprofitable years, &c. Here what the Balance Sheet ought to show is the realisable value of these investments, because that is really the extent to which they are a Reserve Fund available for such purposes. In such cases the figures given in the working columns of the Balance Sheet are generally, and, after all, ought to be, the cost price of the investments, and there is no necessity or logic in debiting to Revenue Account any shrinkage in market value; and the depreciation or shrinkage in value can best be shown, and generally is shown, by means of a note made against the item in the Balance Sheet, stating the market value at the date of the Balance Sheet, or the depreciation from cost prices which has taken place to that date. An appreciation in value ought to be recorded in exactly the same way.

In company bookkeeping the only statement which deals with "wealth" as capital is the Balance Sheet, and the basis of the statement of such "wealth" in money is cost price. The right-hand side of a company's Balance Sheet shows all expenditure charged to Capital Account—that is, expenditure on fixed assets, the benefits of which are not exhausted in one year; and expenditure may quite properly appear here, even although it has not produced any asset having a realisable value. In addition there are shown on this side of the Balance Sheet the stocks and book debts which represent the working capital of the company, and the cash or other assets which represent the profits undistributed among the shareholders.

Modern industry consisting as it does of the destruction of capital in one form in order to create capital in another form, no record of a company's operations is complete

154

which takes account only of the value of the capital created and does not also show the value of capital destroyed, and not solely a statement of the cost price of the assets which originally constituted the capital. The manner in which the capital destroyed is to be ascertained and recorded is best considered by turning to the Revenue Accounts, in which are recorded the flow of "wealth," and the ultimate object of which in the bookkeeping of companies should be to arrive at the profit or loss during a given period, stated in terms of money. There can, I think, be only one definition of profit—viz., the assets which can be withdrawn from the undertaking of a company, leaving the parent or old wealth untouched. For example, a man has at the commencement of a period of time a machine as his capital, and at the end of the period that machine, plus a piece of cloth. I assume he has been able to exchange some of the cloth produced for the money equivalent of the material and wages consumed in producing the whole of the cloth, and that he has still some cloth left over. Well, the piece of cloth left over is profit only if the machine at the end of the period is of the same value to the user—market value does not come in at all—as at the beginning. This is very rarely the case, even where it has been possible to make good the effects of wear and tear by repairs or renewal of parts.

To quote again from Professor Smart, "The course of "manufacturing progress is strewn with the wrecks of fixed "capital; it presents a history of wealth produced, turned "into capital, embodied and embedded in mills and "machinery, and then superannuated and superseded— "that is, to a considerable extent lost."

The value of a machine (or means of production) to the user, as has been already stated, is the present value of its prospective earning power. In process of time, however, the earning power is gone, and then the machine is valueless as a means of production, and its value is the aggregate of the values of its component parts, usually called its scrap value. The difference between the original

155

cost price and the ultimate scrap value is part of the cost of production of the material produced by the machine, and ought to be recorded as such in any correct Revenue Accounts. This difference is the depreciation or exhaustion, effluxion, or expiry of value, to which I wish to direct your attention particularly to-night.

The principal difficulties which face us in dealing with this depreciation in the Revenue Account arise from the necessity of the preparation of periodical accounts. As you know, the Revenue Accounts of companies are in practice periodically brought together, usually yearly, but occasionally half-yearly or quarterly, into an account called the Profit and Loss Account. The sums placed to the debit of the Profit and Loss Account are the costs of the labour, material, and capital wealth consumed in obtaining the products (less the costs of that portion of the products still on hand and unsold), and the costs of sale and distribution ; the sums placed to credit are the sale prices of the products disposed of.

It is easy to arrive at the costs of sale, distribution, labour, and material, because these are usually paid for according to time, quantity, or weight ; but the proportion of the cost of buildings, machinery, and plant, or fixed capital, used or exhausted in a certain period of time, or in producing a certain quantity or weight of the finished product, cannot be accurately measured and in consequence must be estimated.

Let there be no doubt in your minds that these fixed assets are consumed in the manufacture of the products. Modern industry, as I have said already, consists of the destruction of wealth in one form to produce wealth in another form.

In some cases the buildings, plant, or machinery are allowed to wear out, but in by far the greater proportion of cases their efficient or productive life is brought to a close by advances in science and discovery, the alteration of accepted standards of efficiency, shifting of population,

and such causes. If we could wait until the use of such
fixed assets was finished before framing the Profit and
Loss Account, it would be possible to state accurately the
portion of the original cost of these assets to be included
among the outgoings as a cost of production. This we
cannot do in practice, although when the use of the asset
is finished we have the means of correcting the estimates
debited to Profit and Loss Accounts.

If, then, we must estimate this charge against the
profits, what are the factors we ought to consider? First,
undoubtedly, the cost of the building, machine, or whatever asset we are dealing with ; and, second, its probable
value when its efficient life in the particular industry is at
an end. The difference is the charge on Revenue Account
to be spread over the years of the efficient life of the asset,
and a close approximation to accuracy would be impossible, were it not that the scrap value of all but a few
classes of assets is small.

The efficient life itself must next be estimated, and
there are a number of factors which operate in affecting
the duration of this life, and which do not apply with
similar force to every asset, nor even to identical assets in
the same factory.

Firstly, there is the effect of the class of work performed.
This may affect the efficient life of an asset (1) according
to the use taken out of it, or according to the volume of
material treated by it; (2) according to the nature of
the material treated by it ; (3) in the case of machinery,
according to the speed at which it is run.

Secondly, the upkeep plays an important part in determining the effective life, and this depends not only upon
the amount of repairs and renewals of subsidiary parts
executed, but very largely upon the personality of the
individual who looks after or works the asset.

Thirdly, the expected life may be curtailed by the operation of exceptional causes—such as violent storms, serious

157

breakdowns, and disasters of various kinds. But, lastly, and independent of all these factors, the efficient life may be terminated by the progress of science and discovery, or, to put much the same thing in another way, by an alteration of the accepted standard of efficiency.

It is this tendency to obsolescence that is nowadays forcing itself upon the consideration of all accountants who have to do with trading concerns. For the vastly greater classes of productive plant this is the real cause of the termination of effective life, and no amount of expenditure upon repairs, or even renewals of parts, does much to postpone the date of that termination. Think for a moment what frequent changes have occurred in the great industrial processes during the last hundred years. Take transit. In long distance transit horsed vehicles have given place to railway vehicles, and with the development of motor vehicles the supremacy of the latter may soon be challenged. In railways themselves changes have been constantly going on—permanent way has been relaid with heavier material; bridges have been strengthened by reconstruction, in many cases long before the original bridge was worn out; stations, still as good as new, have been pulled down to admit of larger and more up-to-date ones being built; and rolling-stock has gone through a constant succession of changes in type. Again, take power. Until, say, twenty years ago steam power had no rival. To-day it is being gradually ousted from many industries by electric power, and by power produced by gas engines. Even where steam power does remain the most suitable, old methods of generating steam have given place to newer and more economical methods.

It seems to me, and I want to put this very strongly to you, that this tendency to obsolescence is the main factor in determining the estimated efficient life for the vast majority of assets. No amount of care in use, no expenditure on upkeep, and no freedom from exceptional disasters will postpone the day when advancing science takes away from our asset its earning power. That this is so renders it upon the whole more easy to make an estimate of the probable efficient life, because it is indefensible optimism to hope that it can extend to any very long period of years.

The questions to be asked and answered are (1) How long will the machine or other asset last if properly looked after, subjected to average use and with minor parts repaired or renewed? (2) Is the period so arrived at too long an effective life to assign, having in mind the tendency of all machinery, &c., to obsolescence?

Having found the sum which has to be charged against Revenue Account by deducting our estimate of scrap from the actual cost, and having also to the best of our ability made an estimate of the efficient life that may reasonably be expected, there remains the question how this charge is to be apportioned over the Revenue Accounts relative to the years of this efficient life.

The method which obviously suggests itself is the simple one of spreading the charge equally over these years which has the practical advantage of simplicity; and while at first sight this looks a mere rule of thumb method, it can be defended upon theoretical grounds, certainly in those cases where the limit of life is fixed by the probability of obsolescence. It seems, indeed, quite a fair assumption that the tendency to obsolescence affects the subject equally in each year. Where, however, the limit of life will be reached before there is any probability of obsolescence, some other apportionment may be more correct. The apportionment may be according to distance traversed, time in operation, or quantities produced in each year; and, indeed, in many cases methods apparently less logical may fairly be adopted, but in all cases the whole charge should be made against the Revenue Accounts of those years which constitute the efficient or useful life of the asset, and these years alone. In practice a very frequent method is to charge against Revenue Account a percentage of the original cost of the asset, or of that cost as decreased by the sums previously so charged. My own opinion is that the very general adoption of this

H

method tends towards a fixing of these percentages without a proper consideration of the real factors, which I have just tried to indicate to you, as governing the amount of depreciation. It becomes, indeed, too much accepted as a fact that, say in the case of machinery, 10 per cent. on cost is a fair depreciation provision.

There is one other method in pretty general use, and that is to charge renewals against Revenue Account. The origin of this practice seems to have been the old-fashioned belief that buildings, plant, and machinery could have an unlimited efficient life. In practice, however, a machine is hardly ever replaced by an identical one; a building even destroyed, say, by fire is never re-erected precisely as it existed at first. But if the expenditure is sufficient in amount, this method would suit in such cases as, say, a stock of tramway cars. The principal matter, after all, is to get the proper debit made in Revenue Account for the use (or exhaustion or consumption) of the fixed assets, and whether this debit is obtained by charging the amount of actual expenditure on renewals or not is a minor matter If the amount spent on renewals, however, is not equivalent to the proper charge for such use (or consumption), and no depreciation charge is made to bring the total debit up to the proper charge, then a true profit will not be arrived at.

It is perhaps necessary to say a word upon the selection of the unit in respect of which an efficient life is to be calculated, in order to arrive at a depreciation charge, because this is a matter which must be considered, and upon which depends the legitimacy of charging expenditure upon renewals to a fund reserved for renewals and created by transfers of estimated depreciation charges from Revenue Account. In a steamship, for example, the engines, boiler, and hull will all have different efficient lives, and it may be advisable to regard the steamship as composed of three units, and the depreciation charge therefore as the sum of three amounts separately calculated upon different assumptions; but in such a case it must

160

not be forgotten that, in the end, all three units become obsolete as one unit. Thus, suppose we begin from the assumptions that boilers will last ten years, engines fifteen, and hull thirty ; if we can assume that the effective life of the steamer as a whole will be thirty years, there is no difficulty, as we shall exhaust three sets of boilers and two sets of engines in that time.

But if thirty years is too long a life to assume for the particular use to which we intend to put the steamer—and this will depend upon such considerations as whether it is to be used as an ocean grey-hound or as a tramp—the problem is not so easy. We may best deal with it by taking as the efficient life the shortest life of the three units, that is, ten years. This will probably mean that the scrap value of the hull and engines, and what remains of the boilers, may be put fairly high, because the steamer, though out of date for one particular trade, may still suit another. In this case we would cal-culate our depreciation provisions upon all three units, allowing a life of ten years. If at the end of these ten years the steamer is still good for trade, the boilers may be renewed, and the original cost of the old boilers written off against the fund reserved to meet depreciation, and a fresh life and reduced scrap value estimated, bearing in mind that the engines will not now be good for more than five years.

The renewal of minor parts, if it has to be frequently made during the assumed lifetime, should be charged as repairs, and, of course, such minor parts ought not to be regarded as units. If infrequently made, it should be pro-vided for by laying aside each year in fair proportions a Renewal Fund for these minor parts.

Having now treated of the factors necessary to be con-sidered in estimating the charge for depreciation, let us consider the entries to be made in the books to record that charge. There will be debit and credit entries amounting to the same total. With the debit entries there is no option ; they must be recorded in some account representing a

H 2

branch of the Profit and Loss Account, as part of the cost of production ; but with the credit entries there are clearly two alternatives, either (1) to carry the amount to the credit of an account as a provision against the depreciation of the fixed assets, from which may be transferred the amounts necessary to provide the ascertained depreciation in the case of individual items, such as machines, &c., as these are put out of use and scrapped ; or (2) to reduce the figures representing particular assets by sums amounting in total to the charge on Revenue Account.

I do not think we need spend much time discussing which of these two methods is the more correct, although in theory the creation of this earmarked provision or Reserve Account is probably the better, where we are dealing with figures based upon estimates alone. The result in such a case is that fixed assets always appear in the Balance Sheet at cost, and on the other side is shown the provision made to date against the final loss which must be borne when they have become of value as scrap only. In the second case the figures in the Balance Sheet repre-sent the amount of expenditure on fixed assets capitalised and carried forward to be charged upon the profits or revenue of future years, with this qualification, that there will generally be included in these figures sums which will be recovered by realisation of scrap, and the amount of which therefore will form no charge to Revenue Account.

It may be of interest that I should quote the views expressed upon this subject by the Committee which reported in July last as to the form of accounts of local authorities.

"We are strongly of opinion that original cost, when "known, is the only satisfactory basis for the statement of "the values of assets on the Balance Sheets ; and this view "is supported by the evidence given, and is, in fact, acted "upon by almost all local authorities. Any system of "periodical valuation, apart from the question of the "expense involved, would, in our opinion, be open to

162

"serious objection: it would be more liable to variation
"than the usual method, while the Balance Sheet would
"lose one of its most important characteristics as a
"historical record of the actual cost of the assets.

"There is, however, considerable divergency of practice
"in writing off wasting assets, the permanent retention of
"which on the Balance Sheets would be undesirable; and
"a necessity thus exists for regulations under which a
"uniform method of dealing therewith may be ensured.

"The Committee consider that, in regard to all capital
"assets having an abiding or realisable value, it is
"desirable to preserve a current historical account. For
"this purpose the original cost of such assets should be
"shown on the Balance Sheets from year to year, and *per
contra the loans and the repayments (or other provisions,
"if any) in respect thereof.

"Only in the case of an asset passing out of possession,
"or becoming valueless, would its original cost on the one
"hand, and on the other the provision already made for
"the redemption of debt, disappear from the accounts.

"In the case of expenditure out of borrowed moneys
"upon works such as street improvements, paving, or
"sewers, or for such matters as the promotion of Bills in
"Parliament, or compensations, the cost of which has to
"be borne by the rates over a sanctioned number of years
"and may therefore be described as deferred expenditure,
"it is obvious that it cannot be regarded as being in the
"same category with expenditure which has produced
"abiding or realisable assets. Consequently the indefinite
"retention of the original costs of such items would be
"misleading and without compensating advantage. The
"Committee consider, therefore, that under each head of
"such expenditure the amount shown in the Balance Sheet
"should be that portion of the original cost which would
"remain after deducting the loan repayments or other pro-
"visions, and that the liability shown *per contra* should be
"only the outstanding unpaid amounts of the loans.

"But, on the other hand, as regards each separate
"trading undertaking, the whole of the assets and capital
"outlays of the local authority should be shown in the
"Balance Sheet at their original cost, and *per contra* the
"full amounts of the loans and the provision for their
"repayment."

I am using the word "depreciation" to-night because it
is that most usually employed to designate the charge on
revenue, of which I am treating, but one has to admit that
it is a word apt to convey a wrong significance. One recent
writer has used the expression "expired capital outlay,"
which undoubtedly more accurately indicates the nature of
the charge; but, on the other hand, it is not a phrase in
general use.

To this point I have dealt with the question from the
only point of view that is theoretically correct. I now wish
to explain how it comes that so many companies do not
attempt to frame their accounts upon this basis. You are
all, of course, familiar with the constitution of a joint-
stock company. There is, first of all, the fund contributed
by the shareholders and called the share capital, or often,
and to my mind rather confusingly called "the capital."
This is a fund of money which may be employed in
making certain expenditure, and there is no obligation
upon anyone that it be kept up to its original value or
returned to the shareholders at any time. There is, therefore, no legal obligation to provide out of revenue depreciation of capital, even in so far as that arises solely from
use. Capital which has become dead or valueless is not
required to be replaced from revenue, although where
this is not done it must be clear that the rate of return on
the capital must, as time goes on, dwindle away, and on
what are called "junior securities," where such exist, may
vanish. Numerous examples could be given, and a very
clear illustration is to be found in the accounts of the
Central London Railway Company in connection with the
loss on realisation of certain locomotives broken up as
unsuitable for modern conditions. Here everything is

164

strictly legal, and yet expenditure which should theoretically have gone against revenue as a necessary outlay
in earning the profits has not been so charged.

The reason for not making a charge for depreciation is
in certain other cases different, and is best illustrated by
what is known as a single-ship company—that is, a company owning one ship. Such companies rarely set aside
any provision for depreciation, because it is argued that
it is better to pay over all cash earnings to the shareholders
and let them provide from these depreciation against the
ultimate and inevitable drop in the value of the assets,
and which will be reflected in the value of their shares,
rather than to retain a large sum which would be of no use
to the company, and the investment of which would create
unnecessary difficuities. In such cases, and in all cases
where depreciation is not wholly charged against profits,
the dividends consist not solely of the economic profits,
but are in part a return of capital, and should be so
regarded by the shareholders.

But while it is without doubt our duty as accountants in
the broad meaning of the word to study the phenomena of
depreciation from all possible points of view, what in
practice most concerns us is the duty of an auditor in
regard to the amount provided from profits for depreciation or expired capital outlay, and the manner of stating
same in the Balance Sheet of a company.

An auditor is a person appointed to test the correctness
of entries in accounts, and to certify that abstract statements of the same, in the majority of cases the Balance
Sheets only, correctly represent the result of these entries.

He is virtually in the position of a Judge, but he is a
Judge who has to make his decisions on questions of fact
without being able to order before him all the evidence
which might be necessary to arrive at an absolute
assurance as to the position of affairs—evidence which in
many cases would have to be that of parties unconnected

165

with the concern whose Balance Sheet and accounts were under audit.

His duties are defined by the Companies Clauses Act, 1845; the Railway Clauses Act, 1867; the Building Societies Act, 1894; and the Companies Act, 1900, the provisions of the last of which, however, will soon give place to those of the Companies Act, 1907.

Now, as regards audits under the Companies Act, the first important thing to be noticed is that the Balance Sheet is not framed by the auditor, but by the directors; and it is a most desirable advance which has been made in the Companies Act, 1907, and one which should emphasise the fact that the directors are primarily responsible for every figure in the Balance Sheet, and for the way in which that document is stated, that they are now to sign the Balance Sheet issued to the shareholders. The next point to be noted is that the only certificate an auditor is called on to give is in regard to the Balance Sheet. This certificate is one as to fact—that the Balance Sheet is correct, and drawn up so as to give a full and correct view of the company's affairs as at a certain date.

An auditor may also report to the shareholders anything that he considers they ought to know in connection with the accounts.

Where the auditor is a professional accountant, and therefore presumably acquainted theoretically with the factors occasioning depreciation of assets, he generally does ascertain whether these factors have been recognised and considered, and whether an allowance for depreciation based upon the results of such consideration has been made; and where they have not been properly considered he does generally press upon the directors the extreme desirability of a full and careful consideration of all the factors, and the propriety of charging against profits from time to time a fair sum to meet the exhaustion or expiry of value that is taking place. But in doing this he goes beyond the statutory duties imposed on him. He is not in

166

any way responsible to the shareholders and creditors of
the company for the policy pursued by the directors in the
management of the company's affairs, and if they decide
to make an inadequate provision for this depreciation, or
none, he is in no position to insist on such a provision
being made. He is bound, however, to see that the items
in the Balance Sheet are so stated that the average business man can tell that provision has been made, or that no
such provision has been made. This latter is very simply
achieved if against each item of fixed asset in the Balance
Sheet it is stated that such item appears at cost. Where
an allowance for depreciation of expired capital outlay
has been made, and is shown as a deduction from the value
of the asset, no question as to its sufficiency or otherwise
arises, or has to be decided by the auditor when framing
his certificate, if the balance of cost still treated as an
asset is described so as to show that it is expenditure
capitalised and carried forward to be charged against the
profits of future years. In such a case persons reading the
Balance Sheet can form their own opinion as to the depreciation provided, although, owing to the absence of details
from most abstracts of accounts, they can only do so upon
some rough and ready plan. Where the directors refuse
to state the facts sufficiently clearly, then the auditor is
bound to make them clear in his report to the shareholders.
In fact, what he is there for is—not to secure that anything which in his opinion is correct is done, but that what
has been done is truly and correctly stated. In cases where
the figures that appear against fixed assets are unqualified,
the assumption must be that these figures are fair valuations on the basis of a going concern ; and the auditor who
is of opinion that factors occasioning depreciation have not
been considered, and that proper allowance has not been
made in arriving at these figures, is undoubtedly to be
blamed if he does not report his opinions to the shareholders, even if he is in no danger of incurring legal
penalties by keeping silence.

One word in conclusion. I am well aware I have broken
no new ground in what I have said to-night, and I am

painfully conscious that I have not been able to put the
subject before you in the coherent and logical manner
which has been my ideal. If, however, anything I have
said has the result of making you, or of making some of
you, think out for yourselves this question of depreciation
—going right down to bed-rock principle, and not dismiss-
ing it with a study of tables of standard rates of depreciation such as one sees given in many books on accounting—I shall feel I have not been altogether unsuccessful
to-night.

———

A hearty vote of thanks was accorded to Mr. Rintoul, on
the motion of Mr. Alexander Moore, Junr., C.A.

THE LATE JOHN B. WARDHAUGH, C.A.

We regret to announce the death on March 27 of Mr John B. Wardhaugh, C.A., senior partner of Messrs Wardhaugh & McVean, C.A., 194 West Regent Street, Glasgow. After completing his apprenticeship with Messrs Alexander Sloan & Co., C.A., Glasgow, Mr Wardhaugh commenced business on his own account, and two years ago he celebrated his jubilee as a practising accountant.

Mr Wardhaugh was widely known in accounting circles, largely through his interest in the tutorial activities of the Institute, and for the authorship of professional books. For the long period of forty-six years he tutored candidates for the final examination of The Chartered Accountants of Scotland, the last twenty-eight years being under the auspices of the Institute. In 1944 his valued services to the profession were recognised when he was the recipient of a presentation from the Glasgow members. It is not an exaggeration to say that no one has done more for the apprentice chartered accountant in Scotland than Mr Wardhaugh.

He was the author of "The Accountants' Digest" which became a standard work, and was used not only by qualified members, but by students in preparation for their examinations. The sections of "The Accountants' Digest" dealing with Company Law and Accounts, Trust Law and Accounts and Bankruptcy were later published as separate text books.

Mr Wardhaugh was interested not only in the publication of books on professional matters, but he was widely read in general literature. His appointment as convener of the Library Committee in Glasgow was one which appealed to him, and he held that office for a period of twenty-one years. Before he relinquished the convenership in 1955, the re-cataloguing of the library in Glasgow was carried out, under his personal supervision.

He was a member of Council of The Institute of Accountants and Actuaries in Glasgow (now merged in The Institute of Chartered Accountants of Scotland) from 1930 to 1934, and served for some years as a director of The Accountants' Publishing Co. Ltd., the publishers of THE ACCOUNTANTS' MAGAZINE.

Mr Wardhaugh had many interests outwith the profession. He was Honorary Secretary and Treasurer of the Town and Country Planning Association (Scottish Section) for a number of years, and up to the time of his death acted as Honorary Treasurer. He was interested in water-colour painting and was regarded as an authority on philately, having been President of the Caledonian Philatelic Society in the year 1947-48. At the date of his death, he was Honorary Vice-President of the Glasgow Civic Society.

Mr Wardhaugh was an elder of Giffnock Orchardhill Church, a former Vice-Chairman of the First District Council of Renfrewshire, and a member of Whitecraigs Golf Club. He is survived by twin daughters, one of whom, Miss Susie Wardhaugh, became a chartered accountant and was in partnership with her father until she married Mr William H. Marshall, now a partner in the firm.

Mr Wardhaugh's death is mourned not only by his colleagues in the profession, but by a large circle of business and personal friends, by whom he was held in the highest esteem.

John B. Wardhaugh, 'The Legal Limitations of an Auditor's Duties
and Responsibilities' (1908-9)

Wardhaugh was best known for his work on Scottish bankruptcy and trust
accounting. However, this paper represents a significant statement of the
aims and duties of the company auditor, and reflected the growing maturity
of the audit function in the twenty years since the lecture given by
Hutton. Wardhaugh's lecture made explicit the 'ground rules' which had or
were being laid down for the auditor then and for many decades to come.

Wardhaugh advised his student audience of the general role of the
auditor - that is, as a 'check' on company directors, whilst retaining in
his approach a reasonable balance between the latter and the shareholders.
The auditor was not to be bound by the letter of the law, and Wardhaugh
suggested that the auditor could give advice to management when necessary.
Interestingly, he saw the independence of the auditor impaired if the
latter was responsible for writing up the company's books and records as
well as auditing them - that is, unless the former function had been
sanctioned by the shareholders.

The audit report was regarded by Wardhaugh as an important document
and, with no prescribed format, he advocated lengthy reports (particularly
when these contained audit qualifications). Much of the lecture described
the means by which these reports should be supported by available evidence -
the concept of reasonable care and skill in the circumstances being central
to this theme.

Other aspects of the then audit practice, and particularly its related
case law, were dealt with by Wardhaugh - the reliance on company officials
for verification of such matters as inventories and irrecoverable debts;
the acceptability of secret reserves if allowed in the company's regulations;
and the lack of an accepted practice of depreciation.

THE LEGAL LIMITATIONS OF AN AUDITOR'S DUTIES AND RESPONSIBILITIES.

By JOHN B. WARDHAUGH, C.A., Glasgow.

Read to the Chartered Accountants Students' Society of Edinburgh on 18th November 1908.

I SHOULD like to make it perfectly clear that while attempting in this paper to define the legal limitations of an auditor's duty and responsibility, I do not for one moment suggest that an auditor will fulfil the high claims of his honourable profession if he rests content with compliance with the mere letter of the law. An auditor's duties are too multifarious to be bounded by statutory restrictions or legal limitations. With his thorough knowledge of accounts and the experience of men and affairs gained from his association with a large variety of businesses, he is frequently in a position to suggest improvements in administration, and even to give advice on matters of general policy which is entirely outwith the legal requirements of his position. I need hardly remark that the high respect in which our profession is presently held is in a large measure due to the broad view which most accountants take of their duty, and I think you will agree with me that it is just as we get away from calculating carefulness and become an intelligent factor in the progress of the various businesses for which we act, that we derive true pleasure from our work, and have the

A

173

satisfaction of knowing that we are doing something more than acting solely as the brake upon the industrial machine. Keeping this in view, however, it may be profitable for us to consider what are the fundamental principles which have guided the Courts in determining the minimum measure of an auditor's duty. Most of the cases which have come before the Court have had reference to auditors of public companies. Let us therefore consider shortly the essential difference between the position of a public company auditor and an auditor to a private firm.

In the case of a limited company, the shareholders (who may be described as the sleeping partners in the concern) are far removed from the management, the latter being devolved upon directors. The auditor occupies a sort of judicial position between the shareholders and the directors, and while no doubt exercising a check upon the other officials of the company, and thus assisting the directors, his primary duty is to act as a check upon the latter. He therefore at times occupies an exceedingly delicate position, having on the one hand to beware of interfering with the directors in matters of policy, and on the other hand to beware that he does not incur liability through failing to advise the shareholders of the true financial position of the company, or of any breach of its constitution, or of the statutes affecting the accounts.

In the audit of a private firm's books there may be matters which the auditor would feel justified in passing without comment, in view of the fact that the partners in the business take an active part in the management and are necessarily aware of the position, while the same matters would call for reference in a report to shareholders in a limited company, where the parties interested have no immediate control of the management nor any direct means of keeping themselves fully advised as to what is going on. Again, it may be possible to get the individual consent of the partners in a private firm on any matter of accounting which the auditor has reason to question, while in a limited company as a rule such a course is impracticable.

Then a private firm is free from statutory restrictions as

to accounting, whereas the Companies Acts have many provisions relating to the accounting of public companies— *e.g.*, to mention only a few at random, the provision that a company cannot reduce its share capital without the necessary consents; the provision of Table A in regard to payment of dividends; the provisions of the Companies Act, 1900, in regard to the application of capital monies in paying brokerages and commissions.

The responsible duties of the auditor to a public company and the time necessarily occupied in the audit are frequently not fully appreciated by the shareholders who may see only the short docquet on the accounts, but the provisions of the Companies Act, 1907, make it possible for the auditor, without overstepping the apparent limit of his duties, to report at length to the shareholders, and this, while adding somewhat to the responsibilities of the position, is a right which I think the auditor should freely embrace and thus render customary.

Proceeding now to consider the nature of an auditor's liability, we have, at the outset, to distinguish between criminal liability and civil liability; the former need detain us only a short time. To establish criminal liability it is necessary to prove not only that the auditor has been careless or negligent in the performance of his duties, but also that he has been fraudulently so. It must be proved that he has wilfully misrepresented the position. Auditors to public companies may be prosecuted under sect. 84 of the Larceny Act, 1861 (24 & 25 Vict. c. 96), which provides that—

Whosoever being a director, manager, or public officer of any body corporate or public company shall make, circulate, or publish, or concur in making, circulating, or publishing any written statement or account which he shall know to be false in any material particular, with intent to deceive or defraud any member, shareholder, or creditor of such body corporate or public company, or with intent to induce any person to become a shareholder or partner therein, or to entrust or advance any property to such body corporate or public company, or to enter into any security for the benefit thereof, shall be guilty of a misdemeanour, and being convicted thereof shall be liable at the discretion of the

Court to any of the punishments which the Court may award as hereinbefore last mentioned.

You will note the words "intent to deceive or defraud any member, shareholder, or creditor." It is therefore necessary under this section to prove not only that the auditor has knowingly published a false statement, but that he did so with intent to deceive a shareholder or creditor. What amounts to "intent to deceive" may be a fine point to determine, and the summing up of the judge in the Whittaker Wright case, 1904, should be read in this connection (Accountant Law Reports, 1904, p. 13).

Action may also be taken against an auditor under sect. 28 of the Companies Act, 1900. This section provides that any person knowingly making a false statement shall be liable on conviction on indictment to imprisonment for a term not exceeding two years, and on summary conviction to imprisonment for a term not exceeding four months, in either case with or without hard labour, and to a fine in lieu of or in addition to such imprisonment. This section, however, applies only to documents required for the purposes of the Companies Act, 1900. It will be noticed, however, that it is not necessary to prove "intent to deceive"; the mere fact that the person knows the statement to be false is sufficient.

Some years ago a Bill was introduced into Parliament containing a provision similar to the above, but making it apply to any written statement relating to the financial affairs or property of a company. The Bill, however, did not become law.

Almost the first and only instance of criminal conviction in Great Britain was the well-known case of Dumbell's Banking Company, Ltd., Isle of Man (Accountant L. R., 1900, p. 181). The action was raised under sect. 221 of the Manx Criminal Code, 1872, the terms of which I understand are identical with the terms of the Larceny Act, above quoted. The auditors had certified as correct a balance-sheet in which there was a sum stated as cash in hand which, to their knowledge, was made up of, *inter alia*, £15,000 of unissued notes and a loan of £65,000 in respect of which no cash had ever been paid, the account being squared by a corresponding liability; further, they had allowed large overdrafts which were confessedly and hopelessly bad to appear as good debts in the balance-sheet year after year. It is true that the auditors had on more than one occasion remonstrated ineffectually with the managers as to these, but they allowed the balance-sheet to go forward to the shareholders docquetted without qualification. The jury returned a verdict of guilty, and the prisoners were sentenced to various terms of imprisonment, the auditors to twelve and six months' hard labour respectively.

Now all this sounds very alarming, but such cases are happily rare, and can only arise where there is wilful fraud. An auditor who acts honestly need not fear criminal responsibility; the auditor who acts dishonestly is a person for whom we have no sympathy.

We come now, however, to the question of civil liability. Here there is much to make an ignorant auditor hesitate, but nothing to daunt a fully qualified practitioner.

It has been decided that the auditor appointed by a company is a regular officer of the company and is liable to the summary remedies provided by the Act of 1862 against the officers of the company. Thus under sect. 165 the Court may in Scotland, on application of the liquidator or any creditor or contributory, examine into the auditor's conduct and compel him to repay any monies for which he has become liable, together with interest, or to pay a sum in name of damages. As regards England this section was repealed by the Companies Winding Up Act, 1890. Actions in England are therefore now taken under sect. 10 of the latter Act.

It has been held that under this mode of proceeding it must be established that there has been breach of duty that has resulted in some actual diminution of the assets of the company (Liverpool and Wigan Supply Association, Ltd., in Liverpool Court of Bankruptcy—'Acc. Mag.,' 1907, p. 460). How far, if at all, an auditor may be liable for negligence where such has not involved any loss of assets to the company was not decided. The action was for damages under sect. 10 of the Companies Winding Up Act, 1890.

It was alleged here that book debts had been repeatedly included as assets, which the auditor, by the exercise of reasonable care, might have ascertained were worthless. His Honour, Judge Thomas, said—

> In this case I think that the auditor was negligent in the sense that he relied on statements made to him by the directors, and did not put in his certificate the fact that he was relying on the statements of the directors. . . . But none of these acts appear to me to have diminished the assets of the company as such. What may have happened is that the creditors went on dealing with the company longer than they otherwise would have done; but I have no evidence before me that satisfies me that even that was the case, and with respect to creditors, this is not the proper form of procedure, if they have any remedy at all.

The question, therefore, appears to be still open as to whether an action will lie against the auditor on the part of creditors where they alone have suffered loss. The question to be determined, so far as I can see, is whether the auditor is in a position of trust towards the creditors. In the case of a private firm, I should say he certainly is not, unless there happens to be any expressed or implied contract with the creditors. In the case of a limited company the position is somewhat different, because it is now, under the Act of 1907, part of the obligation incurred in receiving the benefit of limited liability that the company shall for the benefit of the public lodge with the Registrar of Joint Stock Companies a duly certified balance-sheet. It is possible, therefore, that creditors of a company may have a right of action, even although there is no loss of assets to the company.

To determine the auditor's civil responsibility we must consider what is the measure of his duty. In the words of Lord Justice Lindley—

> It is no part of an auditor's duty to give advice either to directors or shareholders as to what they ought to do. His business is to ascertain and state the true financial position of the company at the time of the audit, and his duty is confined to that.

But then comes the question: How is he to ascertain such position? The answer is: By examining the books of the company. But he does not discharge his duty by doing this without inquiry and without taking any trouble to see that the books of the company themselves show the company's true position. He must take reasonable care to ascertain that they do. Unless he does this his duty will be worse than a farce. Assuming the books to be so kept as to show the true position of the company, the auditor has to frame a balance-sheet showing that position according to the books, and to certify that the balance-sheet presented is correct in that sense. An auditor, however, is not bound to do more than exercise reasonable care and skill in making inquiries and investigations. He is not an insurer; he does not guarantee that the books do correctly show the true position of the company's affairs. . . . Such I take to be the duty of the auditor. He must be honest—that is, he must not certify what he does not believe to be true, and he must take reasonable care and skill before he believes that what he certifies is true.—(*In re* London and General Bank. Acct. L. R., 1895, p. 173.)

This, then, I would ask you to note as the first point—"reasonable care and skill." What amounts to this can only be determined on a review of the whole circumstances of each case.

The main determining circumstance is "suspicion." Has the auditor reason to be suspicious? Then he must probe matters to the bottom.

In the Kingston Cotton Mills case, 1896, 2 Ch. 279, the *dicta* of Lord Justice Lopes are instructive.

It is the duty of an auditor to bring to bear upon the work he has to perform that skill, care, and caution which a reasonably competent, careful, and cautious auditor would use. An auditor [he says] is not bound to be a detective, or, as has been said, to approach his work with suspicion or with a foregone conclusion that there is something wrong. He is a "watch-dog," but not a "bloodhound." If there is anything calculated to excite suspicion, he should probe it to the bottom, but in the absence of anything of that kind, he is only bound to be reasonably cautious and careful. Auditors [he says] must not be made liable for not tracking out ingenious and carefully laid schemes of fraud when there is nothing to arouse their suspicion.

How far an auditor's suspicion is to be deemed to have

been aroused by the books he has examined will be an interesting point to decide, but in the meantime it is instructive to note the remarks of Lord Davey. Speaking as a member of the select committee appointed by the House of Lords in 1896 to inquire into Company Law amendment, he remarked, "Is not the sounder principle this—that the auditor is bound to know everything the books tell him, to have all the suspicions that the books suggest, and to make all the inferences to what he finds the books would lead him?"

Thus in the case of the Irish Woollen Company, Ltd. (*infra*), it appeared that the ledger accounts had been dealt with in a suspicious manner which was bound to have come to the notice of the auditor had he exercised reasonable care, and that, having come to his knowledge, he was bound to have pursued the matter to its foundation and exercised a fuller check than ordinary circumstances would require. You will therefore observe that suspicious circumstances increase the auditor's responsibility.

Another important circumstance in determining what is reasonable care and skill may be the auditor's knowledge that special reliance has been placed upon him. Thus the fact that it had been left to the auditor to say what books a company ought to keep, and that it was not a business to which any of the directors could have been expected to devote anything like their whole time, a business where, to the auditor's own knowledge, the clerical staff was cut down to a very low point, and where in consideration of a monthly audit the auditor's fee had been increased—circumstances from which the auditor must have known that there was more reliance placed upon him and upon the audit than might be expected in the case of an ordinary company—was held to be an element in determining what in that case was the measure of reasonable care and skill. It may be observed here in passing that the amount of the auditor's remuneration is no factor in determining his responsibilities. His duty, if he considers the remuneration too small, is to refuse the appointment.

Another element which must be taken into consideration

is the facilities at the auditor's hands for checking the transactions of the company. Thus, it being the practice in the woollen trade to require from creditors a statement of their accounts at the balancing period, and the auditor having ample time for the audit, it was decided that, given suspicious circumstances, he should have called for these statements and availed himself of this means of checking the outstanding liabilities. Opinions differ as to how far in ordinary circumstances an auditor may be liable in this regard. It is expedient, however, that he ask for the statements and examine a number of them. In practice I find the examination of the creditors' statements brings to light many points which would otherwise be lost sight of.

Another circumstance to be reckoned with may be the provisions of the articles of association of the company. It is no excuse for an auditor to say that he has not seen the articles. His duties may be regulated thereby, and it should be one of his first steps to possess himself of a copy. If there are no articles it will be observed that Table A (the original or the revised as the case may be) will apply unless expressly excluded. It is the duty of the auditor to ascertain this and see that the terms of the articles are complied with. Further, the auditor is presumed to have knowledge of the provisions of the various Acts of Parliament affecting his particular duties, and the articles of association cannot absolve him from such obligations.

The terms of the special contract with the auditor, expressed or implied, may have an important bearing on the interpretation of reasonable care and skill. In the case of Wilde and others *v.* Cape and Dalgleish, 'Times,' 28th May 1897, the auditor was by mutual arrangement held liable for half losses occasioned by his not fulfilling his contract to make a complete audit of his clients' books. It had been proved that his failure was owing to a misunderstanding on his part as to the existence of such a contract. To be perfectly safe in undertaking a restricted or partial audit, the auditor should see that the instructions are clearly and definitely committed to writing, and also that, in documents subsequently issued—*e.g.*, in his statement of fee—the work is not referred to in such terms as to suggest a complete audit. (Smith *v.* Sheard, 1906, 34, Acct. L. R., p. 65.) It may be difficult in all cases to get written instructions, but it is open to the auditor before entering upon his duties to write to his clients acknowledging the appointment and setting forth the terms of the arrangement, and such a letter might be of considerable weight in the event of proceedings being subsequently instituted against him. It is also advisable to make perfectly clear in the docquet the extent to which the audit has been restricted.

The auditor may render himself liable by undue delay in carrying out the audit. In the case of Martin *v.* Isitt (Acct. L. R., 1898, p. 41), it appeared that the auditors had undertaken to check the books monthly, but that in 1896 the work had been so delayed that in December of that year they were still engaged on the accounts for the summer months. Several defences were adduced, but ultimately the defenders practically admitted liability by consenting to a judgment against them for the share of the loss attributable to the delay.

A further important consideration is the purpose for which the audit is expressly instituted. This was emphasised by the decision in Teacher *v.* Calder, H. L., 24th July 1899 ('Acc. Mag.,' vol. iii. p. 584). The particulars were that Teacher and Calder had made an agreement whereby in respect of an advance the former was to receive 5 per cent interest and half profits after Calder had taken 25 per cent as manager's salary, the accounts to be annually audited, the docquet to be binding upon both parties. In the action Teacher averred that the auditors had acted in ignorance of the existence of the agreement, and that therefore the audit was not binding upon the parties, and he claimed that the accounts be submitted to an accountant for revision. The First Division dismissed the action, but on appeal the House of Lords reversed this judgment, holding that a mutual mistake as to the auditor's knowledge of the agreement, for which neither of the parties to it was responsible, was as good a ground in Scots Law for disregarding the audit and allowing an action as if the mistake had been occasioned by the fault or negligence of one of the parties. The auditor should therefore ascertain the real object of the audit, and having done so he will be responsible for the exercise of reasonable care in making the audit effectual. It may be that the audit is instituted with a view to acting as a check upon suspected fraud, and in such a case it is obvious that the amount of care necessary, at least in verifying the accuracy of the book entries, would be greatly increased.

These, then, are some of the chief circumstances qualifying the meaning of this oft-repeated phrase, "reasonable care and skill," — viz., suspicion, special reliance placed upon auditors, facilities for audit, provisions of Articles of Company and Statutes, special contract with auditor, specified object of audit. It only remains to remark here that in all cases the auditor should beware of being hurried into signing the balance-sheet before he has completed the audit to his own satisfaction.

Turn with me now to consider for a little the auditor's responsibility for the form or nature of his docquet or report and for the submission thereof to the shareholders.

Much discussion has raged round the question how far qualifying phrases in an auditor's docquet are effectual to protect him. No one now thinks that the phrase "as shown by the books of the company" has any effect in protecting an auditor who has not been careful to take the necessary evidence outside of the accounts. Were it necessary to remove any doubt on this point, the terms of sect. 19 of the Companies Act, 1907, set the matter at rest. It is now required of auditors that they certify that the balance-sheet is correct not only as shown by the books but also "according to the best of their information and the explanations given to them." Previous to the 1907 Act, however, the courts had made it perfectly clear that the phrase was only introduced into docquets to relieve the auditor from any responsibility as to affairs of the company kept out of the books and concealed from them, and not to confine the docquet to a mere statement of the correspondence of the balance-sheet with the entries in the books.

An auditor does not discharge his duties by examining the books without taking any trouble to see that the books of the company themselves show the company's true position; he must take reasonable care to ascertain that they do. He is not, however, legally bound to seek for knowledge outside the company, as, for example, to communicate with customers or creditors, however desirable such a course may be in certain circumstances.

In the case of the London and General Bank, Ltd., 1895, 2 Ch. 673, the auditor qualified his docquet to the effect—"The value of the assets as shown on the balance-sheet is dependent upon realisation." A fully detailed report had been made to the directors showing the very unsatisfactory state of certain loans and securities, and the auditors were held to have failed in the discharge of their duties in certifying the balance-sheet without any reference to the report which had been laid before the directors and with no other warning than was conveyed by the above words. Lord Justice Lindley in his judgment in this case remarked—

It is a mere truism to say that the value of loans and securities depends upon their realisation. We are told that a statement to that effect is so unusual that the mere presence of those words is enough to excite suspicion. But, as already stated, the duty of an auditor is to convey information, not to arouse inquiry, and although an auditor might infer from an unusual statement that something was seriously wrong, it by no means follows that ordinary people would have their suspicions aroused by a similar statement, if, as in this case, its language expresses no more than any ordinary person would infer without it.

The Companies Act, 1907, provides that the auditor shall report to the shareholders on every balance-sheet laid before the company in general meeting during his tenure of office. It must be noticed that an auditor does not discharge this duty by simply giving the shareholders so much information in his report as is calculated to induce them to ask for more. It has been judicially remarked that there might be circumstances under which the printed report circulated among a large body of shareholders would by its consequent publicity be very injurious to their interests, in which case the auditor's duties might be discharged if, instead of publishing his report in such a way as to insure publicity, he made a confidential report to the shareholders and invited their attention to it and told them where they could see it. It was, however, added that there was great danger in acting on such a principle, and that an auditor who gives shareholders means of information instead of information in respect of a company's financial position does so at his peril.

Further, you are aware that the Companies Act, 1907, sect. 19 (5), subjects officers of the company to a fine not exceeding £50 if they are knowingly a party to the issue of a balance-sheet which has not been signed by two directors as required by the Act. I hardly think that the auditor is responsible for seeing that the balance-sheet is so signed, but it is highly expedient that he see to this formality before adhibiting his docquet, and if he acquiesce in the issue of the balance - sheet unsigned he would certainly render himself liable.

The question has arisen as to how far, if at all, an auditor is responsible where his report is not submitted to the shareholders. In the case of Joseph Hargreaves, Ltd., 1900 (see Appendix, Dicksee's " Auditing "), the auditor had refused to sign the balance-sheet. No meeting of shareholders had been held, but he knew that certain sums were paid to the shareholders as dividend, and had protested to the directors and suggested that a meeting be called, and he had not charged or received any fee. It was sought to hold him liable for misfeasance in having acquiesced in the payment of dividends out of capital. Justice Cozens-Hardy, in giving his judgment, remarked—

It is sought really, I think, when one gets to the bottom of the case, to render the auditor liable because he did not require a general meeting of the shareholders to be summoned, to which he could make a statement as to the improper conduct of the directors. Well, how could he have summoned a meeting? He had no more power to summon a meeting than I have. It would be startling, I think, to say that an auditor who knows that dividends have been improperly paid out of capital is to be rendered liable because he does not commence an action on behalf of himself and all the other shareholders, I suppose, against the directors who have improperly paid these dividends, or does not do that which he really had no power to do— get the general meeting together and inform them of the facts.

It would thus appear that an auditor's duties are completed when he has audited the accounts and sent his report to the registered office of the company. At the same time I can conceive circumstances under which it may be expedient for the auditor to send his report direct to the shareholders by post, but such does not come within the limits of his statutory duties or legal responsibility. It is rather a matter for the shareholders to see that their statutory rights of meeting together to hear the reports of both directors and auditors are recognised by the directors whose duty it is to summon meetings. I note, however, before leaving this point, that the auditor of a railway company is expressly empowered by Statute to issue independently to the shareholders at the cost of the company any statement respecting the financial condition of the company which they think material for the information of the shareholders.

Another interesting point arises as to how far an auditor is safe in writing up the books of the company. In the case of small companies such a proceeding is by no means uncommon. It has to be noted, however, that sect. 21 of the Companies Act, 1900, provides that "a director or official of the company shall not be capable of being appointed an auditor of the company," and it has also to be noted that the original Table A provides that "no person is eligible as an auditor who is interested otherwise than as a member in any transaction of the company." The acceptance of additional remuneration from the directors in respect of performing the work of secretary or book-keeper is apt to detract from the independent position which an auditor should occupy as between the shareholders and the directors. As pointed out in the pages of 'The Accountants' Magazine,' it is advisable, in order to fully protect himself, that an auditor should see that such additional remuneration is voted by the shareholders, and on no account accept any such additional fee on the authority of the directors alone.

Having now tried your patience in dealing with the general principles underlying the liabilities of auditors, I would ask your attention to the application of these to a few of the common items in the balance-sheet, delaying, however, until later, the general consideration of the legal principles underlying the valuation of the assets and the framing of the profit and loss account.

Take to begin with "stock in trade." How far is an auditor responsible for the value of the stock in trade as shown in the balance-sheet? The position of the auditor is clearly laid down in two cases I have in mind—viz., The Kingston Cotton Mill Company, Ltd. (1896, 2 Ch. 279), and the Irish Woollen Company, Ltd. (Acct. L. R., 1900, p. 13). It is no part of an auditor's duty to take stock or verify its actual existence by a visit to the store, although such a step may occasionally be advantageous. He is entitled to rely upon the returns made by competent and trusted experts where there is nothing to excite his suspicion and where there is no apparent conflict between the interests and the duties of the parties certifying the stock. The duty of the auditor may therefore be put in this way. He is bound to see that the stock is taken by a responsible party, and that such party certifies the stock sheets, to inquire as to the principle upon which the stock has been valued and satisfy himself that such is right, and to test the arithmetical accuracy of the stock sheets. Where suspicion is aroused, however, it will be necessary for the auditor to go somewhat further and test as far as he reasonably can, from invoices, &c., the entries in the stock sheets.

Take next the item of "book debts." How far is the auditor responsible for the value of these? This point was raised in the latter of the two cases above referred to. As to the provision for bad debts, the auditor is dependent for information upon the officials of the company. He is not presumed to have any personal knowledge of the customers, and I take it that in ordinary circumstances the auditor's duty is satisfied when he checks the customers' accounts in the ledger with the subsidiary books, and makes inquiry at the responsible officials in regard to accounts of old date. As to the provision of an estimated sum for cash discount, this is a matter of expediency and not one for the neglect of which the auditor would be found liable, but it should be noted that all trade discounts must be deducted. Inquiry should be made as to the method of treating sales for future delivery and goods out on approbation.

Next take the item "trade creditors." In the case of the Irish Woollen Company, Ltd. (*supra*), while the auditor was exonerated on the first two charges—viz., as to stock and book debts—he was held liable for loss through defalcation of an official on the ground that he had not exercised reasonable care and skill in proving the accuracy of the amount stated as trade creditors. It is instructive to note the particulars of this case. A large number of invoices applicable to the year of audit were carried forward and inserted in the invoice book in the new year, but, after the balance, were entered in their proper place in the ledger accounts. The auditor had once or twice noticed something of this sort and asked an explanation. He was told that the goods were not taken into stock, an explanation, if true, satisfactory so far as the trading account was concerned, but insufficient when considering the accuracy of the statement of liabilities at the date of balance. An examination of the ledger accounts, and in particular one of these accounts brought to the notice of the Court, would have shown that there was something wrong, and would have put the auditor on his guard. Thus in the account of a single customer, items totalling £600 had got into the books after the trial balance was struck under dates going back two months prior to the ascertainment of the trial balance. The position was aggravated by the fact that the auditor had undertaken to make a monthly audit, thus giving him plenty of time to check the accounts thoroughly. It was further pointed out that owing to the custom which prevailed in the woollen trade, creditors' statements of account made up to the date of the balance were available, and the auditor's suspicions having been aroused by the appearance of the ledger accounts, he ought to have called for these statements, in which event the true state of matters would have been brought to light. An auditor should therefore examine the entries in the invoice book for a period following the close of the year, paying attention to the dates of the invoices, and at least occasionally call for the creditors' statements. Immediately his suspicion is aroused, he should leave no stone unturned to get at the true state of affairs.

What is the auditor's duty in regard to the item "cash on hand"? The same rule applies here. The auditor is bound to exercise reasonable care and skill in satisfying himself that the cash balance actually exists. This may consist in counting the cash, generally the most effective way, or by certificate, or by other means at his disposal. Frequently the balance is small, and the verification of it is a matter of little moment. Where it is large it may be due to the fact that cheques have come in on the closing day and not been lodged in the bank. This may be verified by an examination of the books at the opening of the new year. There is no absolute obligation upon the auditor to actually count the cash, but he must be reasonably careful, and consider in each case what is a sufficient check. Personally, I think that the auditor should make a practice of counting the cash if possible. The liability of an auditor for the misstatement of cash on hand was the subject of a decision in the case of the London Oil Storage Company (Acct. L. R., 1904, p. 1). What was called a petty cash book was kept at the city office, and the amount of the cash balance appearing therein was entered in the balance-sheet, but the auditor never troubled to find out whether the cashier had the balance in hand or not until, the latter being invalided, his duties were taken over by another who found in the cash-box £30 while the book showed £796, the balance having gradually increased over the period of the last five years. The case was tried before a jury, and after a lengthy advising by Lord Alverstone, the jury held that there was breach of duty, and assessed as nominal damages the sum of five guineas. In this case the increase of the balance to such large proportions was no doubt a matter

B

calculated to arouse suspicion, but even apart from suspicion the auditor has a *prima facie* duty to verify the assets, and probably should have at least called for a certificate from the secretary.   Lord Alverstone said, "It cannot be disputed that when the auditor returns to the shareholders an entry of cash on hand, he must have taken reasonable steps to ascertain that the cash was on hand."   But "there may be cases in which he would be justified in acting on the representation of a cashier or a servant whom he had no reason to distrust, and on the other hand there may be cases where he ought to go further and examine."

In regard to the verification of the item "cash," where the amount is made up of several balances due by different branches, the auditor should endeavour to check same simultaneously, otherwise the one amount of cash may be made to serve on more than one occasion.   The auditor should also be careful to see that the balance is truly a cash balance and not made up partly of I.O.U.'s or acknowledgments for loans which may be irrecoverable.   In the case of the Astrachan Steamship Company, Ltd., 1900 (Appendix, Dicksee, "Auditing"—'Acc. Mag.,' 1900, p. 190), circumstances such as these arose.   Counsel, describing the manager's peculiar mode of dealing with cash balances, explained that what he did was to present the accounts of various companies for audit at different times, and by keeping in hand a sum of money which went all round he contrived to balance each company's cash account for a short period in turn.   "The sum of money went round while it lasted, but it was first under one thimble and then under another." Further, it appeared that the manager had borrowed from the various companies large sums of money.   The case was ultimately withdrawn under a private arrangement, but the evidence of experts called in the case agreed that the auditor should either (1) have called upon the manager for his special authority for borrowing the money, or (2) have reported the position to the shareholders, or (3) have altered the item in the balance-sheet from "cash in manager's hands" to "cash borrowed by manager at 4 per cent interest."

The items "bills receivable" and "bills payable" call for the auditor's special attention, particularly where transactions have taken place in accommodation bills. In such a case the auditor should walk warily and be most careful to see that each transaction is fully recorded, it being a common thing to find defalcations covered up by partial entry of a transaction in accommodation bills. 'The auditor should see the bills receivable on hand and ascertain that none of them are overdue. Such should not be included under this heading, but be debited to the customers and provision made for any estimated loss. In regard to bills discounted not yet due, the contingent liability on these must be shown at the foot of the balance-sheet, the amount, of course, not being carried out into the balancing column. This, however, will not apply to accommodation bills, the liability on which is already appearing among the liabilities in the body of the balance-sheet unless in the case of cross bills, when, of course, the contingent liability must be stated. Where accommodation bills are numerous the auditors should see that the liability thereon is not included under the general heading "trade creditors," but shown separately as "cash creditors." The same would apply to accommodation bills granted by the firm, which obviously do not form an asset of the same value or realisability as trade debts.

In regard to the securities for investments, the auditor is responsible for seeing that these exist and that they are *ex facie* in order. He is not, however, expected to bring to bear on this part of his duty any special legal knowledge such as would fit him to judge of the validity of the securities. That is a matter for the company's solicitors, from whom he may reasonably require a certificate. In this connection you will recollect that under the Building Societies Act, 1894 (57 & 58 Vict. c. 47), the auditor has to certify that he has at the audit actually inspected the mortgage deeds and other securities belonging to the society, and to state the number of properties in respect of which deeds have been inspected by him.

Before considering the auditor's responsibility for the values of the Fixed Assets, such as Ground and Buildings,

Plant and Machinery, &c., I would draw your attention to one other point—viz., the liability of the auditor in connection with secret reserves. This was the subject of an interesting decision in the case of the Birmingham Small Arms Company, Ltd., 1906 (2 Ch. Div. 378). The Company's Articles had been altered. The new provisions were that an internal reserve fund might be constituted and not disclosed in the balance-sheet, and that the directors need give no information to the shareholders regarding the same, they to have absolute discretion as to its application subject to the disclosure of all particulars to the auditor. The latter's duty, however, was described as being "to see that the same is applied for the purposes of the company in accordance with the provisions hereinbefore contained, but not to disclose any information with regard to the same to the shareholders or otherwise." It was sought to have it declared that these provisions were *ultra vires* of the company. Mr Justice Buckley held that it was competent for the statutory majority of the shareholders to say that as to particular items of their business it was in the interests of the company that there should be secrecy, and that the auditors, who for the purposes of their audit must know all the details, should not disclose them to the members, unless their duty under the Statute made it necessary to do so. . . . But these resolutions went too far. Any regulations which precluded the auditors from availing themselves of all the information to which under the Act they were entitled as material for the report, which under the Act they are to make as to the true and correct state of the company's affairs, were inconsistent with the Act. While, therefore, in ordinary circumstances an auditor would be going beyond the limit of his duties in disclosing particulars of a secret reserve, it is his bounden duty to call attention to anything that is wrong.

It had been a matter of much discussion how far an auditor was justified in stating that a balance-sheet, in which assets were thus entirely omitted or understated, showed "the true and correct view of the state of the company's affairs." It is now clear that the auditor is justified in doing so provided the articles authorise the creation of a secret reserve, and the fact of its existence is made clear in the balance-sheet. Mr Justice Buckley in the case referred to remarked that if the balance-sheet were so worded as to show that there was an undisclosed asset which made the financial position of the company better than was shown, such a balance-sheet would not necessarily be inconsistent with the provisions of the Act. The purpose of a balance-sheet was primarily to show that the financial position of the company was at least as good as was stated, not to show that it was not, or might not be better.

We come now to the vexed question as to the responsibility of the auditor where depreciation on assets has not been provided for. How far is an auditor liable for dividends paid before making good out of profits losses on assets through depreciation or otherwise? That he may be rendered liable for dividends illegally paid is beyond doubt, in view of the decision *in re* the Leeds Estate Building and Investment Society, Ltd. (1887), 36 C. D. 787, where the auditor was held liable for the amount of dividends paid over the six years preceding the action, it having been proved that the balance-sheet contained fictitious information and that the dividend had in point of fact been paid out of capital. But how far is it legally necessary for a company to make good losses of assets? The first consideration is the terms of the company's articles of association, so far as these are consistent with law. The auditor is bound to report any breach of these. Failing definite provision in the articles, or in determining whether these are *ultra vires* or not, he will be confronted by a long series of decisions which it is by no means easy to reconcile. The general result may be summarised in this way—viz., that while a loss of floating or circulating capital or assets must in all cases be made good out of revenue, it is not necessary, subject of course to any express provisions of the articles of the company, to make good out of revenue losses of fixed capital or assets. Although the latter proposition may not hold good in all circumstances, the auditor, I think, will be safe in acting on this basis as a reasonable interpretation of the cases, at least in the meantime. The leading case in this connection is Lee *v.* the Neuchatel Asphalte Co., Ltd. (1889), 41 C. D. 1.

I cannot do better than quote to you from the opinion of Lord Justice Lindley therein.

> If a company [he says] is formed to acquire or work properties of a wasting nature—*e.g.*, a mine, a quarry, or a patent—the capital expended in acquiring the property may be regarded as sunk and gone, and if the company retains assets sufficient to pay its debts, any excess of money obtained by working the property over the cost of working it may be divided among the shareholders. . . . It is not true, as an abstract proposition, that no dividends can be properly declared out of moneys arising from the sale of property bought by capital. But it is true that if the working expenses exceed the current gains, profits cannot be divided, and that, if in such a case capital is divided and paid away as dividend, the capital is misapplied.

In certain circumstances, then, it is evident that a company formed to work a wasting asset is not bound to make good out of revenue a loss on that wasting asset. At the same time we cannot rely on these decisions as an authority for the proposition as a universal negative—viz., that no company owning wasting property need ever create a depreciation fund. In a later case, the Barrow and Hæmatite Steel Company, Ltd., 1902 (1 Ch. 353), a large smelting company, by way of economy acquired leases of mines in order to supply themselves with their own ore instead of buying it as required. The case was distinguished from the Neuchatel Asphalte Company in that the money invested in these mines had to be regarded as circulating capital. It was considered that the mines simply represented an enormous stock of ore which the company had bought in advance instead of buying it as required.

In the Scottish Courts we have the case of Cox *v.* The Edinburgh and District Tramways Company, Ltd., 1898 (see Appendix to Dicksee's "Auditing"), which bears on this same question. Lord Kyllachy, in giving judgment, remarked that, while not perhaps bound by the English decisions, he had no difficulty in accepting not only their

194

results, but their general doctrine. As you may recollect, the case arose owing to the conversion of the tramway system from horse traction to cable traction, and the point at issue was whether or not the loss on horses and rolling stock must be made good out of profits before declaring dividend. The case was decided in the negative on the principle that capital sunk—*i.e.*, capital not represented by tangible and available assets—is not in all cases to be considered as capital lost, but that, in the case before the Court, the scheme on which the company had been embarked was presumably for the benefit of the undertaking, and although it involved a sacrifice in one direction, such sacrifice would at least presumably be compensated by a corresponding gain in some other direction. The judgment did not proceed on any law or doctrine established by the recent decisions, but on the principle that on matters necessarily of estimate and opinion a company was presumably the best judge of its own affairs.

The position of an investment trust as affected by these decisions is interesting. On the one hand Verner *v.* the General and Commercial Trust, 1894 (2 Ch. 239), an English case, decided that where the business of the trust does not consist in trafficking in shares but was purely an investment business, the investments must be looked. upon as fixed capital, and that dividends could be paid although there was a large depreciation on the investment. On the other hand, in a Scotch case, the City Property and Investment Trust *v.* Thorburn, 1897 (25 R. 361), it was held that as the trust was trafficking in its securities, these therefore represented circulating capital, and that actual or estimated loss thereon was properly chargeable to revenue account.

Closely allied to the above question is the question whether accretions to capital are available for the payment of a dividend. This was first the subject of a decision in Lubbock *v.* the British Bank of South America, Ltd., 1892 (2 Ch. 198), where the sum sought to be divided was the surplus ascertained on the asset side after the liabilities and capital were placed on one side of the account and the assets on the other. It must be noticed, however, that an accretion

195

to capital on one asset cannot be treated as revenue without reference to the value of the other assets of the company. This distinction was made clear in Foster *v.* the New Trinidad Lake Asphalte Co., Ltd., 1901 (1 Ch. 208), where it was held that an appreciation in the total value of capital assets, if duly realised by sale or getting in of some portions of such assets, may, in a proper case, be treated as available for purposes of dividend. In an earlier case, the Natal Land and Colonisation Company, Ltd., 1892 (2 Ch. 124), the further principle was laid down that the fact of a company having written up the value of its assets and credited the increase to profit, did not place them under an obligation to bring into account in every subsequent year the increase or decrease in the value of their assets.

Some doubt would appear to have been raised as to whether a company could write off revenue losses to capital, and in a subsequent year, if the receipts for that year exceed the outgoings, pay a dividend without making up the capital account. Such a proposition is obviously entirely wrong, and the decision of the House of Lords in the National Bank of Wales case, 1899 (2 Ch. 629, H. L. (1901) A. C. 477), makes this perfectly clear.

The auditor must exercise reasonable care and skill in ascertaining that the sum stated as " profits " in the balance-sheet which he certifies is arrived at after making the allowances necessary in view of the foregoing decisions. If he fails in that duty he may be held liable for any dividends which, owing to his negligence, have been paid out of capital. There are, however, certain limitations to this liability—*e.g.*, shareholders who have received a dividend improperly paid out of capital cannot maintain an action against the directors who caused such dividend to be paid, nor, I presume, against the auditor (African Tug Co., Ltd., 1904 (1 Ch. 558)). Further, immediately the dividend wrongously paid has been made good out of subsequent profits the responsibility of the company's officials ceases (Watchmakers' Alliance and others (Acct. L. R., 1903, p. 23)).

It is not within the scope of this paper to treat this matter of depreciation of fixed assets from the point of view of good accounting, the dictates of which might lead us to results far different from the above; but I must observe that in relying on these legal decisions the auditor must be careful to see at least that capital lost does not appear in the accounts as still existing intact, but that it is stated separately. I would also remind you that auditors of railway companies have a particular responsibility laid upon them. By the Railway Companies (Scotland) Act, 30 & 31 Vict. c. 126, the duty is devolved upon the auditor of certifying that the dividend proposed is *bonâ-fide* due on the shares after charging revenue for the half-year with all expenses which ought to be paid thereout in the judgment of the auditor.

This lecture would not be complete without at least a very short reference to the duty and responsibility of auditors as regards the Report to the Statutory Meeting of shareholders and also as to statements made in the prospectus.

In regard to the first of these I would draw your attention to the provisions of sect. 22 of the Companies Act, 1907, which modifies the corresponding section of the Companies Act, 1900. It will therefore now be necessary for the auditor to see that the report contains an abstract of the receipts of the company on account of its capital whether from shares or debentures and of all payments made thereout, presumably whether capital payments or payments which in the nature of things will subsequently fall to be paid out of revenue when earned, and further to see that particulars are inserted as to how the balance of the money received is accounted for.

The liability of an auditor certifying the profits at the inception of a company is considerable. He should be careful to certify only as to facts, and while entitled to make calculations upon the facts which he has found established and to arrange these facts in such a way as to best exhibit the true position, he should be careful not to make estimates or prophesy as to the future. In the case of Maynard's Ltd. (Acct. L. R., 1900, p. 24) the accountant certified the amount of the sales, and proceeded—

Owing to the absence of figures showing the position of some of the businesses, we are unable to ascertain the exact net profits of the whole of them, but from our knowledge of the extremely profitable nature of the confectionery trade, and from the facts disclosed during the investigations, we are satisfied that the profits of the business are large, and that after payment of the interest on the preference shares there will remain a profit sufficient to pay a substantial dividend upon the ordinary shares.

The opinion of experts called in the case was much against the accountants, but the latter were able to prove the justice of their estimate, and the case, so far as they were concerned, was dismissed. It is, however, to say the least, a dangerous practice to insert an estimate in a certificate.

An important point to be noticed in this connection is that the profits for the individual years under review should be stated as well as the average, otherwise the true position of affairs may be obscured. In the case mentioned it was shown that the annual profits of the various businesses were by no means steady, nor did the profit of each business fluctuate in the same ratio.

Gentlemen, much more might be said under this head, but I am afraid I have already exceeded the limits of your patience. I will therefore come to an abrupt termination, only expressing the sincere wish that none of us may ever fall into the toils of the law.

Note.—The majority of the cases referred to above will be found reported in Appendix to " Auditing " by Dicksee.

The late JAMES ANDREW FRENCH, C.A.

We deeply regret to record the death of Mr James A. French, which took place at his home, 5 Whittingehame Drive, Glasgow, W., on Thursday, 13th December 1934. Mr French had a heart attack seven weeks earlier, and while latterly an improvement in his condition gave rise to hopes of a recovery, he passed away suddenly without suffering in the end.

Mr French, who was the youngest son of the late Mr William French, Ironmaster, Glasgow, was educated in Glasgow. In 1894 he commenced his apprenticeship with

Messrs Reid & Mair, C.A., Glasgow, qualified in 1899, and in 1900 was admitted a Member of the Institute of Accountants and Actuaries in Glasgow. He commenced in practice in 1903, and in 1908 there was formed the firm of French & Cowan, Chartered Accountants, Glasgow, of which Mr French remained the senior partner up to the time of his death.

Mr French was held in the highest esteem and affection by his many personal friends, his profession, and by a wide business circle in the city. He was a man of sterling qualities, honourable and upright in all his dealings, loyal to his friends and just to all. With a keen intellect, an alert mind and a shrewd business sense, his advice and counsel were much sought after. As a Director of several public and many private companies, his services were highly appreciated by his colleagues on the Boards, and one of his personal activities was as a Member of the Board of Governors of Kelvinside Academy.

Mr French took a very active part in the affairs of both the C.A. Institute and the Students' Society in Glasgow, being at one time a member of the Institute Council and holding office as President and Honorary President of the Glasgow Chartered Accountants Students' Society. His lectures before that Society will be remembered for their scholarship and the outspoken vigour of his strong personality.

At the time of his death he was a member of the Parliamentary and Law Committee of the Institute.

His wide knowledge of Law as well as of Accountancy, and his intense interest in legal questions, led to his frequent employment as an expert witness in many important Commercial Cases in Court and Arbitrations, and within recent years his services were sought by the Crown Authorities in Court proceedings, notably in the "Silks" Case, in which he played a prominent part.

His exceptional qualities of heart, his ready sympathy and self-sacrificing nature endeared him to a large circle of friends and acquaintances, who will deeply deplore his loss and will ever gratefully cherish his memory.

To his sorrowing widow and family we respectfully offer our tribute of profound sympathy.

James A. French, 'Some Doubts on the Duties of Auditors Regarding
Procedure, Grouping of Balance-Sheet Items, and Verification of
Assets and Liabilities' (1924-5)

The further development of the audit function is portrayed in this paper.
The author was convinced of the increasing professionalism of the auditor
despite the lack of definition of his legal duties. The truth of this
is to be seen in French's discussion of such matters as the auditor's
reliance of internal check to reduce his detailed checking of records;
and his constant questioning of the quality of reported information. In
particular with regard to the latter was French's questioning of the
meaning of profit (and the effect of inventory valuations on it); and his
awareness of the quality of financial disclosures in the legally-required
balance sheet (lack of information creating a loss of credibility by users
in the balance sheet).

Whereas French indicated evidence of some advance in audit (and
accounting) thought by 1925, he also revealed certain matters which had
not changed since the days of Hutton or Wardhaugh - for example, the
continuing influence of fraud detection as a major audit aim; the auditor's
reliance on evidence from management; and the need for clear audit
reporting.

SOME DOUBTS ON THE DUTIES OF AUDITORS REGARDING PROCEDURE, GROUPING OF BALANCE-SHEET ITEMS, AND VERIFICATION OF ASSETS AND LIABILITIES.

By JAMES A. FRENCH, Esq., C.A.

(Being a Lecture delivered to The Glasgow Chartered Accountants Students' Society on 14th January 1925, and to The Chartered Accountants Students of Dundee, on 6th February 1925.)

THE auditors, of whom I wish to speak to you to-night, are a perfectly modern creation.

No doubt the office of auditor has existed from very ancient times.

The name is derived from the Latin verb " audio," " I hear," from which it may be assumed that the office existed before the days of writing, or, rather, before the reduction of money transactions into writing.

As far as the United Kingdom is concerned, the original auditor, I believe, was the king's servant, who was present when the high sheriffs of the English counties attended twice a year before the King's Chancellor and handed over the exchequer table the king's taxes which they had collected under deduction of the sums they had expended in their district on the king's behalf. The auditor " heard " their explanations, and allowed or disallowed the expenditure, and I have no doubt he heard a great deal of explanation as to the non-collection of items due but uncollected, and on his report to the king would depend whether or not the high sheriff was to be retained in his office.

One can imagine that Cheops and Cephrenes must have employed some such person to check the contractor's "prime cost" of the Pyramids of Egypt, and would have many a row with the contractor as to the components of his oncost charges.

If, on the other hand, the Pyramids of Egypt were built by direct labour, I am much mistaken if equal vigilance was not necessary to check the prices charged for material—both inanimate and animate—with the current market price of stones and slaves.

The origin of the present-day auditor of commercial trading and financial accounts cannot, I think, be earlier than the joint-stock company enterprise as we know it to-day.

That would place the origin of auditors in the modern sense of the word somewhere about the beginning of Queen Victoria's reign.

In a partnership the books and accounts of the firm are open to the inspection of all the partners.

When as in joint-stock enterprise the partners became numerous, such examination by each became impossible, and one or two of the partners would be deputed to examine the accounts, and report to their fellow-partners what they found.

It must have been in some such notion that the office originated.

The transition from the office being executed at the beginning by a partner, then by a person not necessarily a partner, and finally by a person who is not a partner, is well illustrated by the legislation relating to companies.

The Companies Clauses Consolidation (Scotland) Act, 1845, making certain enactments regarding the constitution of companies carrying on undertakings of a public nature in Scotland, provides—

"That the auditor shall hold at least one share in the undertaking."

The Joint-Stock Companies Act of 1856 provides—

"That the auditor need not have any share qualification."

Table A of the Companies Act, 1862, provides—

"That it shall be no disqualification for the office that he holds a share in the company."

The gentleman appointed would examine the accounts

as far as he thought necessary. In a word, he would do exactly what a partner in a firm does to-day to the books of his firm—look at the transactions he has not personally carried through, and on which he wishes information, see where the profit came from, and how the finance of the firm stands.

He might examine the sales at one time, the purchases at another, the bank account at a third.

He would examine nothing that was within his own knowledge, and he would report to his co-partners what he had found.

His office was probably a gratuitous one for the reason that he did not wish to be paid, not being a professional man.

I fancy the audit would be rather perfunctory. It would certainly not be systematic.

Thackeray wrote ' The Newcomes ' in 1855, and in the fine description he gives of the failure of the Bundlecund Banking Company, the following rather uncomplimentary reference to our profession occurs :—

> " It was found that one of the auditors of the Bank, the generally-esteemed Charlie Condor (a capital fellow, famous for his good dinners and for playing low comedy characters in the Chowringhee Theatre), was indebted to the Bank in £90,000."

If this is indicative of anything, it shows that in 1855 the check of an audit was not thought much of.

I hope and believe the public estimation of our functions is higher to-day.

When the Companies Act of 1862 was passed, there was no provision in it for the appointment of auditors. The model set of articles, which are now sometimes referred to as " Old Table A," contained optional provisions for the appointment of auditors, and it also assumed that they would be remunerated for their services.

It is obvious from the clauses that the framers of the Act did not anticipate that they would be professional men. Certainly that they would not be accountants, because, for the purpose of carrying out their office, they were expressly empowered by Article 92 at the expense of the company to employ accountants to assist them in investigating the accounts.

Matters remained on that footing until 1879, when, following on the failure of the City of Glasgow Bank, banking companies were compelled to appoint auditors.

It was not till 1900 that companies registered under the Companies Act were compelled to employ auditors. The Companies Act of that year, in addition to appointing them, laid down the main lines of the report they had to make to the shareholders.

Further alterations regarding their appointment were made in the Companies Act of 1907, and the present Statutory form of docquet was laid down by that Act, and remains unaltered to this day.

The Act of 1907 provided for the first time that the auditor could not be removed from office unless notice of the intention to propose another in his place was given in the notice calling the meeting, and also by express notice to the person holding the office.

The necessity of having some independent check on the balance-sheet submitted to the shareholders, and incidentally to the public in the case of a banking company, was brought out very prominently when the City of Glasgow Bank failed in the autumn of 1878.

There were several points in connection with the bank's balance-sheet which should have been perfectly obvious if even a very perfunctory examination of the books had been made by any impartial person.

The directors of the bank apparently just issued such a statement as they thought would satisfy the bill-brokers in London, that the bank was in a flourishing state, and conducted with prudence.

The balance-sheet, as matter of fact, was as bad as bad could be.

It was grossly disconform to fact and it did not even conform to the books of account.

The directors were criminally charged with fabricating, concocting and uttering it, and the chief grounds on which the conviction was got were, as I have said before—

(1) That the balance-sheet was not conform to the books of account—*i.e.*, that it did not show the position disclosed by the books of account, while very much less attention was paid to the fact that the books themselves were disconform to fact in the sense

that debts that were notoriously bad were retained
in the books as good, and interest added to them
year by year; and

(2) The faulty grouping of accounts.

What the directors did was to set debtor balances against
creditor balances shown by one ledger, and carry only the
difference into the balance-sheet, there being, of course,
no *concursus debiti et crediti* between such debtors and
creditors.

They also had a pleasant way of taking great blocks
of bad debts and entering them up under the head of
" Government Stocks," which looked far better, but I
think you will agree could hardly be called " fair description."

The duties of an auditor of a company registered under
the Companies Act are entirely undefined by Statute, and
I think it is unquestionable that the present state of procedure has been built up entirely by auditors who felt
that they had a professional reputation to sustain, and it
is from the usage of our profession as regards procedure
that the liability for neglect of duty arises.

It is very important to observe that the auditor is the
servant of the shareholders.

He is appointed at the annual general meeting of shareholders. His remuneration is fixed by the shareholders in
general meeting, and requires to be fixed annually, and he
can only be removed from his office by a majority vote in
general meeting.

His duties, therefore, are to be critical of the transactions
of the executive officers of the company and the Board of
Directors.

His first duty is to read the memorandum of association
of the company, so that he can judge that the transactions
entered into by the company are within its objects clause.

He must read the articles of association of the company
to see that the Board of Directors have carried out any
special enactments laid down therein.

In small private companies these articles often contain
the only information available as regards the fixed salaries
of the managing director or directors, the remuneration
which they are to receive by way of commission, and the
borrowing powers of the company.

The articles may also, but in practice generally do not, lay special duties on the auditor as regards the accounts supplementary to what he may himself consider necessary to make his statutory report to the shareholders.

On his appointment the auditor requires to be furnished with a complete list of books kept by the company.

The Act of 1907, now embodied in secs. 112 and 113 of the Companies (Consolidation) Act, 1908, gives right of access to "the books," and this, I believe, is understood to mean all books, which, of course, includes, besides books of account, letter books, order books, register of members, register of transfers.

On the ordinary procedure of auditing the books, I will now try to indicate some doubts.

You are going to examine the company's sales, and find out the total of these.

Are you to treat the sales book itself as your starting-point, and treat that as your book of original entry ?

You know that the transactions themselves have probably passed through the following prior books :—

1. The order book.
2. Sold contract book.
3. The dispatch book.

Is the auditor under any obligation to compare the sales book entry with these ?

It is obvious that if he does *not*, goods may have been delivered and the proceeds collected, and no trace of the transactions left in the books of account proper.

Sales may be entered at a different price from which the bargain was made for delivery, and an astute clerk or department manager have collected the proceeds on the true bargain made, but recorded a different one in the books and pocketed the difference.

As a matter of ordinary practice, I do not think auditors go beyond the sales day book. If, however, the auditor has access to all the books, is he not under obligation to make inquiry further back than the sales book as regards sales transactions ? What would be his position if it were subsequently found out that something on the lines which I have indicated had been done with the company's affairs, which even a cursory examination of these prior books would have brought to light ?

208

Has the auditor been remiss in his duty, with the result that he would be liable for the amount of the shareholders' monies which has been lost through the fraud, or the transactions being *ultra vires* of the company?

Something of the same sort arises in connection with purchase books. What is the auditor's duty here?

Must he compare all the entries with the invoices?

Has he to check the invoices themselves as regards arithmetic?

Is he under any obligation to check the invoice prices with the purchased contracts made, against which the invoices are part delivery?

In an extensive business it is a practical impossibility to examine all the invoices in detail, but it is perfectly obvious that if the auditor does not examine every invoice, that a subordinate servant, whose duty it is to pass invoices, could do so at different prices to the contract fixed by the Board.

Purchases of goods obviously outside the scope of the company's objects could be passed through, or invoices not in the company's name at all could be passed through, the goods being supplied to a director or servant of the company, or if the transactions were of the nature of a speculation, the goods have been sold at a loss *per contra* through the sales book.

Thus if in auditing the accounts of a cotton-mill you found pig-iron warrants purchased, you would not say that that was a purchase authorised by the articles, and whether on resale the transactions resulted in a profit or a loss, it is equally *ultra vires* of the objects clause, and should be so reported to the shareholders.

The difficulty, you will see, is that unless every invoice is examined, you cannot say with certainty as regards purchases the company has traded within the objects clause of its articles.

As a matter of practice, I do not think in large audits it is usual to examine every invoice, but in a large audit you almost always have internal check—one department checking another,—the invoices as regards quantity being passed by the stores department, as regards prices by the purchasing department, and very often on the top of that the initials of a managing director.

209

But what I want to ask is, in considering this question of internal check : if any such transactions should be ultimately brought to light, with loss to the company, has the auditor been remiss in his duty if, say, he examined four months at random out of the year and no such transactions occured in these ?

Transactions such as the foregoing are not as uncommon as one would think.

I myself found in a small limited company that very considerable transactions were entered into on the Stock Exchange which were clearly beyond the objects clause of the memorandum of association, and I so reported to the shareholders.

The contract notes were all regularly passed in the name of the limited company, were effected on the Stock Exchange, and as a matter of fact for two years running resulted in substantial gains.

The thing that struck me as curious was that the stockbroker concerned had apparently made no inquiry as to whether or not the company had power to enter into these transactions, and had he been unable to recover his contango balance, I doubt very much whether he could have constituted his claim against the company.

We now come to a consideration of the audit of the cash transactions.

A careful examination of the cash book is, I consider, one of the most important parts of an audit.

Many old businesses still keep what is called " a clean cash book "—that is, a clean copy of the book in which the entries are originally.

For my own part, I had very much rather see the scroll cash book.

No matter how dirtily it is kept, it is often much more important to examine it than the clean one.

We will assume that the summations on both sides have been checked, and that the cash book has been vouched with the usual vouchers, pay rolls, subsidiary cash book, and then, if there are any irregularities, the difficulty of an auditor's duty arises.

You know that there are numerous methods by which cash entries can be manipulated.

The most difficult thing in the audit of a commercial cash book is to vouch the incoming cash or cheques.

Where the incoming cash is partly currency and partly cheques, the cashier's opportunities of manipulating the balance are enormously increased.

It is too long a subject to deal with here, but I think it is very important to insist that the whole of the incoming cash—*i.e.*, the gross receipts—are daily lodged in bank.

When this is not done the check on the cashier as regards proper accounting is very difficult.

I will just instance this with one example.

If the cash receipts of the day consist of two transactions—

John Smith's account paid by cash   .   . £10
William Brown's account paid by cheque .   10

the correct contra entry, of course, is—

Lodged in bank £20

but what a defaulting cashier can do is, debit himself with £10 received from John Smith, and to square it pay into bank William Brown's cheque, £10.

His cash thus balances, and he puts the £10 in his pocket.

The entry is challenged later. He says, " Oh, yes. I have made a mistake, but you see I have put Brown's cheque in the bank, although I have forgotten to debit myself with it."

You turn round to him and say, " Oh yes, but what about John Smith's account ? "

He says, " You see I debited myself all right with that."

And so the matter goes on, and if any proceedings are ever taken against the cashier you have no idea how difficult it is to explain such a transaction to a British jury. I have tried it, and I fear I failed.

An effort should certainly be made to trace the lodgments in bank with the amounts debited *per contra*. This can be done by comparing the components of the " paid-in " slip with the entries of incoming cash on the debit side of the day.

I don't say it is the usual practice of the profession to

do this, but it is a very valuable check, particularly at end of month and at balance periods. If no such check is applied, it is quite possible that the cashier has paid into bank cheques to reduce his balance on hand to a reasonable amount, and not debited himself *per contra* with the cheques received.

If all incoming cash is banked and none retained on hand, an excellent check exists for the monthly total, as banked should agree with the collection from sundry debtors shown *per contra*.

In the same fashion, if all payments are made by cheque, the amount drawn in a month will correspond with the payments *per contra* to sundry creditors and for wages.

If some such check is not done systematically, a bank lodgment here and there at random should be verified with the debit side of the cash book, and where the voucher shows "an account paid" was settled by cheque before marking it, you must see the amount is shown *per contra* as drawn from bank.

This, of course, is easier to check, because it comes out of the verification of the bank balance.

Now in verifying the bank balance with the bank's certificate, very great care must be exercised on the reconciliation with cheques outstanding or bills collected after the actual date of the certificate, that the cash book entries are complete on both sides of the book.

Now consider the responsibility of the auditor in regard to the register of members of the company.

Is he to examine this book showing alterations in the proprietorship of the capital, and if so with what ?

1. The transfer deeds themselves ?
2. The passing of same by the Board ?

It is obvious that if he does not, and the register has been improperly altered, a dividend may be paid to a person who is not a shareholder, and the true shareholder would have right of action against the company, or a forged transfer if passed would involve even more serious consequences.

Does an auditor in practice check these ?

If he has no responsibility, why should he ?

On the other hand, it is a book of the company, and

from the shareholders' point of view a very important book.

I do not think in practice these books are examined at all. I have done so myself on odd occasions where the transfers were few.

Then a less question, but arising out of the same book, is dividend warrants.

What is the auditor's duty here ?

Is he to check the names to see that *ex facie* of the register the payments are proper ? I believe this is sometimes done, but I think the more usual course is to accept the list of shareholders prepared by the secretary with the warrants themselves.

Then as regards the stock sheet or stock book of the stock-in-trade, is this an inventory or a book of account ?

The auditor's duty in regard thereto may be generally taken as—

1. To check the summations.
2. To check the more important extensions.
3. To verify the prices at which the stock is entered with invoices and market price lists.

The verification of quantities is, generally speaking, beyond the auditor, and in the Kingston Cotton Mill case, which I will refer to later, the Courts held that, although in this particular case it might have been done, they were satisfied that the auditor had not acted negligently through not doing so, which is a very consoling judgment for us.

Incidentally I may say that arising out of the Kingston Cotton Mill Company case arose the now very common statement you see in an auditor's docquet : " The stock is entered on the inventory, and at the valuation of your own officials."

We now come to the company's letter books.

The doubt I have is : Is the auditor under any duty to examine these ?

Many important matters affecting the books of account may be found in them, such as—

1. Solvency or insolvency of debtors.
2. The admission of claims for bad or short deliveries.
3. The admission of abatements of prices.
4. Agreements to purchase goods or raw materials made

and cancelled with profit not disclosed by the books.

5. Guarantees undertaken by the company on which liability may emerge.

If it is the wish of the Board or the officials of the company that none of these matters be recorded in the books of account, the auditor at the time of his audit may have no chance of knowing anything of them unless he examines the letter books.

Yet we all know it is not the practice to examine letter books, certainly systematically, but if the Statute gives the auditor the right of access to the books and the information is there, and he does not even attempt to look at them, is he remiss if liability to the shareholders emerges?

The last book I will mention is the Minute book, the book containing Minutes—

1. Of the meetings of the Board.
2. Of the shareholders.

It is certainly essential that the auditor read the latter carefully to see that the dividends, if falling under the articles to be declared by the company in general meeting, are so declared, that the directors' remuneration is fixed under the Minute, and that he himself has been competently reappointed.

As regards increases of capital and the terms of issue thereof, he will also find these matters dealt with in the Minutes of the company in general meeting.

It is also considered that the Minutes of meetings of the Board should also be examined, but I understand that this is resisted by some companies, who hold that they are only bound to give certified excerpts on matters (if any) which the auditor expects should be in the Minutes and on which he raises specific question.

I think myself the auditor is bound to examine the Board Minutes.

It is usually not a voluminous matter, and certainly it is there that very many important matters are recorded.

The whole of the foregoing points I have raised not so much with a view to giving you direct guidance as to what your duties are, but merely to show that in conducting an audit it is important to think what you are doing, and not content yourself with making a list of blue marks on the books and shutting your eyes to the vital facts which they contain or should contain.

To pass now from the audit procedure to one of the principal objects of an audit, the ascertainment of the balance of profit and loss which is to form the directors' warrant for declaring or not declaring a dividend, first let me say there is no legal definition of profit.

What is profit?

It is something like truth, and you no doubt all remember a momentous occasion on which a great Roman Pro-Consul asked the question: "What is truth?"

Well, I am afraid I cannot answer the question, "What is profit?"

In many cases profit seems perfectly obvious.

For example, a transaction on the Stock Exchange, any single transaction when it is finally closed—the profit on the voyage of a ship, the profit on holding a football match.

I would commend to your careful perusal on this difficult subject a White Paper, issued on 5th December 1918, and presented to Parliament in 1919, entitled, "Report of the Committee on Financial Risks attached to the holding of Trading Stocks."

A definition of profit, in the sense that we have to deal with it, is "the usual method adopted by traders or manufacturers to ascertain profits," and in the White Paper Lord Justice Farwell is cited as saying: "On the expression profit of a trade depends its ordinary significance as used by business men in business."

An eminent Glasgow iron-master, now deceased, is credited, when examining a balance-sheet that showed very rosy profits pretty much on paper, with asking the question: "Whaur's the siller?"

He evidently considered there was no profit until it was reduced into money, and certainly it is a very safe maxim to work on.

Stock-in-trade always presents a complication.

The fair value of it at the beginning and end of the period is essential, but where the stock is only turned over, say, twice a year, the valuation of stock-in-trade assumes ominous proportions in ascertaining whether or not there is a profit on the year's working.

K

215

The same difficulty arises with work-in-progress, if it is a heavy figure in proportion to the turnover.

The genuineness of capital expenditure, where open to considerable debate, whether on revenue or capital account, presents another difficulty, and, of course, the solvency of debtors when involving very large amounts and the balance has been outstanding more than the ordinary terms of trade credit.

Little help is got f.om legal decisions on these points.

In considering legal decisions students are very much inclined to take a lot of parrot cries from them, such as—

1. The auditor must exercise reasonable care.
2. The stock must be valued at cost or market, whichever is the lower.
3. The capital expenditure must be *bona fide* incurred on capital account.

I know these parrot cries well.

They form a fine stock-in-trade for answering the questions on auditing.

If a candidate does not know what a question means, he generally entertains the examiners to a dissertation of " cost or market value," which is anything but illuminating.

Reasonable care is a truism.

The expression " Cost or market value," what exactly does it mean ?

Is it the whole stock on cost basis or on market basis, or part on one basis and part on the other, with the implication that the less is chosen in all cases ?

In solving these points as regards stock, work-in-progress, and capital expenditure, after having used all the tests that he can find in the books as regards arithmetic and verification of prices and proportion of oncost charged, I think the auditor has to rely on a certificate obtained from the trusted officials of the company, and concurred in by the Board of Directors.

As regards the solvency of debtors, this is a very important matter.   The auditor must watch the ledger balances very carefully to see that no items—

1. Have been outstanding too long ;
2. Have been settled out of their turn ; and
3. That all discounts and rebates have been put through to credit.

All that appear as irregular should be queried and carefully gone over with a responsible servant of the company other than the ledger-keeper, and the auditor must be satisfied in his own mind before passing the amounts as truly resting owing to the company.

Any items if the amounts are vital and the auditor is not quite satisfied he should bring to the special notice of the Board, and get their reasoned statement as to why the items are retained in the books at their face value.

It is an excellent plan to bring the audit of the cash book down beyond the date of the balance-sheet, and the auditor can thus test the actual collection of the sundry debtors, and reduce the outstandings in doubt to very small dimensions.

In Scotland it is not common to send to sundry debtors a stamped postcard asking them to confirm the amount due by them at the balance date, but I understand this practice obtains in England in larger concerns dealing with equally large concerns. In the ordinary case I do not think the practice has much to commend it, but, of course, one must not overlook that it is done in banking, where customers confirm the state of their accounts by signing the bank's ledger, or signing a separate docquet slip.

Balances due by consignment agents abroad can be verified by their signed accounts current brought down to the balance date. It is important to do this, so as to see that no account sales or charges debits outlayed by the agents have been omitted from the books of account.

This question of verification of sundry debtors is just one of the cases where the correspondence passing between the company and the debtor may show by an examination of the letter books that matters are in a much worse position than is disclosed by the books of account and the officials of the company wish him to believe.

To verify the balance-sheet item sundry creditors. Here again it is an excellent plan to continue the cash audit beyond the balance date, and ascertain by the actual vouchers that the sundry creditors have all been settled, *and at the figure shown by the trial balance.* If any invoices which should have been through the purchase book prior to the balance-sheet have been omitted either by mistake or by intention, the subsequent settlement will show the error.

It is common in Scotland for business concerns to obtain from their suppliers what are called "stocktaking statements." These are invaluable for checking the ordinary trade creditors outstanding.

It would almost appear from the Irish Woollen Company case that in the normal case the auditor must verify the sundry creditors outstanding, either by stocktaking statements or the subsequent settlements. In delivering judgment against the auditor, Holmes, L.J., said :—

"There is no doubt that both the suppression and carrying over of invoices would have been detected if the auditor had called for the creditors' statements of accounts upon which payment was ordered, and compared them with the ledger. I should have thought this was part of the auditor's duty."

The only other point I will mention on the verification of assets is property held on a registered title.

The practice as regards stock or share holdings in public companies is to accept the certificate issued by the company, without verifying that the shares, in fact, stand registered in the register of members of the company.

In the case of shipping property, is it the auditor's duty to verify at the Custom House that the vessel or vessels owned by the company stand registered in the company's name?

I believe the professional practice varies.

Some auditors make a practice of doing so ; some don't.

At least that was the position about twenty years ago, when I made inquiry round certain of the offices in Glasgow as to their practice.

I think it is desirable that the company's title to the ship should be verified by examining the Custom House Register, or by getting a certificate from the Registrar of Shipping that the ship is registered at the date of the balance in the company's name.

This certificate should also cover the mortgages or other encumbrances affecting the hull of the vessel disclosed by the register.

In Scotland a ship is the only considerable form of moveable property which can be pledged in support of debt without delivery.

I wish to emphasise just one other point. The Statutory

report must deal with the position at the date of balance of the books in the light of all the circumstances and information in the knowledge of the auditor at the date he signs his report.

Thus if at 31st December 1923 a large debt due to a company shown by the books was at that date believed to be good, the debtor suspended payment grossly insolvent on 1st February 1924, and the audit was not completed and the report signed till 28th February 1924, then either the balance-sheet presented to the shareholders must deal with the item as a bad debt, or the fact must be brought to the shareholders' knowledge by the auditor's report.

The earlier judgments of the Courts of Law fixing liability on an auditor for breach of his duty are all based on a finding, in fact, that he had knowledge of the true state of matters, yet failed to have the courage to report it to the shareholders.

The judgments were given entirely in cases where the rights of creditors were involved—that is, where, through the failure to report the true state of affairs, a dividend was paid out of capital, and thus resulting in loss to the creditors on the company suspending payment.

That the auditor knew the true state of affairs was found proven from his own admissions in writing or in confidential reports to the Board of Directors.

That was the principal ground of judgment in the Leeds Building Society Company case and the London and General Bank Company case, which you will find reported in 'Dicksee on Auditing.'

The Courts have always shown a very considerable contempt of an auditor hinting in reports by vague and indefinite language that the balance-sheet is not correct, or of the auditor indicating that if the shareholders care to carry the matter further they will find the true facts.

The auditor's duty as laid down in these cases is to report to the shareholders, not to the directors, what he finds—not to hint where information may be found, but to impart it ; and if he fails to do so, he is guilty of negligence, with all the consequences which flow from such negligence.

The Kingston Cotton Mill Company case, to which I have referred before, was also a case where the rights of creditors were involved.

The stock-in-trade had been heavily and apparently increasingly overstated in the balance-sheet of the company for a number of years.

The auditor in the witness-box stated that he had checked the summations and some of the extensions at random, and thereafter relied on the manager's certificate, although from the report it is not clear that this certificate was ever in existence, and from the auditor's cross-examination some of the sheets showed no trace of his blue pencil, but he stated that even if the blue ticks were not there, the stock must have been examined.

The judge who heard the case first held the auditor liable, on the ground that in this particular case from the manner in which the bought and sold books were kept, if he had examined them by taking out the totals, he would have found that the stock as entered on the balance-sheet was grossly overstated as regards quantity, and that in these circumstances the auditor had no right to rely on a certificate which was furnished to him by the officials of the company.

In the Court of Appeal this judgment was reversed, and the auditor was freed from liability, the principal reason for the judgments of that Court reversing the earlier judgment being that they were satisfied that, while in this particular case such an examination of the stock was possible, it was not the practice of auditors to check quantities against quantities, and that the auditor had followed the ordinary course of his profession in accepting the certificate supporting the quantity and value placed on the stock in the balance-sheet.

There was not in the case the slightest suggestion that the auditor had any knowledge of the overstatement of the stock, which only came out on investigation by liquidators, which is a very different investigation from an investigation by an auditor, and, of course, is from an entirely different angle of view.

Another case you will find of considerable interest and instruction is the Irish Woollen Company case.

This was settled in the Irish Courts in January 1900.

The auditor there was held liable for the under-entry of liability in the balance-sheet certified by him, but the pecuniary amounts of same was left over until it was ascertained if the rights of creditors were involved, as only in that event was liability to attach to him. The ground of judgment of the Court apparently was that he had failed to examine invoices, and that a perusal of the company's invoice files would have distinctly shown the liabilities omitted.

Liability appears to have attached to the auditor in this case on the ground that in the circumstances of his employment the Board looked to him doing a very full audit, and in these circumstances his professional fee as auditor was considerably larger than it would otherwise have been.

The most recent case of all bearing on the liability is the *City Equitable Insurance Company* v. *The Directors and Auditors*.

The whole evidence of the accountant witnesses is reported in 'The Accountant' in February and March of last year, and the judgment of Mr Justice Romer, who heard the case, will be found in the issue of 31st May 1924, and the judgments of the Court of Appeal will be found in issue of 19th July 1924.

I do not know whether the case is going further, but in both Courts the auditor was completely assoilzied of liability.

Under Mr Justice Romer's judgment, he found in the first instance that he had been negligent in accepting certificates from brokers for securities held by them on behalf of the company, without seeing the documents showing that the brokers were, in fact, in possession of the stock ; but he was able in law to exonerate the auditor in respect that he believed that he had acted honestly throughout, and therefore came within a clause in the company's articles excluding " officers " of the company from all liability for negligence if they have, in fact, acted honestly.

This clause will be found at the end of the articles of association of many companies, and there has been a good deal of expression of opinion that as regards an auditor at least the clause should not be applicable.

For my part, I cannot quite see why the auditor should be put in a worse position than the directors of the company if he acts honestly.

221

The question of whether or not the auditor in that case was entitled to rely on the certificates he obtained is a very narrow one, and the judges in the Court of Appeal, in adhering to Mr Justice Romer's judgment, expressly stated that they did not consider it necessary to decide whether or not, apart from the clause in the articles, they would have reached the same judgment as the judge of first instance.

There was a great deal of evidence led regarding the faulty grouping of the balance-sheet items, and what is fair description under which to class the various assets —no question appears to have arisen as regards the classing of the liabilities.

I wish to consider now, with the time left at my disposal, the question of grouping of balance-sheets—that is, the arrangement of the assets and liabilities under proper headings.

To take a violent case. It would be perfectly improper to enter under the head " Government Stocks " a holding in a speculative gold mine, or under the head "Sundry Debtors " a claim for breach of contract which had been repudiated, and which has not been constituted at law by legal action.

At the risk of tiring you, I am going to repeat the very words of sec. 113 of the Companies (Consolidation) Act, 1908, regarding the balance-sheet :—

> "The auditor has to report whether in his opinion the balance-sheet referred to in his report to the shareholders is properly drawn up, so as to exhibit a true and correct view of the state of the company's affairs—
>
> (a) According to the best of his information.
>
> (b) According to the explanations given to him.
>
> (c) As shown by the books of the company.

Here the first question that arises is, " What is a balance-sheet ? "

In the first place, I do not think it is a piece of paper with the words " balance-sheet " written at the top of it, and then with sets of figures, liabilities, and assets put down at random without proper classification, on which the liability side agrees with arithmetical accuracy with the assets side.

I was once told by a prominent Inland Revenue official

in Glasgow that it appeared to him that every citizen in this country had three sets of balance-sheets :—

1. A very rosy one to show to his banker.
2. A very depressed one to show to the Inland Revenue —and his wife.
3. A fairly accurate one that showed the true state of affairs.

I may be wrong, but it seems to me that the simple meaning of sec. 112 of the Companies (Consolidation) Act is that the balance-sheet which the company have to prepare and to submit to the auditor for his examination before submission to the shareholders is the clearest statement of the company's affairs which the books disclose, supplemented by any explanations which the auditor thinks necessary to obtain from the directors or officials of the company, so as to show its financial position at the balancing date.

I think that was the intention of the framers of the Act, but in practice I fear we have got away from the simple meaning of the words.

In considering this question, " What is a balance-sheet " ? it has to be kept in view that, in addition to the balance-sheet submitted to the shareholders, the Act of 1907 also provides that in the case of companies consisting of more than fifty persons there requires to be lodged annually with the Registrar of Joint-Stock Companies a " statement in the form of a balance-sheet " showing the company's share capital, its liabilities and assets, giving (I am now quoting the very words of the Act) " such particulars as will disclose the general nature of these liabilities and assets, and how the values of the fixed assets have been arrived at."

When the Act of 1907 became law, the English Institute obtained an opinion from eminent counsel, who advised—

Where the balance-sheet does not state how the value of the assets has been arrived at, it would, in order to comply with the section, have to be supplemented by a note or memo. stating how the value of such assets is arrived at. In whatever form the " statement " is lodged, it must be audited by the company auditor, and the result of the audit should be certified at the foot of the statement.

This statement, in the form of a balance-sheet, it will

be observed, is kept on the company's file with the Registrar of Joint-Stock Companies. The file is open to the inspection of the public, which, of course, includes creditors and possible creditors of the company, as well as possible shareholders, and from the details specified in the Act and as advised by counsel, gives considerably more information than is disclosed by the published balance-sheets of many companies as issued to the shareholders.

As an example, " goodwill," according to the opinion of counsel, requires to be entered separately. Now we all know as a matter of practice, in published balance-sheets this item is generally jumbled up with ground and buildings and machinery and plant.

Surely shareholders of a company are entitled to as much information in the copy of the balance-sheet furnished to them (with the report of an auditor employed and paid by them) as is given to members of the public.

This question of " What is a true balance-sheet ? " was examined by the Court of Session in the year 1911—that is about three years after the Act of 1907 came into force— in the case of *Young* v. *Brownlee & Co., Ltd.*, 5 Session Cases, 10th March 1911.

Mr Young was an individual shareholder of the company, and complained that the stock of the company was not entered in the balance-sheet at its true value. He appears to have been a member of the Board of the company, and it was admitted that he had never attempted to raise the question of the true value at a general meeting of the shareholders. He expressly disclaimed any suggestion of fraud or impropriety against either the directors of the company or the auditor, but his point was that the stock on the basis of cost or market value was about £50,000 greater than the value at which the directors in their discretion saw fit to include it in the company's accounts. He suggested that the object which the directors had in understating the stock value as they did was to conceal the amount of profits being made in the business.

As far as he was concerned as an individual shareholder, his wish was that the stock should be shown at its cost or market value as an asset, and any reserve which the directors saw fit to make for contingencies or possible loss in actual realisation of same should be shown *per contra* as a Stock Reserve Fund.

The stock was apparently in fact under-valued, and the £50,000 of under-valuation was apparently a percentage deduction of about 31 per cent on the total cost or market value, and it appeared that the directors caused certificates to be furnished to those shareholders who desired to sell their shares of the amount which had been deducted from cost or market value in arriving at balance-sheet value of the same.

The Court refused to interfere in the matter, largely, as I can read the case, on the ground that the pursuer himself made no suggestion that the directors were actuated by any dishonest or selfish motive in stating the accounts as they did, and further, that the auditors were, in the exercise of their discretion, satisfied in passing the balance-sheet stated as above without comment.

In his case against the company, Mr Young made no allegation against the auditors, and in Lord Kinnear's judgment you will find these words : " Sec. 113 deals only with the duty of auditors, and it is not said that the auditors have not performed their duty."

Lord Skerrington, the judge of first instance, in delivering his opinion, puts the matter thus :—

" Though it is no part of an auditor's duty to value a stock of timber, it is his duty to inquire on what principle the valuation in the balance-sheet has been arrived at, and if he is dissatisfied with the explanations of the directors he should mention the matter in his docquet."

When dealing with the question, " What is a balance-sheet ? " Lord Kinnear uses these words :—

" The sole purpose of preparing a balance-sheet is to show the financial position of the company, and among other important features in their financial position is the amount of profits earned."

One would say from this case that a very great responsibility is laid on the individual auditor's shoulders in deciding whether a balance-sheet in its form complies with the requirements of sec. 112.

There is for trading companies no statutory form of

balance-sheet. The original Table A—old Table A—the model set of articles of association in the Companies Act of 1862—gives a form, copies of which are in your hands.

The articles of association laid down in Table A were, of course, optional, but even before the table was abolished and the present Table A substituted in 1906, which laid down no form of balance-sheet, the form was not in general use.

I am inclined to think that it was a backward move to abolish this form of balance-sheet.

It is certainly a model of clearness, shows a distinct and definite grouping of the assets and liabilities arranged under proper heads.

You will notice curiously that a very favourite item among the assets of a modern company, " goodwill," is not provided for.

All properly drawn balance-sheets contain the information grouped generally under the heads shown there, and I think it is a pity that the form has disappeared from the Statute Book.

The form even in its wording is not yet quite extinct. Some of the old Dundee jute companies still publish their accounts in this 1862 form.

Let us now consider one or two points arising out of the grouping in a balance-sheet.

It is not correct to group under the head "Sundry Creditors ":—

1. Creditors on simple contract.
2. Liabilities for contingencies more or less remote and very much matter of opinion.
3. Wild estimates of liabilities not yet definitely ascertained.

The fault here is lack of specification.

In a " full and fair " balance-sheet these should be shown separately.

I have in my mind's eye a balance-sheet showing under heading "Sundry Creditors and Credit Balances," say, £1,020,000.

A knowledge of this concern's credit, the manner in which their business is conducted, the high repute they have for prompt settlement of their ordinary trade accounts, would tell any one that the £20,000 was about the true "simple contract" creditors, and the balance under this heading was really reserve.

An example of over-specification is to show in great detail sonorous and indefinite names on the liability side of the balance-sheet, which no one can say whether the figures represent liability to creditors, or are simple reserves.

My complaint on these two groupings is that no one looking at the balance-sheet can form the slightest idea of what are the true liabilities of the company.

They know in a general way that all the liabilities are in these heads, but how much of them are liability and how much of them reserve no one can say, and there is no reason why it should be so.

The shareholder of a company is surely entitled to know what are the liabilities as distinct from the reserves which the directors in their prudence have made.

I am inclined to think that stockbrokers and other people who are in the habit of looking at balance-sheets as showing the position of a company have lost all faith in them, and it is for that reason that a stockbroker tells you—

1. "There's a great deal of money tucked away in the company not shown by the balance-sheet."

2. "The company's got a very big reserve fund; we don't know how much, but it's somewhere under the head 'Sundry Creditors.'"

3. "The directors are believed to have written-off the whole of the capital expenditure during the year to revenue account."

Now turning to the assets side of the balance-sheet, in stating, a distinction should be drawn between—

1. Fixed capital expenditure.
2. Floating assets.

As regards fixed assets, it is desirable that there should be a distinction between—

1. Capital expenditure on tangible assets, such as ground and buildings.

2. Capital expenditure on intangible assets, such as goodwill, trade marks, and designs.

And I think these assets should be shown at their gross cost less gross depreciation written - off since they were acquired.

You will observe from the sheet in your hands that the framers of that balance-sheet apparently held this opinion.

The practice of writing-down assets by amounts far in excess of ordinary wear and tear, where ordinary wear and tear is all the depreciation that has taken place, gives a quite fallacious idea of their worth to the company from which one can form an opinion of their present value.

If both total cost and total writings-off are shown, one can form a notion of the extent of the expenditure.

I have now completely exhausted my time, and I hope I have not equally exhausted your patience.   The late Poet Laureate wrote :—

> " There lives more faith in honest doubt
> Than in one-half the creeds."

Can we say in our case—

> " Than in half the Counsels of perfection
> That Lecturers and text-books give."

I have tried to indicate to you that there is no royal road to success as an auditor by a meticulous observation of blue tick marks, and doing summations of cash books and finding the odd 10s. 2d. that the trial balance is out.

An auditor must, in addition to thoroughly knowing the art of book-keeping, understand the terms and conditions of the trade or business carried on by his clients, and, of course, he must read and thoroughly grasp the constitution of the company as laid down in its memorandum and articles of association.

Mere arithmetical comparison of the balance-sheet with the books of account, without consideration of the transactions at the back of these figures, will not now enable him to fulfil the duties of his office with usefulness to his clients—the shareholders—or be sufficient to free him from legal responsibility to them if the balance-sheet be not " properly drawn up so as to exhibit a true and correct view of the state of the company's affairs shown by the books," supplemented with any additional information or explanations which he thinks necessary or desirable to communicate to them.

APPENDIX.

BALANCE-SHEET OF THE

CAPITAL AND LIABILITIES.

I. CAPITAL.
    Showing—
        The Number of Shares .   .
        The amount paid per share   .
        If any Arrears of Calls, the nature
          of the arrear, and the names of
          the Defaulters   .   .   .

        The Particulars of any forfeited
          Shares .   .   .   .   £

II. DEBTS AND LIABILITIES OF THE COMPANY.
    Showing—
        The Amount of Loans on Mort-
          gages or Debenture Bonds . £
        The Amount of Debts owing by
          the Company, distinguishing—
        (a) Debts for which Acceptances
            have been given   .   .
        (b) Debts to Tradesmen for sup-
            plies of Stock in Trade or
            other Articles .   .
        (c) Debts for Law Expenses   .
        (d) Debts for Interest on Deben-
            tures or other Loans .   .
        (e) Unclaimed Dividends .   .
        (f) Debts not enumerated above
                          £

III. RESERVE FUND.
    Showing—
        The Amount set aside from Profits
          to meet Contingencies .   .   £

IV. PROFIT AND LOSS.
    Showing—
        The disposable Balance for Pay-
          ment of Dividends, &c. .   .   £

                                £

      CONTINGENT LIABILITIES.
        Claims against the Company not
          acknowledged as Debts .   . £
        Moneys for which the Company is
          contingently liable .   .   . £

                              £

230

Table A of the Companies Act of 1862.

COMPANY MADE UP TO   18

PROPERTY AND ASSETS.

I. PROPERTY HELD BY THE COMPANY.
  Showing—
    Immovable Property, distinguishing—
      (a) Freehold Land .   .   . £
      (b)   „   Buildings .   .
      (c) Leasehold   „   .   .
    Movable Property, distinguishing—
      (d) Stock-in-Trade .   .   .
      (e) Plant   .   .   .   .
                                        ———— £
          The Cost to be stated with
          Deductions for Deteriora-
          tion in Value as charged to
          the Reserve Fund or Profit
          and Loss.

II. DEBTS OWING TO THE COMPANY.
  Showing—
      Debts considered good for which
      the Company hold Bills or other
      Securities   .   .   .   . £
      Debts considered good for which
      the Company hold no security .
      Debts considered doubtful and bad
                                        ———— £
          Any Debt due from a Director
          or other Officer of the Com-
          pany to be separately
          stated.

III. CASH AND INVESTMENTS.
  Showing—
      The Nature of Investment and
        Rate of Interest   .   .   . £
      The Amount of Cash, where lodged,
        and if bearing Interest   .   .
                                        ———— £
                                        ———————
                                             £
                                        ———————

George L.C. Touche, BA, FCA

The editor wrote to Mr Touche for biographical details, and the following is an extract from his response:

' .... I was born on 23 January 1903, was educated at Marlborough and University College, Oxford. I got firsts in Classical Moderations and Litterai Humaniores (Greats).

My father, Sir George Touche Bt, was well known in the City of London, and was a Chartered Accountant of Edinburgh. He founded the accounting firms of George A. Touche and Co. in England and Canada, and the firm of Touche Niven and Co. in the USA. These firms are now part of Touche Ross and Co.

I joined the family firm and qualified as a member of The Institute of Chartered Accountants in England and Wales in 1928. I was on the Council of the English Institute from 1950 to 1958, and was senior partner of the firm for many years.

In 1952, my brother Donovan Touche died, and I took his place as director of several investment trusts, in which field my father had been a principal figure in London. From this date, investment became my main activity, and in the late sixties .... the Touche investment trusts and others were brought together in a firm called Touche, Remnant and Co., which is one of the large London groups.

I retired from business bit by bit during 1970 to 1973. I have no honours or awards, and have held various directorships and committee memberships which arose out of my business position.'

George L.C. Touche, 'The Form of the Balance-Sheet' (1932-3)

Few lecturers to the Students' Societies dealt with the growing importance of financial reporting. Touche's paper is an exception to this general rule and is refreshingly modern in its outlook. It concentrated on the balance sheet as this was the then legally-required financial statement. The central theme of the lecture was the inadequacy of the traditional balance sheet in terms of its role of giving a reasonable picture of the financial position of the reporting entity. According to Touche, the main reason for the inadequacy appeared to be the bookkeeping or double-entry influence on balance sheet composition - leaving the statement as little more than a detailed trial balance.

Touche reported on the dissatisfaction of investors and financial journalists at the state of balance sheet reporting, thus emphasising the growing importance of report users in discussions of financial statements. In particular, Touche saw the need to provide a clear, unequivocal and reliable view of financial position with which investors could 'reasonably adventure their money' (an explicit statement of investment decision making and its relationship to financial statements).

The major problems associated with financial reporting were seen by Touche as, first, the unnecessary detail often given in balance sheets; second, the adequacy of depreciation when measuring profit; third, the relevance of using unallocated costs to depict fixed asset values; and, fourth, the lack of adequate classification of fixed and current assets. The latter topic formed an important part of the lecture, and Touche illustrated the effects of poor classification. He also emphasised the importance of liquidity measurements, although using the somewhat static working capital ratio for this purpose. Nevertheless, the paper described many topics which remain problems for present-day financial reporters.

THE FORM OF THE BALANCE-SHEET.

By GEORGE L. C. TOUCHE, B.A., A.C.A.

(Being a Lecture delivered to the Chartered Accountants Students' Society of Edinburgh and the Glasgow Chartered Accountants Students' Society on 23rd and 24th March 1933.)

THE NEED FOR BETTER BALANCE-SHEETS.

I HAVE chosen as my subject " The Form of the Balance-sheet," because I think this is a respect in which the traditional type of Balance-sheet to which we are accustomed in this country is most defective. A great deal of time is spent by auditors and accountants in exact calculation of numerous items, which are then grouped under certain traditional headings, with little thought of the effect of the statement as a whole. The result of this practice is that Balance-sheets are frequently open to the criticism that they do not give the information they should give, that is, the salient facts of the financial position, and are encumbered with figures which afford a great deal of miscellaneous information of small relative importance which is inappropriate and obstructive in such a condensed form of statement as a Balance-sheet must inevitably be.

As evidence of my statement that the traditional Balance-sheet is an inadequate document, I need only adduce the fact that it is not used for any serious business where accuracy is of importance. In questions of the valuation of businesses for purchase or sale, of taxation, of cost accounting, and, in general, in cases where accuracy is essential, the accounts presented to the shareholders, although they may be used as a basis, are usually adjusted by the addition and subtraction of so many items as to render the final result often widely different from the original picture.

236

Herein lies the distinction between Accountancy and Bookkeeping. I do not think it unfair to say that many Balance-sheets of important companies still amount to little more than bookkeeping. But there is a growing pressure within our profession and a rising clamour on the part of the investing public and the financial press to produce Balance-sheets which mean something; Balance-sheets which do not get so far out of touch with reality that it is possible for a company to reach a condition where the greater part of the ordinary capital has to be written off, without any direct and adequate warning, intelligible to the non-technical, having been given in the Balance-sheet. Wherever this sort of thing happens, it is a black mark against our profession.

Let us begin by considering what a Balance-sheet is, and what information it is intended and can be expected to afford.

ARITHMETICAL CONVENTIONS.

Historically, the Balance-sheet is a development of the list of balances left on the ledger after making the closing entries. As a result of its origin in the double-entry ledger, the Balance-sheet has two sides. There is no intrinsic reason why the Balance-sheet should have two sides, and a Balance-sheet in statement form (with one side only) could be prepared with perfect propriety from a double-entry ledger.

I should like to consider, in passing, this question of double entry, because I think the text-books are apt to create a rather misleading impression about it in the minds of students. The text-books either leave the impression, or state in so many words, that " every transaction has two aspects which are reflected in the debit and credit side of the entry." In so far as such statements appear to imply that this double aspect of commercial transactions is a law of Nature in the economic sphere, which has been discovered by accountants in the same manner as discoveries are made in the sphere of physics, they are responsible, in my opinion, for much of the difficulty experienced by accountancy students in those first baffling months of study. It is, of course, nonsense to imagine that a transaction has fundamentally two aspects. Any concrete historical transaction has exactly as many aspects as the points from which it is viewed.

The purpose of double entry is to provide a purely arithmetical check and afford additional analysis. You enter every transaction in the ledger twice, in different columns, in such a manner that the balancing of the columns proves the correctness of the arithmetic. This provides a single check ; if a double check is wanted, there is no reason, other than the great labour involved, why the books should not be kept on a treble-entry basis. At the same time, double entry affords an analysis of receipts or expenditure which is of value for business management.

I fear this digression may have seemed rather elementary. What I wanted to make clear was : in the first place, that the two sides of the Balance-sheet are an historical accident arising out of the form of the double-entry ledger ; and secondly, that in the double-entry ledger this duality has largely an arithmetical purpose.

This arbitrary feature of the modern Balance-sheet is unfortunate, and leads to much confusion in the minds of those who are not trained accountants. Even in our own profession the arbitrary nature of the arrangement is not fully recognised, and some accountants endeavour to import some significance into it by labelling the two sides 'Assets' and 'Liabilities.' The layman naturally asks how accumulated losses can be an asset, and how a general reserve can be a liability. The truthful answer is : they cannot. The accountant then juggles with words in the endeavour to make the headings a true description of the items listed under them. We are all familiar with such headings as the following : 'Capital and Liabilities,' 'Liabilities, Capital and Reserves,' 'Assets and Debit Balances.' But in the last resort the only true headings are 'Most Debit Balances less Some Credit Balances' and 'Most Credit Balances less Some Debit Balances,' which, in the language of the geometricians, is absurd.

WHAT SHOULD A BALANCE-SHEET SHOW.

Leaving these rather academic questions, let us consider what a Balance-sheet may be expected to show. It is the final summary into which all the other accounts of the business are ultimately merged. A large industrial combine operating in a number of allied but distinct industries, employing many thousands of men and women and trading in many distant parts of the world, has to record its financial position at a given date on a piece of paper about a foot square. Clearly the amount of information which can be given on this piece of paper is not one-hundredth part of that which is available; and yet this information, combined with that given in the Profit and Loss Account and other published statements, must be sufficient to enable investors, bankers, creditors and other interested parties to obtain a clear and unequivocal view of the financial position of the concern, upon which they feel they can rely and upon which they can reasonably adventure their money.

Now, this is a very difficult problem, and indeed, if it were not being done every day, it would appear at first attempt an almost insurmountable problem. The difficulty of selection, when one has to reduce in the ratio of 100 to 1, appears to be such as to render the result quite arbitrary and dependent upon the caprice of the selector.

The burden is, however, very much lightened by the fact that there are a small number of points about the financial position of a company (I am speaking throughout of the normal industrial undertaking) which are so important as to overshadow everything else, and if these points are clearly presented in the Balance-sheet, the financial position of the undertaking can, within very fine limits, be accurately ascertained.

What are these points? I think it would not be contested that in normal cases the most important thing to know about a company is the profit or loss it is making. This should be shown by the Profit and Loss Account, but I am only speaking on this occasion about the Balance-sheet. My reason for that, apart from a desire to limit the subject to what can be handled in the time at my disposal, is that I do not feel the shortcomings of the Profit and Loss Account to be problems of form so much as questions of honesty. What the investor wants to know from the Profit and Loss Account is: What is the profit? And when we find the figure of profit, we scrutinise the account to see if the profit has been struck at the right place, or if depreciation, interest and other charges have been left out. We scrutinise the provision for depreciation not so much because we want to know what depreciation the company actually suffers, but to see whether the provision made appears generous or niggardly. This gives us a guide to the degree of honesty with which the accounts have been drawn up, and I think that if the investor could always be sure that the published figure of profit was a genuine and honest net profit for the year, there would be very little of the clamour we now hear for increased information in the Profit and Loss Account, the details of which are after all of interest primarily for the management.

I trust, therefore, that you will make the necessary mental reservation when I speak of certain items as being of great or little importance, and understand that I am speaking of the Balance-sheet as showing the financial position at a date, and not of the Profit and Loss Account which shows the results over a period. I do not belittle the Profit and Loss Account, but I regard its problems as more in the field of morality than of accountancy. The question of form is not so pressing.

THE LIQUID POSITION.

Reverting, therefore, to the important points which the Balance-sheet should demonstrate, I think there is nothing which will so surely cause a company to founder, in spite of an apparent sufficiency of total assets, as the inability to meet liabilities as and when they fall due. When this happens, it is a common experience to see the control of a company with a large total of assets passing out of the hands of the shareholders, for no adequate consideration, into those of a group who come forward with the small amount of money necessary to relieve the company from its temporary embarrassment.

I do not think, therefore, that we shall be far wrong in putting as the most important factor in the financial position of the ordinary industrial concern, the proportion of current assets to current liabilities—more shortly described as ' the liquid position.' From an analysis of a large number of industrial Balance-sheets it has been found that a proportion of 2 to 1 may be considered normal, and a company with a ratio of less than this would not be regarded as in a strong position. Many powerful companies have a proportion in the region of 10 to 1. These figures are not intended to be dogmatic. It is clearly a matter in which the special circumstances of each trade intervene. I have, however, found the 2 to 1 ratio a useful test in the case of an ordinary industrial concern.

If we agree the importance of the liquid position, it remains to ask in what manner is this vital factor illustrated in the statements which the accountants of this country prepare. I think it is safe to say that in four cases out of five this ratio can only be ascertained by taking a pencil and doing a little sum, and in the fifth case it is often found that the classification into fixed and current assets has been made so unintelligently as to amount to serious error. One often meets the view that the word 'fixed' in the expression 'fixed assets' means rooted to the soil and therefore only applies to land, buildings and plant, while all other assets are 'floating,' because they are not attached to the soil. This view is utterly absurd, and I would not have mentioned it here at all but that it dies so hard, and I have had it advanced to me even by leaders in our profession who ought to know better. The distinction between 'fixed assets' and 'floating assets' is not a physical distinction but a financial one. I prefer to use the American term 'current,' which has a well-defined meaning, rather than the ambiguous term 'floating.'

I have said above that even where separate totals for fixed assets and current assets and liabilities are shown on a Balance-sheet, the classification is often so unintelligently made as to amount to error. Items are included in the total current assets which are not liquid funds available for the general purposes of business. The following items, for instance, should not be classed as current assets :—

Stocks of material for the construction or repair of capital assets.

Advances to customers and others which are really for the purpose of financing their businesses, or

> though not originally made for that purpose
> have become frozen. This is often the case with
> amounts owing by subsidiary companies.
>
> All investments except those that represent the
> temporary investment of surplus cash.
>
> Cash and securities in the hands of the trustees for
> debenture-holders, or otherwise earmarked for
> purposes other than the discharge of current
> liabilities.

The list could be multiplied. I mention a few to illustrate the principle.

On the liabilities side the same care must be taken to see that the current liabilities are properly stated. The American rule in this matter is that nothing should be included in current assets which will not be turned into cash within a year from the date of the Balance-sheet, and that any liability that is due for payment within a year from that date should be classed as a current liability. It follows that if there is an issue of debentures or short-term notes which falls due for repayment three months after the date of the Balance-sheet, the total of current liabilities would be incorrectly stated if it did not include such debentures or notes, and a misleading idea of the liquidity of the company would be obtained by comparing the current assets and current liabilities.

I have laboured this question of current assets and current liabilities because I think it requires very careful consideration if the accountancy profession is to evolve a form of Balance-sheet which is reliable and intelligible to the ordinary investor.

To illustrate this and later points I have prepared three imaginary Balance-sheets (see pp. 64-68). They are all composed of the same items, but are in different forms. The company whose financial position is portrayed in these Balance-sheets is really in a very precarious condition.

Balance-sheet ' A ' is what I call the traditional type of English Balance-sheet, which is still the most common. I do not think it unfair to say that this form of Balance-sheet discloses practically nothing about the financial position until one has done a good deal of mental arithmetic. To the many shareholders who cannot do mental arithmetic and are too lazy to get pencil and paper and do a small sum, I do not think it unfair to say that this Balance-sheet fails to disclose that the concern is in a precarious condition.

Balance-sheet ' B ' is what I consider to be a more correct Balance-sheet, without departing too much from the conventional form. From this Balance-sheet it is at once apparent that the company is not solvent. It cannot meet its liabilities, as and when they fall due, without selling its fixed assets (which means going out of business) or procuring new capital.

Although the items are the same in Balance-sheets ' A ' and ' B,' I would draw your attention to certain important details brought out by the more correct construction of the second Balance-sheet.

You observe that the secured loans are in fact repayable on 1st April 1933, that is, three months after the date of the Balance-sheet, and are therefore classed as current liabilities.

You will also observe that the reserve for taxation is a provision for an actual liability, and is not a free reserve.

The value of the buildings at the London and Glasgow depots shows an increase in Balance-sheet ' B ' of £10,000. This represents the construction of a new building in London, the lease of the original building having expired. At the date of the Balance-sheet the building was in process of construction, and only £15,000 of the total price of £25,000 had been paid to the contractors. In Balance-sheet ' A ' only the amount actually paid has been brought on to the books. The failure to disclose the liability for the final instalment, which actually fell due in February, gives a misleading view of the liquid position.

Another point you will observe is that the investments shown in Balance-sheet ' A ' at £107,500 turn out to be composed as to £102,000 of unmarketable investments, while only a small balance of £5500 represents genuinely liquid resources.

In Balance-sheet ' B ' I have placed the current assets and liabilities at the top of the Balance-sheet in order to emphasise their importance. This leaves the fixed assets

A.—BALANCE-SHEET

Liabilities.

	£	s.	d.	£	s.	d.
Share capital, authorised and issued—						
200,000 shares of £1 each, fully paid . . .		.		200,000	0	0
6 per cent First Mortgage Debentures .	100,000	0	0			
Less : Redeemed to date . .	28,810	5	0			
				71,189	15	0
Secured loans	15,000	0	0			
Interest accrued	2,052	12	6			
				17,052	12	6
Sundry creditors		.		189,047	16	2
Bills payable		.		14,106	13	4
Reserve for taxation		.		9,250	0	0
General reserve—						
As per last Balance-sheet . .	12,000	0	0			
Transfer from Profit and Loss Account .	3,000	0	0			
				15,000	0	0
Profit and Loss Account—						
As per last Balance-sheet . .	2,209	17	4			
Profit for year	5,020	12	1			
	7,230	9	5			
Less : Transfer to general reserve . .	3,000	0	0			
				4,230	9	5
				519,877	6	5

AS AT 31ST DECEMBER 1932.

Assets.

	£	s.	d.	£	s.	d.
Freehold property, Coventry, at cost—						
As per last Balance-sheet . . .	49,857	12	5			
Additions during year	1,749	1	2			
				51,606	13	7
Leasehold properties, London and Glasgow, at cost, less amounts written off—						
As per last Balance-sheet . . .	32,042	5	9			
Additions during year	592	6	4			
	32,634	12	1			
Depreciation for year	749	0	2			
				31,885	11	11
Plant and machinery, at cost less depreciation—						
As per last Balance-sheet . . .	104,052	10	0			
Additions during year	10,561	3	6			
	114,613	13	6			
Depreciation for year	9,642	1	9			
				104,971	11	9
Loose tools and equipment, at cost less depreciation . .				5,085	16	2
Furniture, fixtures and fittings, at cost less depreciation—						
Coventry, per last Balance-sheet . .	3,841	0	5			
Additions during year	169	10	6			
	4,010	10	11			
Depreciation for year	200	10	0			
	3,810	0	11			
London and Glasgow, per last Balance-sheet .	1,571 13 0					
Additions during year .	37 10 0					
	1609 3 0					
Depreciation for year .	80 10 0					
	1,528	13	0			
				5,338	13	11
Stock and work in progress, as certified by the managing director				82,456	5	9
Investments, at cost .				107,500	10	6
Sundry debtors	74,506	1	4			
Less : Reserve for bad and doubtful debts	2,000	0	0			
				72,506	1	4
Payments in advance				146	7	9
Amounts due from directors . . .				75	8	7
Bills receivable				5,000	0	0
Discount on debentures				10,000	0	0
Preliminary expenses				13,289	7	6
Cash in hands of trustees for debenture-holders .				24,500	10	0
Cash at bankers	5,142	7	2			
Cash in hand	372	0	6			
				5,514	7	8
				519,877	6	5

E

B.—BALANCE-SHEET,

	£ s. d.	£ s. d.
Current liabilities—		
Bills payable for goods supplied . .	14,106 13 4	
Trade creditors and expenses . . .	189,047 16 2	
Income tax	9,250 0 0	
Final instalment on rebuilding of London premises	10,000 0 0	
Secured loans, repayable 1st April 1933, and accrued interest . . .	17,052 12 6	
		239,457 2 0
Funded debt—		
6 per cent First Mortgage Debentures, repayable 1st January 1935, at par		71,189 15 0
Total liabilities . . .		310,646 17 0
Invested capital—		
Share capital, authorised and issued—		
200,000 shares of £1 each, fully paid .	200,000 0 0	
General reserve	15,000 0 0	
Unappropriated profits	4,230 9 5	
	219,230 9 5	

		£ s. d.	
Less : Unproductive capital expenditure—			
Discount on debentures . . .	£10,000 0 0		
Preliminary expenses	13,289 7 6		
		23,289 7 6	
			195,941 1 11
			506,587 18 11

at the bottom opposite the invested capital, which I also consider appropriate.

I have now dealt with the first, and what I consider the most important, of the points which reflect a company's financial position; that is, the proportion of current assets to current liabilities or 'the liquid position.' Let us pass on to the second point.

THE DEBT POSITION.

In my view, the second point in order of magnitude is this: How much of the assets belong to the shareholders, and how much represent creditors' moneys. We may term this 'the debt position.'

I would like to illustrate the connection of this point

31ST DECEMBER 1932.

	£	s.	d.	£	s.	d.
Current assets—						
Cash	5,514	7	8			
Securities, at market value . . .	5,500	0	0			
Amounts due from customers . . .	77,506	1	4			
Amounts due from directors . . .	75	8	7			
Payments in advance of current expenses .	146	7	9			
Stocks of raw materials, and partly and wholly manufactured goods . . .	82,456	5	9			
				171,198	11	1
Cash in the hands of the trustees for the debenture-holders .				24,500	10	0
Fixed assets—						
Freehold factory and manufacturing plant at Coventry, at cost less depreciation .	165,474	2	5			
Leasehold depots and distributing equipment at London and Glasgow, at cost less depreciation	43,414	4	11			
Trade investments, at cost . . .	102,000	10	6			
				310,888	17	10
				506,587	18	11

with the preceding one. A company with a poor liquid position can doctor it by increasing its funded debt and using the proceeds to pay off its current liabilities. This improves the liquid position, but leaves as bad a dislocation in the debt position as before, and is in fact liable to lead to worse.

The proportion of creditors' to shareholders' money illustrates the pressure of debt on the concern. In times of good trade and high profits a large volume of debt may result in increased profits for the shareholders, owing to the rate of profit earned in the business being higher than the rate of interest on the debt. A company in this position is, however, very sensitive to changes in trade, and is exceptionally vulnerable in times of depression. In those times the company continues to have an advantage over companies with less heavy debt until the rate of profit

C.—BALANCE-SHEET.

31st December 1932.

	£	s.	d.	£	s.	d.
Current assets—						
Cash	5,514	7	8			
Securities, at market value	5,500	0	0			
Amounts due from customers	77,506	1	4			
Amounts due from directors	75	8	7			
Payments in advance of current expenses	146	7	9			
Stock of raw materials, and partly and wholly manufactured goods	82,456	5	9			
				171,198	11	1
Current liabilities—						
Bills payable for goods supplied	14,106	13	4			
Trade creditors and expenses	189,047	16	2			
Income tax	9,250	0	0			
Final instalment on rebuilding of Glasgow premises	10,000	0	0			
Secured loans, repayable 1st April 1933, and accrued interest	17,052	12	6			
				239,457	2	0
				68,258	*10*	*11*
Fixed assets—						
Freehold factory and manufacturing plant at Coventry, at cost less depreciation	165,474	2	5			
Leasehold depots and distributing equipment at London and Glasgow, at cost less depreciation	43,414	4	11			
Trade investments, at cost	102,000	10	6			
				310,888	17	10
				242,630	6	11
Funded debt—						
6 per cent First Mortgage Debentures, repayable 1st January 1935, at par	71,189	15	0			
Less : Cash in the hands of the trustees for the debenture-holders	24,500	10	0			
				46,689	5	0
Balance being invested capital				195,941	1	11
Represented by—						
Share capital, authorised and issued—						
200,000 shares of £1 each, fully paid	200,000	0	0			
General reserve	15,000	0	0			
Unappropriated profits	4,230	9	5			
				219,230	9	5
Less : Unproductive capital expenditure—						
Discount on debentures £10,000 0 0						
Preliminary expenses . 13,289 7 6				23,289	7	6
				195,941	1	11

earned falls to the point at which it equals the rate of interest on the debt. Every further fall beyond this point results in an increasing burden. The pressure may in a surprisingly short time become intolerable and lead to a receivership or other crisis, resulting in the control passing out of the shareholders' hands.

I think then that this feature may fairly be described as the second great point in the financial position of a company. To illustrate it, I will ask you to return to our two Balance-sheets 'A' and 'B' and appraise their success in recording this feature.

Let us look first at Balance-sheet 'A.' What we want to know is the value of the total assets, the amount of the shareholders' interest in those assets and the amount of debt.

In the first place, this Balance-sheet gives a figure of total assets which includes two items representing expenditure on capital account which does not involve the acquisition of corresponding assets and may be called 'unproductive capital expenditure.' I refer to "Discount on Debentures, £10,000" and "Preliminary expenses, £13,289." I think it a most undesirable thing that lost or expended capital should be shown on the assets side of a Balance-sheet. This is one of those conventions which is most puzzling to the layman, and rightly so, as it appears to be based on no more intelligent principle than the mere arithmetic of double entry.

Having made the necessary adjustment for these two items, and arrived at a figure of total assets, we want to know the total debt and the total amount of the shareholders' interest.

On Balance-sheet 'A' the total debt is not apparent, but has to be picked out and added up; and when you come to the item "Reserve for taxation," you are in two minds as to whether to include this or not. It may be a liability or it may be a free reserve.

When you come to reckon up the amount of the shareholders' interest, you are in worse plight. You have to add together the issued capital, the general reserve and the balance on Profit and Loss Account, and you have the same ambiguity with regard to the reserve for taxation.

Having arrived at this figure you have to deduct the dead wood still carried among the assets in the form of "Discount on Debentures" and "Preliminary expenses."

Balance-sheet 'A' cannot therefore be regarded as a success in supplying this particular piece of information. What of Balance-sheet 'B'?

In this second Balance-sheet the true total of assets is shown, and the true worth of the shareholders' interest is shown, assuming that the assets have been correctly valued. The total of the debt is also shown.

You will observe that the capital and free reserves have been added together. This is following American practice in which all proprietors' funds are grouped together under the heading of "Net worth." I think this practice is an advance on the traditional English presentation. The language of the American heading is neat but barbarous, but I have not been able to think of an equally neat substitute.

Effect of Form in Balance-sheets.

With regard to the proportions between the various figures on a Balance-sheet, I am going to confine myself to-night to the two already discussed : first, the proportion of current assets to current liabilities ; and secondly, the proportionate interests of shareholders and creditors. These two are of such significance that by themselves they take one a long way towards assessing the financial position of the normal commercial undertaking, and a recognition of their importance has direct effects on the "Form of the Balance-sheet," which is the subject of this lecture.

Let us now take the two Balance-sheets 'A' and 'B' and look at them through the eyes of an investor. What do they tell us about the company?

Balance-sheet 'A' would probably be praised in some sections of the press as being a commendably frank and detailed statement. It gives a full analysis of the buildings and plant, showing under each heading the capital expenditure during the year and the amount written off for depreciation. The amount written off plant and machinery is between 8 and 9 per cent, while 5 per cent is written off fixtures. These rates seem quite reasonable and do not suggest any cheese-paring. The amount provided for doubtful debts is shown, and there are large totals against debtors and stocks, suggesting a substantial volume of business. Investments figure at £107,500, and this figure suggests, from its position in the list, comfortable resources in case of need; while cash items of one form or another total £30,000.

On the other side of the Balance-sheet it is seen that the company has redeemed a substantial amount of its debentures, and the amount outstanding will shortly be still further reduced by the application of the funds in the hands of the trustees. The company appears to be gradually building up a general reserve, and the taxation reserve from its position in the Balance-sheet may be an additional free reserve. A profit of $2\frac{1}{2}$ per cent on the capital was made during a year of exceptionally bad trade, and conservative practice is shown by the transfer of the bulk of it to general reserve.

I think we may fairly say that the general impression of this Balance-sheet on the usual inexperienced investor, is that although the company is experiencing, in common with other companies, a period of very poor trade, it appears to be conservatively and conscientiously managed and should be able to keep its head above water until the tide turns.

That Balance-sheet 'A' should give this impression is little short of scandalous. And yet, although it would not in some respects pass the test of the most conscientious views in our profession, there is not, I think, anything in it for which precedent could not be found in our common practice. I think a clean auditors' certificate could be attached to it without incurring any liability on account of negligence.

Now turn to Balance-sheet 'B.' It is at once apparent that the company cannot carry on without the provision of further finance. So far from the current assets reaching the proportion of double the current liabilities, which we postulated as desirable for a sound position in a concern of this nature, they actually fall short of the current liabilities by £68,000. In addition to this, the balance of the debentures falls due for repayment in three years. There is still £71,000 outstanding, against which the company has only provided £24,000.

Applying our second criterion we find that the liabilities exceeded the capital invested by £115,000.

From this Balance-sheet it can be seen, after a short consideration, that the company requires about £120,000 to keep the wolf from the door, without providing anything for working capital.

We have now got to the point where we can ask: Why is it that these two Balance-sheets give such a different first impression? They are composed of the same items, and with the exception of bringing in the outstanding building commitment in Balance-sheet 'B,' which was omitted in Balance-sheet 'A,' the figures themselves are identical.

Why is it, then, that the first casual impression is so different? My answer is that it is due to the form of the Balance-sheet, based upon two totally different conceptions of the relative importance of various aspects.

The Importance of Selection.

As I said at the beginning of this lecture, a Balance-sheet represents a condensation on a tremendous scale. In order to impress this upon you, I will repeat my words: "The Balance-sheet is the final summary into which all the other accounts of the business are ultimately merged. A large industrial combine, operating in a number of allied but distinct industries, employing many thousands of men and women and trading in many distant parts of the world, has to record its financial position at a given date on this piece of paper. The amount of information which can be given on this piece of paper is not one-hundredth part of that which is available, and yet this information, combined with that given in the Profit and Loss Account and other published statements, must be sufficient to enable investors, bankers, creditors and other interested parties to obtain a clear and unequivocal view of the financial position of the concern."

There is no room for haphazard selection. Not only must every item which finds a place on the face of the Balance-sheet justify its position as a vital and important figure, but extreme care must be taken to see that the material is so grouped and arranged that the fundamental facts of the financial position are clearly shown.

It is just on these two points that Balance-sheet ' A ' fails. Look at it, this ' clear and detailed statement.' Detailed it certainly is, but clear it is not, precisely because it is detailed. You cannot have detail on a Balance-sheet without obscuring the proportions between the various parts and the whole, and these proportions are so much more important than any details likely to be disclosed, that the quantity should be cut down to the most that can be given without obscuring the major factors. On the assets side of Balance-sheet ' A ' there are fifteen items in the total column. In my view, the maximum number of items that are desirable in the total column on either side of the Balance-sheet is five, and a smaller number is to be preferred. The mind cannot easily hold a greater number in proper perspective, and what matters is the perspective— the relative and not the absolute size of the figures.

Look again at Balance-sheet ' A.' Look at the great mass of details given in connection with the fixed assets. There are no less than twenty-five figures down to the end of the item " Furniture, fixtures and fittings." All this information is comparatively unimportant. It is not important to know that £37, 10s. was spent on fixtures at London and Glasgow during the year, nor that £80, 10s. was written off. I would even go further and say that it is not very important to know the division of the book value between buildings, plant, loose equipment and fixtures. Industrial plant stands as one, and its value falls as one if it cannot earn profits. There is some argument for showing the value of land separately, as land generally holds its value ; but even this generalisation is subject to numerous qualifications in special circumstances. On this subject I would even go so far as to say that I see little objection to grouping land, buildings, plant, machinery, loose tools, furniture, fixtures and fittings in one item; although I know the text-books regard this as a heresy. Many Balance-sheets I have seen would have had their clarity increased by such a procedure in a degree out of proportion to the value of the detail lost.

I hope I have said enough to indicate that in framing a Balance-sheet one should always be satisfied, first, that one has made the salient points of the financial position quite clear; and secondly, that any detail introduced is relatively more important than other detail left out, and does not obscure the general picture. Balance-sheet ' A ' fails on both these points.

You may think that I have been unfair to Balance-sheet ' A,' that I have loaded the dice against it. You may say that the best accountants would have stated the repayment dates of the debentures and loans, would not have left the ambiguity in the reserve for taxation, and would have included the outstanding liability for the London building. I admit the auditor would probably have liked to remedy all these faults; but supposing the directors had not agreed with him, would he have qualified his report accordingly? This is largely a matter of the individual conscience, but it is a very usual thing for Balance-sheets to be published containing loans and debentures without any reference to the terms of repayment; I might almost say it is the rule rather than the exception. Similarly with regard to the reserve for taxation, the directors could point out that the reserve was earmarked for a particular kind of liability and was adequate to cover that liability up to the date of the Balance-sheet. The omission of the building commitment is in my view a more serious defect, but I do not think that even here I have gone beyond what is commonly done in the Balance-sheets of public companies. It would be argued that at the date of the Balance-sheet the building was still incomplete, and the use of it had not passed to the company. I do not think that a very good argument, but it is one that is often advanced.

You may also say that all this has nothing to do with form, that most of the information could have been given in Balance-sheet ' A ' without altering the form. That is to some extent true, but my point is this : The form of Balance-sheet ' A ' admits of these and similar defects and ambiguities, and still remains a passable Balance-sheet. The form of Balance-sheet ' B ' compels you to face these questions, and the Balance-sheet cannot be made up without committing oneself on these matters.

Do not imagine that I regard Balance-sheet ' B ' as a perfect Balance-sheet. Very far from it. I regard it as a good Balance-sheet within the limits of the existing conventions. It shows the current assets and the current liabilities ; it shows the total debt and the value of the capital invested. The accuracy of this last figure is dependent on the accuracy of the valuation of the assets. There is no great difficulty in valuing current assets, and a reasonable approximation to the truth can generally be made. I have assumed that there is also a golden rule for valuing fixed assets, which is not in fact the case. I have assumed throughout this lecture that the figures set against the assets properly represent their values, for my subject was " The Form of the Balance-sheet," and I did not wish to be involved in the question of valuation, which is a separate subject.

THE VALUATION OF FIXED ASSETS.

I had intended to say something on the question of valuation, under the heading of " The Auditor's Responsibility for Values," but I have dealt with the question of form at greater length than I had intended.

The question of the valuation of fixed assets is, in my view, the most difficult question in accountancy, and I do not mind confessing to you that I do not know what the figures set opposite the fixed assets in a Balance-sheet are intended to represent. What do they mean ? There appear to be two widely held and mutually contradictory views among accountants. On one view they represent present value, and on the other view they represent unamortised expenditure. Against the first view it may be objected that there is no known method of accurately measuring the present value ; and against the second, that if these figures do not represent some kind of present value, it renders the Balance-sheet a comparatively academic and useless document.

THE DANGERS OF ARBITRARY CONVENTIONS.

The science of accountancy is still adolescent, and is still in process of emerging from bookkeeping. We are hampered by bookkeeping traditions and bookkeeping conventions. Balance-sheet ' B ' reflects this in having two sides which add up to the same figure. I would have preferred one side only, as in Balance-sheet ' C.' (It is significant that a similar form to this is used by some statistical services.) The exact balancing of the two sides of the conventional Balance-sheets is a legacy from the double-entry ledger, and adds nothing but mystery and confusion in the minds of those not acquainted with bookkeeping, and even, if we are to believe all we hear, in the minds of learned Judges.

In the field of valuation these conventions are far more serious. It may truly be said that in some businesses the Balance-sheet cannot properly be understood unless one is familiar with the conventions generally used in such businesses for the valuation of their assets. All these conventions militate against a clear and intelligible statement. If our profession is not to become pettifogging, it is our business to develop a concise and lucid accountancy adequate to the increasing complexity of modern industry.

Obituary

McHAFFIE, Arthur Newton Edward, B.COM., died on January 9, 1973, in his 71st year. He was retired and living at Lea Rig, Golf Road, Ballater, Aberdeenshire.

Mr McHaffie was a member of Council of the Scottish Institute from 1955 to 1960 and was also a member of the London Local Committee from 1954 to 1960. He served as Convener of sub-committees set up for the Self-Employed Retirement Benefit Scheme and for the Employees of Professional Firms Retirement Benefit Scheme. He was elected Mayor of the Royal Borough of Kensington in 1958, having been a member of that Borough's Council since 1949, serving on many of its committees.

Mr McHaffie was Group Managing Director of Associated Electrical Industries Ltd. until his retiral in 1956, after which he practised as a financial consultant. Admitted (*Edinburgh*) 1925.

<u>Arthur N.E. McHaffie, 'Rising Price Levels in Relation to Accounts'</u>
<u>(1949-50)</u>

The effects of rising prices were being felt immediately following the
Second World War, and McHaffie's paper is an example of the discussion
which took place in the UK at the end of the 1940s and beginning of the
1950s. It was concerned with a debate on the merits of introducing
some form of replacement cost accounting. In particular, McHaffie
described what he termed the economic concept of profit - that is, profit
after preserving capital having allowed for the replacement of assets.
The major problem was identified by him as the assumption in historic
cost accounting of the stability of the money unit. Thus, he confused
the issue of constant purchasing power (general price changes) with
replacement cost (specific price changes). However, the focus of the
paper was entirely on the latter topic.

   McHaffie's lecture explored certain of the alternatives to
traditional historic cost practice - that is, either transferring lump
sums from historic cost profit to reserve; transferring lump sums from
revenue to capital reserves; or revaluing fixed assets and depreciating
the revalued figure. The first two methods would not disturb the historic
cost basis of accounting but would retain profits in the business; the
last method resembled a form of replacement cost accounting.

   The paper discussed other related issues - the use of actual price
changes or index movements; the need to cope with inventory and fixed
asset price changes; and the effects of these suggestions on taxation.
McHaffie did not provide any definite solutions, although he saw the
need for a form of replacement cost accounting if price increases persisted.
The paper should therefore be taken as an example of a growing awareness
of a long-lived problem.

259

RISING PRICE LEVELS IN RELATION TO ACCOUNTS.

By A. N. E. M'HAFFIE, B.Comm., C.A.

(Being a Lecture delivered to the Chartered Accountants Students' Society of Edinburgh on 13th January 1950.)

In my talk this evening I shall confine myself to the effect of the rising price level on accounting. I use the term " accounting " rather than " accounts "; and if I may venture into the realm of definition, accounting may be termed the principles, and the practice, under which accounts are produced.

In brief summary, my talk deals firstly with what we mean price level; secondly, the impact of a rising price level on industry, as measured by its accounts; and, thirdly, what measures industry should take towards the problem.

PRICES AND PRICE LEVEL.

What do we mean when we refer to a price ?

Price may be defined as the value of goods or services expressed in terms of money. In other words, Price is a measure, but unlike, for example, measures of length or weight, Money, the measure itself, is not a constant.

When we speak of rising price levels, we mean that the value of goods or services has increased in relation to money. We can therefore view the problem which we have before us in two ways: we can say that the price of goods has increased, or we can say that the value of money has decreased.

Price levels are continually changing. An article bought in 1938, the year before the late war, at a cost of £100, would have cost £215-£220 in 1948, and to-day its price would be even higher. During the depression in 1932 you could have bought the same article for £85-£90. In 1920 it would have cost £255-£260, and in 1913 the cost would have been £80-£85.

HISTORY OF PRICE LEVELS.

I would, at this point, refer you to the table of prices (reproduced as Appendix I.), which is based on the Board of Trade Index for General Wholesale Prices. This Index [1] appears to be the most suitable to industrial and accounting conditions, and uses 1938 as the base year. By interpolation, and conversion from an older table, I have carried the data back to 1924 and 1913, which in turn were used as base years, and have set out an index table for the period of approximately forty years—from 1910 to 1948. And if you refer to the reproduction of the index table in chart form (reproduced as Appendix II.), you will see some of the contortions of the price level within our own time. When we speak of price, therefore, it is as if we were trying to measure something with an elastic ruler.

DEVALUATION OF THE POUND STERLING.

My talk this evening would not be complete unless I made reference to devaluation of the pound. As you will recollect, there were persistent rumours during the summer of 1949 that the pound would be devalued, and in September of that year, after the summer recess, the Chancellor of the Exchequer announced the cheaper pound.

Devaluation, and all its implications, is a subject by itself, but I should like to say, in reference to our subject this evening, that devaluation was the official recognition of the *de facto* state of affairs whereby the value of the pound sterling had decreased in terms of goods and services provided by countries with other currencies, especially the dollar area.

The immediate effect of devaluation, so far as price levels are concerned, has not been particularly marked; resulting in a rise of possibly a point or two, but we have still to see the cumulative effect of the time lag in the increase in production costs. Devaluation is undoubtedly inflationary, and adds impetus to those factors which are tending to push prices to an even higher level.

ACCOUNTING ON THE BASIS OF HISTORICAL COST.

In the financial accounts which we draw up periodically we seek to display all the activities of a business; what it has done, what

---

[1] The Board of Trade Index for Intermediate Products is possibly more applicable, but the data for this Index are not available for the whole of the same period.

it consists of, how much it is worth, all measured in terms of the temperamental yardstick which we have been examining.

The accountant's approach to the problem has, generally speaking, until recently been quite straightforward. Metaphorically speaking, he clutched at the pound sterling like a drowning man at a straw. " I cannot allow this to vary," he said, " it makes nonsense of my accounts." So he stuck to the principle of accounting on a historical basis, on the assumption that the value of the pound remained unchanged.

Let us see what this implied. Suppose an asset was purchased in 1938 at a cost of £100. We will assume a life of five years and write off depreciation at 20 per cent on the diminishing value, thus reducing the book value of the asset to £33. If the asset, for simplicity's sake, were then sold for £33 we would now have funds available to replace it according to the historical method of accounting. We have retained in the business £67 by way of depreciation and we have realised £33 on the sale—a total of £100. In the meantime, however, prices have risen, and a similar asset in 1943 would cost £160 or thereabouts, so that we have under-provided to the extent of £60.

Now suppose that over the period of the five years the profits of the business, apart from depreciation, amounted to £200. After deducting the £67 of depreciation there is £133 left available for distribution. If the full amount had been provided to replace the asset at its enhanced price, the amount available for distribution would have been £73. If the whole of the £133 had been distributed as dividends or, for that matter, any amount over £73, there would have been, in effect, a distribution of real capital.

ECONOMIC CONCEPT OF PROFIT.

The economist, that disciple of the dry-as-dust science, is not restricted by the rules of double-entry book-keeping, and his attitude towards profits is generally referred to as the economic concept of profit.

The economic concept of profit may be stated briefly as being that which is left over after paying all the running costs of a business and after allowing for the preservation of its capital fund.

The important point here is the preservation of the capital fund. Under the rules of accountancy as we know it, capital is considered to be intact so long as the balance sheet shows that a given sum, expressed in terms of the symbol " £ ", has not been dissipated. The economist shows that, in abnormal circumstances, a balance sheet, drawn up with all the skill and accuracy expected of the

H

accountancy profession, is still capable not only of concealing facts but even of being misleading—a most disturbing thought.

Reverting to the illustration which I have just mentioned, where the business had an asset which cost £100 and the profits were £200, then the economic concept of the profits of that business would be, in the circumstances quoted, only £73. And even this may be an overstatement if inventories, to which I shall refer later, are stated in terms of enhanced prices.

(a) Accounting on Basis of Historical Cost.

Depreciation for the period	£67	Trading Profits for the period	£200
Net Profit available for distribution	133		
	£200		£200

(b) Economic Concept of Profit.

Depreciation for the period—		Trading Profits for the period	£200
On historical cost	£67		
Provision for replacement cost	60		
	£127		
Net Profit available for distribution	73		
	£200		£200

Traditional Finance.

The traditional method of guarding against distribution of the real capital fund was to retain additional profits in the business by appropriations to reserve. These amounts were not based on any scientific appraisal of the effect on the business of changes in prices, but rather on the state of the business, and of business in general; and, possibly, with one eye on the shareholders.

Where it was conscientiously applied for the good of the business, this method worked quite well until it met with a difficulty, which came to a crux during the war period, and which, for that matter, is still with us. Taxation rose with the rise in the price level, and, as I need scarcely mention to this audience, appropriations to reserve are not allowable charges for tax purposes. Accordingly, the margin of profit after taxation shrank, and industry as a whole began to find increasing difficulty in providing for the replacement of its assets.

The problem was already with us during the war years, when Income Tax reached 10s. in the £, with Excess Profits Tax at 100 per cent, less the post-war refund. Then, however, the position was to a great extent obscured as so many businesses were financing their manufacturing capacity by progress payments on Government contracts, very often granted on a generous scale, and the actual payment of the E.P.T. was not made until a considerable time after the profits were earned.

With the diminution in the system of progress payments, and the nemesis of the tax inspector overtaking the tax liabilities, industry began to find itself in 1946 and 1947, if not in financial difficulty, at least not in easy street, to which it had grown accustomed.

The difficulty was only overcome, in many cases, by making a new issue of share capital, or by borrowing from the banks or the investing public. To borrow a term from Nature, industry was no longer self-propagating. It found itself in the position of requiring to raise new money, not for the legitimate object of expanding its productive capacity, but merely in order to replace its worn-out assets. It should be remembered, also, that the effect of rising price levels was not confined to fixed assets alone. The cost of raw materials also rose during the war, and after. In addition, wages paid to labour, and by that I mean labour in its widest sense, including the higher-paid executive as well as the lower-paid groups, were approximately doubled. As a result, the money-price of inventories increased very greatly. Debtors and creditors, of course, followed the same trend.

FUTURE MOVEMENT OF PRICE LEVELS.

Before we consider methods of counteracting these tendencies in the accounts we must briefly consider what is likely to happen to the price level in the future.

I approach this, however, with some trepidation. The circumstances after the late war are not the same as they were in the 1920-1925 period, either in this country or in the world as a whole, and all that we can do is to consider general tendencies.

In general terms, from the beginning of the century prices rose steadily, but comparatively slowly, up to the time of the 1914-1918 war. This was a period of prosperity in the country. Then, during the war, as you will see if you refer to the chart again, prices rose very rapidly, largely under the influence of scarcity, until by the end of the war they had, on the average, rather more than doubled themselves. This steep rise continued for a short time, rather over a year after the end of the war, and then a sharp fall set in. Apart from a slight tendency to rise in 1924 the fall continued, turning into the slump of the 1930's. At the bottom of the slump, incidentally, prices fell almost to the level at which they had stood just prior to the 1914-1918 war. The slump ended and was followed by a fairly sharp rise which, in turn, broke just before 1938. As in the case of the 1914-1918 war, prices rose during the late war; but the rise was not halted within a short period; in fact it tended to become steeper.

It is a matter of opinion whether we have yet reached the peak. There are some signs that the rising pressure is slackening, but it is too early to give a definite answer one way or the other.

REPLACEMENT COST OF FIXED ASSETS.

We have already seen how the rise in prices has affected fixed assets, rendering normal depreciation insufficient, and leading to possible dissipation of real capital. Several methods have been suggested to overcome this.

The most obvious expedient is a revaluation by a professional valuer, a formidable if not impossible task, if industry as a whole were to undertake it, in view of the load which it would throw on the available skill. A rather more approximate method is to use index numbers, based on suitable published statistics. The index number can be applied in two ways. It can be applied to the original cost of each asset, or suitable groupings of assets, and to the depreciation written off to date, or it can be applied directly to the written-down value of the assets. The final effect is, of course, the same, but the method of writing up both original cost and depreciation does make some pretence at continuity.

An amount equal to the increase in the net total of the fixed assets will have to be carried to reserve, and this reserve should be, of course, regarded as being of a capital nature if it is not, in fact, capitalised by the issue of (in my opinion, misnamed) bonus shares.

There is another method which has been used. The amount by which the net fixed assets require to be written up, as calculated in the foregoing paragraph, is transferred from the General Reserve, or other reserves not specifically designated, to a reserve called Reserve for Replacement of Fixed Assets or some similar title. This is being done to-day by a number of public companies.

Where the last method is adopted it will be obvious that the Reserve will remain a free reserve, and this may or may not be a disadvantage. On the other hand, there is no sudden break in the accounts, which remain on the historical cost basis and are more readily comparable from year to year. Another point is that the charge for depreciation is not altered.

The Index of General Wholesale Prices from 1910 to 1948 (already referred to) can be converted to the 1948 price level by means of a conversion table, and I refer you to the further table (reproduced as Appendix III.).

Industry is now giving thought to this problem and, although not a great deal has so far been published on the subject, I believe that a certain amount of internal investigation has been carried out for managerial information on the fixed asset position.

In the case of one company with which I am associated such an investigation has been carried out, and I submit a columnar balance sheet which gives a comparison of replacement cost with historical cost (reproduced as Appendix IV.). It also shows a column headed " Alternative Method," when a Replacement Reserve is set up.

In order to arrive at the " Replacement Cost " the capital expenditure was analysed from the beginning, assets scrapped were eliminated, and the net balance remaining for each year had the relevant conversion factor applied to it. As you will see, the replacement cost of assets, costing £166,700, came to £302,000. It may be of interest in passing to mention that for insurance purposes the assets, based on schedules prepared quite independently by technical experts, come to approximately £315,000.

We have already seen that prices are not constant. Having revalued the assets of our business, what are we to do when prices either go higher or begin to drop ? Are we to revalue every year or say when the index shows a 10 per cent movement ? If we have capitalised the reserve we cannot, of course, touch it ; so, in the event of the new valuation being considerably lower, are we to write off the difference to Profit and Loss Account ? Again, if we capitalise the reserve, will the business stand the payment in future years of a reasonable dividend on the increased capital ?

DEPRECIATION POLICY—MANUFACTURING COSTS.

Let us now consider the question of depreciation, and how it should be treated if we were to adopt some basis of replacement cost for our fixed assets. If we do write up the assets the annual charge for depreciation will be considerably greater, and this may be a serious matter if profits decline. If we look at this last point in another way we may have Company " A " and Company " B " owning precisely similar fixed assets, being depreciated at the same rate, but whereas " A " is running at a substantial profit, " B " is

just breaking even. Company " A " can stand the increased depreciation charge which, in the case of " B," would result in a loss.
Company " A " might therefore write up its assets, while " B "
obviously would not. Which of the two companies is contravening
accounting principle ?

The use of a machine-hour rate in costing complicates the matter,
in so far as depreciation of the machine enters into it. If the new
depreciation is brought into the computation of the rate, then an
article made on that machine will cost, on paper, more to produce
one day than it did on the previous day. A possible alternative,
or compromise, would be to split the depreciation between " normal "
depreciation on the old basis and " excess " depreciation to adjust
the total charge to the new basis, the excess being applied as general
overhead. The case of a new machine purchased at an enhanced
price is of importance here, since, if the machine-hour rate is applied
strictly to each machine individually, the cost of production of
articles will vary according to the machine used, notwithstanding
that the machines are otherwise identical. What principle of accounting is to be applied to such circumstances ?

I am raising these matters in the form of questions, without
attempting to give answers, as I should like to stimulate discussion.

INVENTORIES AND THEIR FINANCE.

We may now consider the question of inventories, using this
term to cover raw materials, stocks, work - in - progress, and
finished goods. The price of raw materials obviously rises with
the general price level. Labour for this purpose may be considered
as a commodity and, in times of rising prices, the cost of labour
will also rise. The third element—namely, the charge for overheads
—is commonly computed on a basis which will include labour and/or,
in some cases, material. It follows, therefore, that in a period of
rising prices the value of work-in-progress will be inflated by excess
cost of materials, labour, and overhead. If stock and work-in-
progress become inflated in this way it may be, according to the
economic concept of profit, that they will encroach on the capital
fund. Therefore, it is necessary to create a reserve. The question
is how large should the reserve be ?

There is, in any business, what we may call an economic stock
level. That is, the level at which the stocks, using the word stock
in the widest sense to include raw materials, work-in-progress, and
finished stock, should be maintained, in order that the factory may
not be held up through lack of materials, or unduly long delivery

quotations be necessary for the sales force. At the same time, the amount of money tied up in this basic stock should be the minimum compatible with an official production and delivery programme.

The establishment of the basic stock level is a matter of some difficulty. In practice the figures for a year regarded as normal would probably be adopted, or the average of a number of years might be used. This would then be amended to allow for changes in the level or the character of production to give the new basic stock. The excess of actual stocks over this figure represents the amount to be reserved. Obviously, it might well be necessary to spread the creation of the reserve over a number of years. Any such reserve created in this way would, of course, require to be adjusted periodically.

In the case of a new undertaking, or a fundamental alteration in the technique of production, the basic stock would require to be a theoretical estimate.

In the event of a fall in prices taking place, a part of this reserve would become unnecessary and would then be brought back to the credit of profit and loss. What attitude should industry, and the professional auditor, take towards such transfers ?

ACTION ON THE PART OF INDUSTRY.

I have, in my review of the problem, already mentioned a number of courses which are open to industry.

Is industry to drop the historical basis of accounting and adopt the economic concept of profit ? As I mentioned in my introductory remarks, I do not propose to dogmatise on this, but I will go so far as to say that the policy of ploughing back a substantial proportion of the profits arrived at on the historical cost method is imperative, and it is not, as it is so often regarded, ultra-conservative finance.

In order to stimulate discussion I throw out the suggestion that if the price level were to double itself again within the next five years, then industry ought to write up its assets to replacement cost and increase the depreciation charge. Such a writing up has already been done in France and Belgium, and in other countries.

Before we pass on to consideration of action on the part of Government, I would remind the audience that action on the part of Government is unlikely unless it is prodded, and possibly not gently, by industry. Industry, therefore, must take upon itself the task of educating the public, and the Government, that industry in actual fact is not making the excessive profits which we so often hear referred to.

ACTION ON THE PART OF GOVERNMENT.

Assuming now that industry has brought about the necessary change of heart on the part of Government, what positive action could Government take in order to grant a measure of relief to industry ? I make the following suggestions :—

(1) Reduce the burden of taxation generally, so that industry would have a greater margin of taxed profits to plough back into the business. Reduction in taxation would also permit of personal savings, which formerly provided an important source of capital for industry.

(2) In respect of fixed assets, allow increased depreciation, possibly on a notional basis. This principle has already been adopted in France and Belgium.

(3) With regard to inventories, some formula might be worked out, whereby sums placed to a Stock Reserve, within stipulated limits, might receive a tax concession.

If the Treasury considered that concessions along these lines would bear too heavily on the Budget for one year, then the effect might be spread over a period of years, and industry benefit accordingly.

APPENDIX I.

INDEX TABLE OF GENERAL WHOLESALE PRICES
FOR THE PERIOD FROM 1910 TO 1948.

YEAR.	INDEX.	YEAR.	INDEX.
1910	81·1	1931	86·2
		32	84·4
1911	82·5	33	84·5
12	82·5	34	86·9
13	82·5	1935	87·7
14	96·2		
1915	123·7	1936	93·0
		37	107·2
1916	151·2	38	100·0
17	171·9	39	101·4
18	192·5	1940	134·6
19	206·2		
1920	253·7	1941	150·5
		42	157·1
1921	162·2	43	160·4
22	131·1	44	163·7
23	131·1	1945	166·6
24	137·1		
1925	131·3	1946	172·7
		47	189·1
1926	122·2	48	216·2
27	116·9		
28	115·8		
29	112·6		
1930	98·6		

NOTES.

1. The Index Column represents Board of Trade Index Numbers for General Wholesale Prices : 1938 = 100.

2. Index numbers for 1910-1912 inclusive and 1914-1919 inclusive have been estimated, no official figures being available.

APPENDIX II.

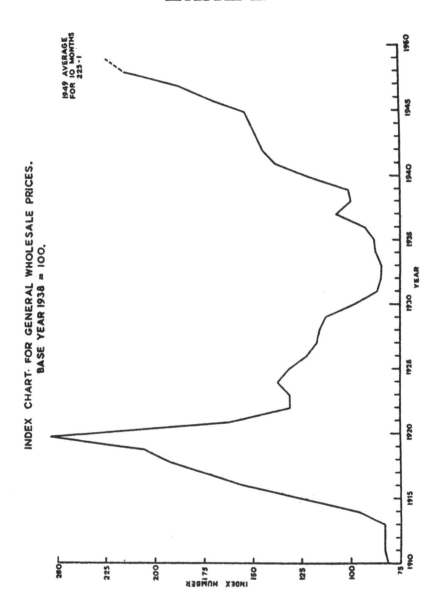

APPENDIX III.

CONVERSION TABLE OF PRICE INDEX.

Year.	Conversion Factor.	Year.	Conversion Factor.
1910	2·67	1931	2·51
		32	2·56
1911	2·62	33	2·56
12	2·62	34	2·49
13	2·62	1935	2·47
14	2·54		
1915	1·75	1936	2·33
		37	2·02
1916	1·43	38	2·16
17	1·26	39	2·13
18	1·12	1940	1·61
19	1·05		
1920	0·85	1941	1·44
		42	1·38
1921	1·33	43	1·35
22	1·65	44	1·32
23	1·65	1945	1·30
24	1·58		
1925	1·65	1946	1·25
		47	1·14
1926	1·77	48	1·00
27	1·85		
28	1·87		
29	1·92		
1930	2·19		

NOTE.

The conversion factors would need to be increased a further 2·82 per cent to obtain replacement costs at 1949 prices. (Calculated on average increase during first six months of 1949.)

273

APPENDIX IV.

THE A.B. MANUFACTURING CO. LTD.

BALANCE SHEET AS AT 31ST DECEMBER 1949.

Redrafted to Show Comparison of Replacement Cost with Historical Cost.

	Historical Cost. £	Replacement Cost. £	Alternative Method. £		Historical Cost. £	Replacement Cost. £	Alternative Method. £
Share Capital	100,000	100,000	100,000	Fixed Assets—			
Capital Reserve	..	46,700	..	At Cost, or Revalued	166,700	302,000	166,700
Replacement Reserve	..	..	46,700	Depreciation	108,900	197,500	108,900
Revenue Surplus	138,900	138,900	92,200		£57,800	£104,500	£57,800
	£238,900	£285,600	£238,900	Current Assets	263,500	263,500	263,500
Liabilities and Provisions	82,400	82,400	82,400				
	£321,300	£368,000	£321,300		£321,300	£368,000	£321,300

274

<u>William T. Baxter, BCom, PhD, DL, CA</u>

Will Baxter was born in Grimsby in 1906. He graduated from the University of Edinburgh in 1929, and qualified as a Scottish Chartered Accountant in 1930.

From 1934 to 1936, Professor Baxter was a Lecturer in Accounting at the University of Edinburgh. He then translated to the University of Cape Town as Professor of Accounting where he remained until 1947 when he took up his Chair at the London School of Economics. He held this position until his retirement in 1973 as Emeritus Professor. In 1945 he graduated at the University of Edinburgh as Doctor of Philosophy for his thesis on the House of Hancock (published by Harvard University Press as <u>The House of Hancock - Business in Boston, 1724-75</u>). Since his retirement, Professor Baxter has continued his academic work - for example, between 1974 and 1976, he held the part-time post at the London School of Economics of Fellow in Latin-American Studies; and between 1978 and 1979, and 1982 and 1983, he has been Visiting Professor at the City University of New York.

Professor Baxter is well-known for his scholarly contributions to the areas of accounting theory generally and income determination particularly. His major written works include <u>Depreciation</u> (Sweet and Maxwell, 1972); <u>Accounting Values and Inflation</u> (McGraw-Hill, 1975); (with S. Davidson) <u>Studies in Accounting Theory</u> (Sweet and Maxwell, 1977); <u>Collected Papers on Accounting</u> (Arno Press, 1978); and <u>Depreciating Assets: an Introduction</u> (Institute of Chartered Accountants of Scotland, 1980). For these and other contributions to accounting thought, he has been awarded honorary doctorates from the University of Kent, Heriot-Watt University and the University of Hull.

William T. Baxter, 'The Study of Balance Sheets' (1950-1)

By 1950 the practice of financial reporting had improved considerably since the times of Brown or Touche. Baxter confirmed the improvement, believing that the needs of the expert report user were tolerably satisfied. His main concern, therefore, was with the needs of the unsophisticated user - a matter which has yet to be coped with today.

Baxter felt the balance sheet should give as good a picture as possible of the reporting entity's assets and liabilities, avoiding wording which was over-technical and providing detailed disclosures in appendices. He identified the reporting entity's owners as the major user group, and distinguished different needs in terms of expertise. He provided examples of explanatory balance sheets and, as such, his lecture was an early indication of an argument for simplified financial statements. It also reflected Baxter's then emphasis on the importance of reporting on liquidity matters - the funds statement was discussed in some detail. And he also favoured multi-column reporting with a vertical format.

277

THE STUDY OF BALANCE SHEETS

BY PROFESSOR W. T. BAXTER, B.COM., PH.D., C.A.

(Being a Lecture delivered to the Chartered Accountants Students' Society of Edinburgh on 13th October 1950)

I. THE SHAPE OF THE BALANCE SHEET

IF a paper on this subject had been written some years before the Second Great War, there would have been no doubt about its content and tenor. Thoughtful accountants of that date were at one in feeling unhappy about published statements; for instance, some of Professor Annan's best teaching was on their shortcomings. The man who had to lecture on style in balance sheets usually began by deploring their lack of style. He would probably illustrate his argument with an imaginary set of figures, arranged as in the usual published balance sheet of the period—*i.e.*, with little attention to order and still less to grouping or completeness. Pointing to this indigestible jumble, he would show how limited were its uses, and how many pencil jottings the reader would have to make in order to see the company's position even in outline. Then he would shuffle the figures into what he regarded as good style; and the company's situation would suddenly emerge from the fog.

Though the general standard was very poor until the late 'thirties, there were some noteworthy exceptions. A number of companies were already—without any legal compulsion—pioneering in better ways. Their example received much praise; conceivably indeed it would have been followed voluntarily even if the law had not stepped in. Be this as it may, the Companies Act of 1948 re-enforced the example of the pioneers and made obligatory what had hitherto been an act of virtue.

So to-day we take it for granted that a balance sheet should be well arranged in groups, with the individual items, marshalled in a helpful order; we also expect candour and full disclosure. Perhaps, indeed, the swing has gone to the other extreme, and the reader may now be confused by the excessive detail that the law demands. Perhaps, too, the completeness and rigidity prescribed by the Eighth Schedule, while admirable for dealing with the laggards, may act as a strait-jacket and cramp further experiment by pioneers.

It may make my later argument clearer if I give simple specimen figures (omitting much of the detail that would be desirable, and indeed compulsory, in practice). I accordingly attach an outline balance sheet— Appendix A. This seems to me to be in a form that is fairly typical of present-day published balance sheets.

FUTURE DEVELOPMENTS

Does the vast improvement of recent years mean that there is now no scope for further steps ?

In general, I think we may say that the needs of the technical reader (*e.g.*, the financial editor, or the accountant on the staff of an investment trust) are tolerably well satisfied already. No doubt further detail is needed—and badly needed—in some directions (*e.g.*, there is still no compulsion to state the bases on which stock is valued or depreciation allowed—often vital matters). No doubt, too, we shall continue to argue about the precise form in which certain items should be presented (*e.g.*, whether the credit for a remote income tax liability should be classed as a long-term liability or a reserve). Further, the revenue picture can hardly be regarded as complete yet; some accountants (including me) can see no very good reason why figures for sales, &c., should not be shown in British (as in many American) accounts.[1] A more extreme view is that the full tax computation should be published, since this gives, in respect of many items of expense and revenue, alternative figures; these figures may be less " right " than those of the company, but have the merit of being drafted by an independent person who follows fairly objective and well-known rules. However, important though such issues are, they are small compared with the victory that has already been won.

My suggestion is that the needs of the non-specialist (the shareholder who knows little of finance and nothing of double-entry) are more clamant. These needs might well be our guides in discussing further developments; we should think of the ignorant shareholder as our employer, or as the customer who is always right. How can the main features of the company's progress be shown to such innocents with maximum clarity ? Are we who have grown familiar with an existing pattern of accounts, and with the intricate apparatus of debit and credit,

[1] Incidentally, the precise definition of turnover is a matter of some difficulty. For instance, what is the " turnover " of a travel agency—ticket sales or commission ?

perhaps apt to ignore our customer's needs and to overlook obvious means for helping him ? What follows is largely concerned with the task of making our figures more suitable for the layman.

WHAT SHOULD A BALANCE SHEET SHOW ?

When we ask what the job of a balance sheet is, we probably all agree that it is to give as good a picture as possible of the firm's property and finances. For instance, we want to know how big the firm is, and whether it owns machinery or shops or mineral seams. This basic work is already done fairly well, so far as the figures go, but a short verbal statement on the nature of the company would often be a useful addition to published reports (which sometimes neglect to give any inkling of the trade carried on).

Before considering how the figures can best be presented, it may be helpful to ask how balance sheets got their present form. They almost certainly began as mere trial balances (*i.e.*, as the book-keeper's private proofs of accuracy). When they came to be employed for external purposes such as testing credit and informing absentee owners, much the same form was still used. With time, less crude and stilted arrangements have been adopted, but our present model still shows its descent very clearly. Only recently have we begun to wonder whether this form is not archaic—a lingering trace of servility to the trial balance—and to ask ourselves whether we need reflect in any way the double-entry structure of the ledger. Might not our two-sided balance sheet be replaced with advantage by a " report form " of account ?

To decide how our figures should be arrayed, we must know what our aims are. We want to focus attention on the more important aspects of the firm's finances. Two approaches seem possible:—

(1) We may feel that the man who consults a balance sheet is more likely to be concerned with the intricacies of the share capital and reserves than with anything else, and that accordingly they should come first. Such would seem to be the general opinion of British accountants; at least, the overwhelming majority of our balance sheets begin, as you know well, by giving this group the place of honour at the top left-hand corner.

(2) We may instead decide that what readers are most likely to look at—particularly if they are the non-specialists—is the liquid position of the company. Nobody can deny that this is important in many contexts. Further, such things as cash and

debts are understood by everyone, and so form a good jumping-off place for the timid reader. Many American reports begin with the liquid assets—and American companies have been far more progressive than others in making their reports palatable to the general public.

On the whole, I am inclined to think that this second view is the better one, and that it should at least guide us in our experiments. As you will see from my later remarks, this treatment also seems to fit in well with some other ideas about the best way to explain the nature of a company's finance.

Certain other desiderata may be taken for granted, and I shall not mention them in any detail. Plainly, the balance sheet should look attractive. Whenever such a device leads to simplicity, complicated sets of figures should be put into appendices. The lay-out should make for easy comparison with the results of earlier years. Perhaps, too, the lay-out should let us show consolidated figures for the group on the same page as the holding company's figures; but I am not sure that this arrangement may not seem too complex.

The Two-sided Balance Sheet

If we feel friendly towards the criteria that I have just suggested, but are not yet convinced of the need to jettison such an old and faithful servant as the two-sided balance sheet, what mild changes in its form might we consider ?

To stress the liquid position more, we might make the connection between current assets and current liabilities closer by deducting the latter on the assets side, bringing out a figure for net working capital. This is already done by many British companies.

Again, we might reverse the vertical order of the items so that the assets begin with cash and other current items (*i.e.*, familiar and important things which the laymen would like to see first), the order of the liabilities being reversed to match. This is the lay-out favoured by Aspro, Ltd.—and, of course, by innumerable non-incorporated firms.

Finally, we might well consider switching the sides round, bringing the assets to the place of honour on the left. I think that this arrangement would on the whole appear more logical to the non-accountant, though it seems to make the British accountant's hackles rise; in this matter, as with the " rule of the road," all countries are out of step except Britain.

NEED FOR CLEARER WORDING

Such changes in design might help the unsophisticated shareholder to understand what has happened to his money. But we could also give him help in another important way—by paying more attention to the *wording* of our statements. At present, our wording is over-technical, and is often out of line with normal speech. If we want to get our meaning across, we may have to scrap our recondite expressions and substitute ones that are well understood. This would probably result in shorter words but far more of them.

I have redrafted Appendix A. in a form that may illustrate my suggestions (Appendix B.). The wording is a fairly close copy of that used in explanatory supplements to the accounts of Jantzen (Australia). Though we may feel that some of the phrases are unfortunate (*e.g.*, " what we were worth " might give rise to some queer ideas), this company's experiment seems a courageous attempt to help its shareholders.

THE ONE-SIDED BALANCE SHEET

If we once admit that our present balance sheet calls for improvement, we must face the question of whether we should not be wiser to go the whole hog and abandon the two-sided statement in favour of the report form (*i.e.*, a single-sided document with suitable narrative).

Such an arrangement gives a welcome elasticity. In particular, it leaves more room for columns in which to show previous years' results, consolidated figures, &c. But it has the demerit of not showing all the liabilities in a compact list; for some purposes, such a list is handy for comparing with the gross assets.

While most accountants will probably not share my predilection for a balance sheet in report form, they must admit that this style is gaining favour for the appropriation account. In such accounts, small groups of debits and credits may with advantage be set off against one another so that we can see, *e.g.*, profit before tax, profit after tax, and so on. The two-sided account is far too clumsy for this purpose. Appendix C. gives a good example of a well-worded revenue and appropriation statement in one-sided form; it is taken (slightly shortened) from the report of the Industrial and Commercial Finance Corporation. The example is interesting in a second way—the statement appears as an integral part of the directors' report, no other profit and loss account being published.

Is this a good plan ? I think so. To give figures twice is surely untidy; also, on meeting the figures for the second time, the layman may well scratch his head and ask, " Is this the same sum that I ploughed through on page one, put in again for fun, or is it new stuff ? "

If we vote for the report style, I suggest that our specimen balance sheet might be arranged somewhat as in Appendix D.

APPENDICES.

I have already said that appendices are a useful means for getting clumsy detail out of the balance sheet. Needless to say, however, they can be used to show any other material that is likely to interest share-holders. In particular, the main figures from the revenue account and balance sheets of a number of years may be given with great advantage; a ten-year summary is likely to cover the whole of a trade cycle. Some American companies also give the profit and dividends *per share*, the more important percentages and ratios (*e.g.*, profit as a percentage of sales), and even the high and low Stock Exchange quotations for the shares. At least one British company does this sort of thing admirably— I recommend you to study the statements of Harding, Tilton & Hartley Ltd.

THE TEST OF SUCCESS

Supposing that we accept, as our ideal, the need for helping the average shareholder to understand our figures, and that we make some of these experiments. How are we to know whether our experiments are a success ? How are we to decide which method is best ?

Adequate tests would be expensive. I suppose professional diviners of public opinion would be willing to conduct a poll on the subject. But, to be convincing, a test would have to be on an almost impossible scale. We should have to take a fairly large sample of persons who know nothing of finance. We should split them up into groups, and give one form of balance sheet to each group. After a suitable time for digesting the figures, each person would sit an examination on the financial state of the company. The group that won the highest marks could be presumed to have received the best form of balance sheet.

As such tests are out of the question, accountants are in a real diffi-culty. With diffidence, I suggest that the views of teachers should carry some weight, for teachers know—all too well—how perplexing a balance sheet seems to beginners. And we must gather what we can from the opinions of the press, and of such shareholders as may volunteer their views; this is not very satisfactory, however, because the man who does not understand is usually shy about showing his ignorance, and he is the man whom we should plan to aid.

II. THE OWNERS' BALANCES

THE PROBLEM OF CAPITAL, &C.

To my mind, the section in our balance sheets that is most hard to explain is that containing the owners' balances (*i.e.*, capital, reserves, profits, and so forth).

Let us start with the balance sheet of a small trader. It will look something like this :—

Creditors . . . 2	Sundry assets . . 9
Capital . . . 7	
9	9

Now, why is it arranged just so ? For no better reason than because such an arrangement echoes the ledger balances. If the trader had never heard of a ledger, he would most likely have put down the data thus:—

Sundry assets 9
Less Creditors 2

Net assets—*i.e.*, capital . . . 7

This is short, direct, and free from confusing repetitions. The figure 7 is shown in its simplest guise—as the (net) total of the other items. From the viewpoint of the owner, 7 is the answer to the whole sum, not a step in the calculation. A book-keeper must unhappily in his ledger treat the 7 as an item in its own right, because he needs such a counterweight to balance his books; but to show it as a separate item in balance sheets is to drag in complication needlessly. Much ingenuity has been expended on explaining to students why capital is like a liability; a rather more truthful plan is to say that it is nothing of the kind (in the owner's eyes, at least), and that its appearance on one side of a balance sheet is just a quaint survival of early practice. Or am I over-stating my case ?

No great harm may be done where the small trader is concerned. The capital section of his balance sheet can remain simple; each year, profits (less drawings) are merged with opening capital. But company law makes the position much worse. A company's " capital " may be changed only if great formalities are observed, and therefore growth in real capital—in the form of profits, &c.—must not be merged with the figure for share capital. The quantity corresponding to the sole trader's 7 gets elaborated into a series of items—share capital, various reserves, profits, and so on—sometimes not even put next to one another in the balance sheet. A lay reader may well be pardoned if he is confused— if, for instance, he supposes that a reserve betokens the existence of wealth over and above what is shown among the assets (a common mistake among not unintelligent people).

This is not to suggest that our re-analysis of the owners' wealth serves no useful end. In other fields, a double analysis of data is often helpful; thus the trucks in a railway yard might be classified twice—by:

(1) physical type (*e.g.*, size) and
(2) their place of origin. (*i.e.*, the station that may be able to claim them back).

In the same way, we analyse the given net asset figure *first* by asset type and *second* by source (and here, too, the source may, in the eyes of the law, affect the destination). The point I am striving to make, then, is not that we should scrap the analysis, but that we should make clearer what we are doing—namely, examining the same wealth from different points of view. Whatever the faults of Appendix D., it does at least grapple with the problem.

DESCRIPTIONS OF THE GROUP

How are published statements trying to meet the difficulty of describing the ownership group ? Some of the headings are:—

Shareholders' Capital, Reserves, and Profits.
Shareholders' Interest.
Net Worth.—This otherwise convenient Americanism conveys a suggestion of revaluation, which is most unfortunate.
Ownership evidenced by.
Sources of Net Assets.
Members' Funds.—Perhaps " funds " may be ambiguous (cf. " reserve fund ").

Lever Bros. start their balance sheet with:—

> *Capital Employed.*—The share capital, &c., follows. Next comes:
> *Employment of Capital.*—The various assets are then listed.

This is bold, but perhaps over-subtle.

WHO ARE OWNERS ?

We have seen that, if we list the gross assets of a firm, and then strip off the claims of " outsiders," we are left with the answer that interests the owner (*i.e.*, the total of his wealth in the business).[1] But, you will object, a company may have many types and grades of " owners." What are the tests that we should apply to candidates for admission to the ownership group (*e.g.*, why do we put debentures under some other head, such as " long-term liabilities ") ?

From the standpoint of economic analysis, all persons who are represented by a credit balance can be regarded as contributors of capital, in the sense that all of them—trade creditors, debenture-holders, and shareholders, &c.—make up the structure by which finances are mobilised for business. However, for many purposes we can distinguish at least an outer and an inner group, using the following tests:—

(1) *Permanence.*—The temporary trade creditor is much less likely to be interested in our balance-sheet analysis than the man whose claims have been " funded " into some more permanent form.

(2) *Control.*—Particularly in the eyes of lawyers, the main test is that of control, as expressed by the right to attend meetings and to vote. By this criterion, preference shareholders are owners, whereas the holders of debentures, and of the " notes " that have recently become so important (for reasons not unconnected with the rules of profits tax), are mere creditors. Yet it sometimes happens that preference shares carry no votes. Again—particularly if the company gets into difficulties—the holders of debentures may be given control; thus debenture-holders took over many cotton companies during

---

[1] Of course, the size of the total depends on the method of *valuing* the assets. Whether the balance-sheet method is " right " is a big question demanding separate treatment; but we should be well advised to avoid expressions like " net worth," " what we were worth," &c.

the depression. This test is accordingly not so significant as appears at first sight.

(3) *Deferability of Claim.*—A man's place in the queue for benefits (annual interest and ultimate repayment of capital) gives a better clue to his degree of ownership. A creditor's interest *must* be paid each year; the preference dividend may be withheld. At winding-up, creditors rank before shareholders. However, the preference shares probably rank before the ordinaries, and also may be redeemable; so the position of the preference shareholder is again not free from ambiguity. The ordinary shareholder is normally at the end of the queue (*i.e.*, his is the " residuary claim ").

(4) *Fixed-money Claims* versus *Equities.*[1]—A Stock Exchange security is essentially a set of promises—of yearly payments and a final return of capital. Creditors insist on promises that are defined in terms of so much money. But the ultimate owner cannot promise himself a fixed sum of money; the uncertainties of life make the surplus unpredictable, ·so the last man in the queue merely gets what is left over, be it large or small. An ordinary share's rights must be defined as a promise to pay, not so many £s, but an arithmetical proportion of whatever number of £s may be available.[2] Ordinary dividends and quotations are thus apt to be mercurial, and to jig up and down in tune with the company's fortunes. On the other hand, ordinary shares may have stability in real terms when the value of the £ is changing. The inflation has underlined the enormous difference between " fixed-money rights " and " equities." For instance, companies financed by fixed-money claims have since 1939 in effect carried a shrinking burden, and their fortunate ordinary shareholders have become correspondingly richer (though our balance sheets give no inkling of this change, unless the assets have been revalued). True, the quotations for such equities have appreciated less than might be expected, for two reasons: the first is dividend limitation, and the second is our failure to charge replacement cost provisions, with a consequent rise in tax to a point at which many equities are subject to a yearly capital levy.

[1] " Equity " has unfortunately several meanings, but that of residual claims (in contrast to fixed-money claims) is now widely recognised.

[2] It follows that a *pro rata* issue of bonus ordinary shares to all ordinary shareholders cannot affect their rights in the slightest; the fraction of the total belonging to each shareholder is unaffected.

To-day the distinction between fixed-money claims and equities is often, I venture to say, immensely more important than any other test that can be applied in a balance sheet.

Perhaps the four criteria given above are, at bottom, only aspects of the same test—the amount of risk borne. The man who risks his wealth most deeply will normally insist on having the final say in management, and on getting accounts that photograph the enterprise from his standpoint. However, there are innumerable degrees of risk-bearing; and many schemes of ownership, which at first sight seem surprising, may work quite well. Thus the surplus of a consumer's co-operative goes not to the capitalist but to the customer; and a nationalised industry has no residual owners, unless you and I count as such.

THE UNITY OF ORDINARY CAPITAL AND RESERVES

Ordinary capital, reserves, and profits constitute a unity, whatever statutes may say. The true capital of the ordinary shareholders is thus an elastic figure, rising as reserves and profits accumulate. Its total should be shown plainly.

Our logic suggests that we should put reserves, &c.—not preference shares—next to ordinary shares in the balance sheet. Instead of:—

Ordinary shares	.	.	.	£ —
Preference shares	.	.	.	—
				£ —
Reserves, &c. .	.	.	.	—

we should have:—

Ordinary shares	.	.	.	£ —
Reserves, &c. .	.	.	.	—
				£ —
Preference shares	.	.	.	—

The case for this rearrangement would be weakened where preference shares participate in either profits or surplus on winding-up.

The splitting up of true capital is unfortunate in many ways. For instance, when a student of book-keeping is working on holding companies, the separation of the subsidiary's capital from reserves and profits gives him needless trouble. In most cases, the rule is simple: you add together the three items (as at the date of acquisition), and so find the true capital that must be set off against the cost of the investment—the difference being the so-called " goodwill " (if a debit) or " capital reserve " (if a credit).

Again, the directors of companies with large reserves find it hard to explain to critics—perhaps among their workpeople or in Parliament— that a dividend of, say, 40 per cent on share capital may be only a small yield on true capital. If we always treated share capital, reserves, and profits as an indivisible trinity, the explanations would be a lot simpler. Big Business is usually credited by its foes with great skill at bluffing the public; here it has in fact failed to do itself bare justice.

The cause of all these troubles is the nominal (or par) values with which we endow our securities. What is the meaning of " nominal value," and what good purpose does it serve ?

THE UNIMPORTANCE OF " NOMINAL VALUES "

A security that has £1 printed on its certificate may be issued at 21s. (*i.e.*, at a premium of 1s.), be redeemable at 22s., and be currently quoted on the Stock Exchange at 35s. £1 is not its issue price, or its redemption figure, or its market value. Why, then, should we use the " £1 " at all ?

When label and contents are at such odds, many people are likely to be deluded. They may be confused when buying shares; " it was thought that the engraving of $100 upon a share of stock oftentimes led the investor to pay, if not the full $100, at least a larger sum than he would have paid if freed from the hypnotic effect of the $100 emblazoned upon the certificate." [1] Again, the holder of shares may be lulled into a false sense of security when his investment is sinking in value, or he may fail to recognise its true worth when it appreciates. The longer the time since the original issue, the greater is the extent to which market value may diverge from par. True, with fixed-money securities the divergence tends to be slow and slight (though dramatic moves are not unknown); the chief factors making for price changes are rates of interest in general (*e.g.*, a rise in these depresses prices) and the level of the particular company's earnings (which can push the price to below the normal figure for shares in other companies of the same type, but not raise it much above). Equities are far more sensitive, at least to

[1] Henry Rand Hatfield: ' Accounting: Its Principles and Problems,' p. 189.

the latter of these factors, and their prices go up and down freely; the link with nominal value is here excessively elastic.

Anyone who has tried to explain this matter to, shall we say, an old lady who owns some shares, will know how extraordinarily hard it is to do so. I feel certain that very large numbers of simple people attach a wholly false significance to the printed symbol, and are thereby sorely handicapped in their investment policies.

You may object that nominal value has at least one use from the shareholders' standpoint—it enables the dividend to be stated quickly as, *e.g.*, a dividend of 5 per cent. But the directors might declare a dividend of 1s. per share equally well—indeed, even more conveniently; the *amount*, and the current *yield*, are of far more importance than a percentage based on par, which can at most have a historical interest.

THE SHARE OF NO-PAR VALUE

There seems to me to be an extremely strong case for the share of no-par value. As you know, most American states permit the issue of such shares, and, after a good many teething troubles, the practice now appears to work satisfactorily. A layman, if his shares were not called " £1 shares " but " shares of no-par value," would appreciate far better than at present the nature of his wealth. " A purchaser of such stock, because of the fact that it carries no designated par value, is at once put on notice to investigate the values back of it." [1]

Why, then, does our Parliament not countenance the share of no-par value ? [2] The main argument against it is that some minimum value per share ought to be paid to the company when shares are issued, and maintained permanently, to safeguard creditors. But surely this difficulty could be got over with carefully drafted rules, based on American experience. Shares of no-par value, like other shares, are issued in

---

[1] Roy B. Kester: ' Principles of Accounting ' (New York), p. 352.

[2] The Cohen Committee sets out the case for shares of no-par value extremely well; but it concludes a little lamely: " While there is, in our view, much logic in the arguments put forward in favour of shares of no-par value, there is little public demand for, and considerable opposition to, the proposal. We have also had some evidence that in practice this class of share has given an opportunity to the unscrupulous to manipulate accounts which could be defeated only by a series of elaborate provisions, the substantial effect of which would be to re-introduce a capital account and, with it, most of those same complications which the no-par-value share was designed to avoid. Nor would the proposal bring any of the other major subjects of our enquiry nearer to solution. We therefore refrain from recommending any change in this matter." —' Report of the Committee on Company Law Amendment,' Cmd. 6659, p. 12.

return for a consideration. This can be made subject to a legal minimum; also it can be credited to a special account—as can any premiums on later issues—and then treated as non-distributable. In the event of no-par preference shares being issued, their rights to annual dividends, and final repayment on winding up, could surely be stated without undue difficulty (see, *e.g.*, the rules governing the Mexican Eagle issue). Protection of creditors need not depend on the befogging of shareholders.

One of the few British advocates of no-par shares was the late Lord Melchett.[1] He proposed that, as industrial plant has often little or no value in uses other than those for which it is designed, industrial companies ought to issue no-par shares up to the amount of their fixed assets. For my own part, I should prefer the test to be the legal rights of the shares, &c. If the shares are not to be redeemed within a short period, and at a figure near to par, the use of par is at best rather pointless and at worst a cruel snare.

RESERVES

The layman must surely find that " reserves " are the most treacherous feature in a balance sheet. There seem to be powerful arguments for altering both wording and practice.

To explain reserves to a layman, one would have to trace the steps by which they come into existence. Perhaps the explanation might go somewhat as follows:—

" Suppose a company's balance sheet runs:—

				£					£
Capital	.	.	.	1200	Plant	.	.	.	1150
Profit	.	.	.	200	Cash	.	.	.	250
				£1400					£1400

Legally, £200 of cash may be paid as dividend. But the board does not want to distribute so much, as new plant costing £175 would be a good investment. In other words, the board wishes to plough back £175 of profit, and so expand the permanent ' capital ' by that sum.

Accordingly, by way of a polite indication to the shareholders

---

[1] His plea is reprinted in ' Studies in Accounting ' (editor, W. T. Baxter).

of this plan, the directors recommend that £175 be ' put to reserve.'
The accountant makes a journal entry:—

Appropriation Account . . . . *Dr.*	£175	
Reserve . . . . *Cr.*		£175

The appropriation account appears:—

	£		£
Transfer to reserve . .	175	Profit brought down from	
Balance of unappropriated		Profit and Loss Account	200
profits carried forward .	25		
	£200		£200

The balance sheet will now run:—

	£		£
Capital . . .	1200	Plant . . .	1150
Reserve . . .	175	Cash . . .	250
Profit	25		
	£1400		£1400

If the shareholders take this hint, and at their general meeting
confirm the directors' recommendations and accept a meagre
dividend, the new plant can be bought. Suppose that in fact
they decide to conserve cash by paying no dividend at all. Then,
when the £175 has been spent, the balance sheet will run:—

	£			£
Capital . . .	1200	Plant—		
Reserve . . .	175	Original .	£1150	
Profit and Loss . .	25	New .	175	
				1325
		Cash		75
	£1400			£1400

" Reserve " thus tends to mean that certain profits are not available
for dividend, in the meantime at least. The word helps to make balance
sheets look impressive, for it vaguely suggests strength and stability—
which doubtless explains why it has come to be preferred to " surplus "
or " rest." (" Rest " is the pleasantly unexpected word still used by the
Bank of England and one or two other old institutions.)

We must ask ourselves whether this procedure really indicates what
is happening. What does the man-in-the-street mean when he talks
about a " reserve " in everyday speech ? (I set an examination question

in which I posed this question. One candidate answered that " company reserve " conveyed the idea of " shyness or an unwillingness to talk and mix with others.") In the layman's ordinary usage, the word probably suggests an excess of assets over normal or immediate needs (*e.g.*, he may refer to his spare can of petrol as his " reserve of petrol ") and his daily paper tells him of munition reserves, dollar reserves, and gold reserves. He will therefore tend to look for a company's reserve among its assets, and especially its liquid assets. He has ample justification for doing so. Even persons who are well skilled in accounts use the phrase in this sense; thus, when bankers append a " ratio of reserves to liabilities " to their balance sheets, they mean the ratio of cash, &c., to deposits.

But, in the language of accounts, " reserve " indicates something much more abstract—the line of our re-analysis that shows how much of the total is probably not destined for distribution. Emphatically, the word does *not* guarantee the existence of liquid assets; the savings may be ploughed back into fixed assets as in the above example.

CAPITAL AND REVENUE RESERVES

The position has become even more obscure since the 1948 Act forced us to split reserves into capital reserves and revenue reserves, giving us the following by way of definition:—

> The expression " capital reserve " shall not include any amount recorded as free for distribution through the profit and loss account and the expression " revenue reserve " shall mean any reserve other than a capital reserve.[1]

We are now wondering what " not free for distribution through the profit and loss account " means. Booklets published by the Institute of Chartered Accountants in England and Wales,[2] and by the Joint Committee of Councils of Chartered Accountants of Scotland,[3] discuss the issue and elaborate it somewhat, but end by stating (very properly) that the decision must in each case depend on the views and judgment of those responsible (*i.e.*, the directors and auditors). A wide range of items might be regarded as capital reserves:—

(a) We can be reasonably sure of a minimum meaning: not *legally* free because of some explicit rule in a statute or the company's

---

[1] Eighth Schedule, 27 (1) (c).
[2] The Companies Act, 1947, pp. 51-52.
[3] Memorandum on the Companies Act (1948), pp. 11-12.

E

own Articles. Thus the Act itself forbids the distribution of premiums on shares.

(b) Certain types of receipts may reasonably be earmarked as " capital," in the sense that their distribution would mean the shareholder was in effect getting back his original contribution. Thus, when the company buys up another business, any profit that the latter has already earned at purchase date is no increase in the buyer's wealth; again, profit accrued when shares are bought in a subsidiary is presumably also allowed for in the purchase price.

(c) Gains on sale of fixed assets may be deemed " capital." But the case law on the subject is notoriously elastic, the Courts being reluctant to interfere with the honest judgments of business men. Apart from the hazards of case law, there seem in general no very good reasons why such gains should not be divided.

(d) In (a), (b), and (c) a reserve was labelled by virtue of its *origin*. But " not regarded as free " might also imply consideration of the *purpose* for which the reserve is retained. Once this view is granted, the labelling of reserves becomes part of the directors' budget procedure, and any sum may be dubbed a " capital reserve " when the directors feel that its distribution would be inconvenient. And then, as the Scottish memorandum points out, " there does not seem to be anything in the Act which would prevent a change in the classification in a subsequent year." We might push the matter even further, and suggest that what was at 3 o'clock an entirely sensible estimate regarding the company's surplus cash may by 3.05 have become nonsense (*e.g.*, because of what the bank manager says about overdrafts).

Whereabouts in the above range of possibilities should we draw the line ? Probably we all agree that (a) and (b) are capital reserves; but (c), and still more (d), give plenty of scope for argument. And note how the Scottish memorandum concludes:—

" In the definition a capital reserve is one not ' regarded as free for distribution through the *profit and loss account*.' This does not appear to preclude the distribution to shareholders of a capital reserve. For example, a profit on the sale of fixed assets may be classified as a capital reserve and may subsequently be distributed directly (*i.e.*, not through the profit and loss account) to shareholders by way of capital dividend, provided that the Articles and circumstances of the company warrant such a distribution."

So we are in a pretty pickle. I suggest that no terse statement of reserves is likely to explain all that the balance sheet's readers (expert or lay) want to know about the company's financial policy. A full narrative is desirable, perhaps on the lines of Appendix D. Here is a point on which statute and accountants' "recommendations" may conceivably hamper progress. We must still give much thought to definitions, wording, and layout, and the more elbow-room we have for experiment the better.

III. TESTS OF FINAL ACCOUNTS

ANALYSIS OF BALANCE SHEET CHANGES

Even the best drafted of balance sheets, considered all by itself, cannot tell us much about a firm's progress. A *series* of balance sheets is immensely more informative.

If we take the balance sheets of this year and last year, and wish to analyse the changes that have taken place, we can do so in two ways. First, we may analyse the differences by considering why the changes were made—what sort of services were obtained by the firm from outside, and what it did in return. An analysis of this type is, of course, our old friend the profit and loss account. Secondly, we may consider how each kind of asset and liability has altered.

Various names have been proposed for this second calculation. One American suggestion, unfortunately abandoned, is the "Where-got-gone." More usual is the "Statement of source and disposition of funds." This is, besides being quite a mouthful, very vague. What are "funds"? The phrase can be used to mean almost anything, from cash in the till to reserves that are matched by an earmarked group of securities. Better phrases are: "Statement of balance sheet changes," or "Summary of 1950 financial operations," or "Source of net current assets."

While one associates these statements primarily with American practice (because many United States companies include them in their reports), they are being used more and more here. It would be interesting to know what proportion of our auditors makes a practice of supplying clients with such an analysis.

The method of preparing the statements is simple and is shown in Appendix E.; one merely finds the difference between each of the balance sheet items. In what form could the statement best be served up for presentation ? There is a good deal to be said for sticking to the full layout shown in E., which is self-explanatory. But usually the contents of the right-hand column are presented as an independent calculation. The exact wording of this is still a matter of experiment. Users of such statements may want to tackle the problem from either end—that is, they may be impelled by one or other of two questions:—

(1) The accounts show a profit of £X. Why is there not £X for us to spend ?
(2) Our cash (or net current assets) has gone up by £Y. Where did this come from ?

If you think that question (1) is typical, then you should arrange the calculation in such a way as to answer it, and your statement will run like Appendix F. If the aim is instead to show how the net current assets have been behaving, the figures will be arranged in the reverse order, as in G.

There is, I submit, a great field for accounting skill in adapting these statements to the needs of the particular client. Two examples of possible variations will suffice:—

(a) In F. I have glossed over the problem of depreciation. An alternative (and to my mind confusing) treatment is to add depreciation to profits, describing it as a " non-cash expense."
(b) The general aim is to show what new resources became available to the business during the year, and how they were invested in the plant and similar assets. But should we regard stock as a " similar asset " ? Usually business men do not share the accountant's feeling that a wide gulf separates stock from fixed assets (or such is at least my guess). Therefore changes in stock might well be put beside investments in plant, rather than beside the more liquid assets.

Appendix G. includes both these elaborations.

RATIOS

Appendix H. shows how the figures of E., together with the revenue accounts of the same company (shown in H.), might be subjected to a further analysis with the help of ratios.

Thus line (a) shows the working capital ratio. I suppose that normally we mean, by working capital, what I have been careful to call " the net current assets." The absolute amount of such assets is an important guide to the firm's liquid position. But for some purposes (e.g., if we are comparing a big firm with a small one) the absolute amount is not very helpful; ratios may be more significant. Further, if an extremely exacting test of liquidity is desired, stock might well be deemed too inert for inclusion, and we should deal only with the more liquid assets that make up (b), the quick asset ratio.

A ratio of the owners' balances to other sources of finance may be a useful means of finding whether too great reliance is being placed on temporary sources. Hence (c), the proprietary ratio.

The investor who is anxious to hedge against the effects of the trade cycle will study the gearing of his companies. A highly geared capital structure is one in which the equity capital is insignificant in comparison with the preference and debenture capital. As we have seen, on the up-swing of the trade cycle the holder of ordinary shares tends to get better dividends; on the down-swing his dividends are apt to dwindle. The more highly geared the company, the more pronounced are these gains and losses; with high gearing a small increase in the total earnings means a very high percentage increase in the amount available to the ordinary shareholders. Hence the importance of (d).

The average credit periods can be tested with ratios (e) and (f).

The stock turnover may be shown either as a period of months, as in (g), or as a ratio. The former gives the more concrete idea, but it has one slight fault. Imagine that the various ratios, &c., are arranged in rows across a table, with monthly columns. The director who scans the table hastily can assume, where most rows are concerned, that a *rising* trend is a good sign; there is thus perhaps some risk that, when he comes to turnover, he will fail to note a danger signal.

It may be helpful to compare earnings with the quantity of assets employed. In particular, the comparison may suggest that further expansion of the business is not worth while, as such outlay may be yielding a lower return than can be got from alternative investments. Ratios (h), (i), and (j) try to test this aspect of the directors' policy.

LIMITATIONS OF RATIOS

Ratios, like other forms of mathematical expression, look impressive. One should, however, not be overawed by them, or go to the trouble of preparing them unless one is sure that they will be of some real use.

Perhaps it is hardly necessary for me to stress that any given ratio can, considered all by itself, scarcely be of much significance. The greatest statistician on earth, if told, say, that the working capital ratio is 1·8, could not glean much from this isolated figure. If he knows the corresponding figures for similar firms he may gain a useful impression. He is still more likely to learn something if he is shown how the ratio for this firm has been behaving over several years. Such a series may be the quickest and most reliable pointer to what is happening.

But even a series has its limitations. One can never say, simply because the figures sink (*e.g.*, from 1·8 to 1·5, and then to 1·3), that the position is getting worse. Such a conclusion would only be justified if all other factors had remained the same—and, in particular, if we could be sure that the directors had not embarked on a different trade policy. Thus the directors may have realised that their particular company would gain by holding a bigger selection of stock, or letting debtors pay at a more genteel tempo; in such circumstances an increase in the periods of turnover and credit would be an inevitable accompaniment to the change in policy, and a ratio series that looks deplorable might go hand-in-hand with rapidly growing net profits. In this sense, the net profit trend is more important than anything else. Mathematical fireworks never become a good substitute for commonsense and understanding.

APPENDICES

APPENDIX A. OUTLINE OF BALANCE SHEET
IN PRESENT CONVENTIONAL FORM

Share Capital, Reserves, &c.—				Fixed Assets—			
Capital—				Premises	.	.	£3,500	
Ordinary Shares	.	£3,000		Motor Vehicles	. £3,000		
5 per cent Preference				Less Depreciation 1,500			
Shares .	.	2,000				1,500	
		£5,000					£5,000
Capital Reserve	.	500		Current Assets—			
Revenue Reserves—				Stock .	.	.	£2,500	
General Reserve £1,000				Debtors	.	.	2,200	
Profit carried				Cash	.	.	1,100	
forward	500						5,800
		1,500					
			£7,000				
Long-term Liabilities—							
Debentures .	.	.	2,000				
Current Liabilities—							
Creditors	.	.	1,800				
			£10,800				£10,800

APPENDIX B. OUTLINE OF BALANCE SHEET
WITH FULL NARRATIVE, AND WITH ASSETS ON LEFT

EXPLANATORY BALANCE SHEET

Listing what we owned, what we owed, and what we were worth
at the close of our financial year 19

ASSETS—WHAT WE OWNED.		LIABILITIES—WHAT WE OWED.	
Cash.—This amount is the total of cash, stamps, and bank balances	£1,100	*Trade Creditors.*—Amounts we owed for the purchase of merchandise, supplies, and services . .	£1,800
Debtors.—Total owed us by our customers for merchandise, less estimated amounts which we may not be able to collect .	2,200	*Debentures.*—This is the amount borrowed, at 5 per cent interest, from creditors, to whom we gave a bond over our premises as security . . .	2,000
Stocks.—This is the value of the merchandise on hand . .	2,500		£3,800
Motor Vehicles—Depreciated Cost.—This is the amount we paid for motor vehicles (£3000), less an estimated allowance (£1500) for loss in value because they were gradually wearing out . .	1,500	SHAREHOLDERS' FUNDS— WHAT WE WERE WORTH. *Capital, Reserves, and Surplus.*—This represents the investment in the business by 238 shareholders . . .	7,000
Premises.—This is what we paid for land and buildings . . .	3,500		
	£10,800		£10,800

299

APPENDIX C.

REVENUE ACCOUNT IN NARRATIVE FORM
(Included in Directors' Report)

REPORT OF THE DIRECTORS

The Directors submit their Report for the year to 31st March 1950, together with the audited Balance Sheet at that date and the following Statement of Profit and Loss.

STATEMENT OF PROFIT AND LOSS

Previous Period			Year to 31st March 1950
	Interest and Dividends on Advances and Investments (gross), less Interest on Loan Capital amount to		£536,161
	To which has to be added Other Income (including Net Profits on Sales of Investments) amounting to		128,053
			£664,214
	There fall to be deducted :—		
	Administration Expenses	£106,025	
	Provision for Audit Fee	630	
	Directors' Remuneration—		
	Fees	£4,000	
	Salary	2,500	
		6,500	
	Depreciation of Furniture and Equipment and Amortisation of Expenditure on Alterations to Leased Premises	429	
		£113,584	
	Amount set aside for Doubtful Advances and Investments	190,000	
			303,584
	So that the Profit for the Year before taxation is		£360,630
	The estimated charge for Income Tax, based on the profit for the year after giving effect to relief—£36,506—in respect of losses of earlier years, is		126,226
	Leaving a Net Profit for the year of		£234,404
	The accumulated deficiency brought forward from the previous period has to be deducted		53,585
	Leaving a balance to the credit of Profit and Loss Account of		£180,819
	The Directors have decided to make a transfer to Reserve for Contingencies of		100,000
	So that there is a Surplus on the Profit and Loss Account to be carried forward of		£80,819

(Rest of Directors' Report follows)

APPENDIX D.   OUTLINE OF BALANCE SHEET

IN SINGLE-SIDED OR REPORT FORM

THE COMPANY'S ASSETS ARE :—
1. Current Assets—

Cash	£1,100	
Debtors	2,200	
Stock	2,500	
		£5,800

2. *Less :* Current Liabilities—

Trade Creditors		1,800

3.   Net Current Assets or " Working Capital "   £4,000

4. Fixed Assets—

Motor Vehicles	£3,000	
Less : Depreciation	1,500	
	£1,500	
Premises	3,500	
		5,000

5.   Total Assets less Current Liabilities   £9,000

6. *Less :* Long-term Liabilities—

Debentures	2,000

7.   Net Assets   £7,000

THE ABOVE NET ASSETS HAVE BEEN PROVIDED BY THE SHAREHOLDERS THUS :—
8. Ordinary Shareholders—

Original Capital of 3000 Ordinary Shares	£3,000	
Premium on issue of these Shares	500	
Trade Profits—		
Portion to be retained in business indefinitely	£1,000	
Portion not yet appropriated	500	
	1,500	

9.   Ordinary Shareholders' Interest (the " Equity ")   £5,000

10. Preference Shareholders—

Original Capital of 2000 5 per cent Shares	2,000
	£7,000

APPENDIX E.   SUMMARISED BALANCE SHEETS

Assets—		Last year		This year	Increase in assets during this year
Fixed Assets—					
Premises		£3,500		£3,500	
Motor Vehicles—					
1st Jan.—Cost less depreciation	£1,620		£1,200		
Additions	..		800		
	£1,620		£2,000		
Depreciation for year	420		500		
		1,200		1,500	£300 [1]
		£4,700		£5,000	£300
Current Assets—					
Stock		£3,000		£2,500	— £500
Debtors		1,300		2,200	900
Cash		..		1,100	1,100
		£4,300		£5,800	£1,500
Total Assets		£9,000		£10,800	£1,800

[1] Made up of gross investment £800, less depreciation £500.

								Sources of finance
Less : Liabilities to outside Creditors—								
Short-term Liabilities—								
Creditors	.	.	.	.	.	£1,200	£1,800	£600
Bank Overdraft	.	.	.	.	.	925	..	— 925
						£2,125	£1,800	— £325
Long-term Liabilities—								
Debentures	.	.	.	.	.	..	£2,000	£2,000
	Total Liabilities	.		.		£2,125	£3,800	£1,675
	Net Assets	.		.		£6,875	£7,000	
Ownership—								
5 per cent Cum. Pref. Shares		.	.	.		£2,000	£2,000	
Ordinary Shares	.	.	.	.		3,000	3,000	
Reserve	.	.	.	.		1,500	1,500	
Profit and Loss Account	.	.	.			375 [1]	500	£125
	Total	.	.			£6,875	£7,000	£125
								£1,800

[1] In preceding year, a loss of (£435 — £375) = £60.

APPENDIX F.   ANALYSIS OF BALANCE SHEET CHANGES
(*Simple Form*)

STATEMENT SHOWING HOW PROFIT, &c., WAS USED

Profits shown in Profit and Loss Account		£225
To this must be added money obtained from debenture issue . . .		2,000
Total		£2,225
This has been used as follows :—		
Preference dividend		£100
Increase in motor vehicles . . .		300
Increase in net current assets—		
Current assets	£1,500	
Current liabilities (reduction in) . . .	325	
		1,825
		£2,225

APPENDIX G.   ANALYSIS OF BALANCE SHEET CHANGES
(*Alternative Form*)

STATEMENT SHOWING HOW QUICK ASSETS WERE OBTAINED

Quick assets (net)—		
At close of year.		£1,500
At start of year (deficiency)		825
Increase during year		£2,325
This increase has been obtained as follows :—		
Profits		£225
Add : Non-cash expense—depreciation for year . . .		500
Found from own resources		£725
Debentures issued		2,000
Available resources for year		£2,725
Less : Disbursements—		
Additions to motor vehicles . . .	£800	
Preference dividend	100	
	£900	
Less : Reduction in stock . . .	500	
		400
		£2,325

APPENDIX H. SUMMARISED TRADING AND PROFIT AND LOSS ACCOUNT

Year ended 31st December	Last Year	% 100	This Year	% 100
Sales	£8,000	100	£10,000	100
Stock, 1st January	£2,800		£3,000	
Purchases	5,960		7,000	
	£8,760		£10,000	
Stock, 31st December	3,000		2,500	
Cost of goods sold	£5,760	72·0	£7,500	75·0
Gross profit	£2,240	28·0	£2,500	25·0
Selling expenses	£120	1·5	£125	1·2
Distribution expenses (including depreciation)	545	6·8	750	7·5
Administrative expenses	840	10·5	1,100	11·0
Financial expenses	200	2·5	300	3·0
	£1,705	21·3	£2,275	22·7
Net profit	£535	6·7	£225	2·3

Year ended 31st December	Last Year	This Year
Preference dividend	£100	£100
Ordinary dividend	..	..
Added to carry forward	435	125
	£535	£225

RATIOS

	Last Year	This Year
(a) Working capita ratio—		
$\dfrac{\text{current assets}}{\text{current liabilities}}$	$\dfrac{4,300}{2,125} = 2·0$	$\dfrac{5,800}{1,800} = 3·$
(b) Quick asset ratio—		
$\dfrac{\text{debtors and cash}}{\text{current liabilities}}$	$\dfrac{1,300}{2,125} = 0·6$	$\dfrac{3,300}{1,800} = 1·8$
(c) Proprietary ratio—		
$\dfrac{\text{ownership}}{\text{liabilities}}$	$\dfrac{6,875}{2,125} = 3·2$	$\dfrac{7,000}{3,800} = 1·8$
(d) Capital gearing—		
$\dfrac{\text{pref. and deb. capital}}{\text{equity capital}}$	$\dfrac{2,000}{3,000} = 0·7$	$\dfrac{4,000}{3,000} = 1·3$

	Last Year	This Year

Average credit periods—

(e) (i) Allowed—

$\dfrac{\text{average debtors}}{\text{sales}}$ $\dfrac{1,300^{1}}{8,000} \times 12 = 2 \text{ months}$ $\dfrac{1,300 + 2,200}{2 \times 10,000} \times 12 = 2\cdot1 \text{ months}$

(f) (ii) Taken—

$\dfrac{\text{average creditors}}{\text{purchases}}$ $\dfrac{1,200^{1}}{5,960} \times 12 = 2\cdot4 \text{ ,,}$ $\dfrac{1,200 + 1,800}{2 \times 7,000} \times 12 = 2\cdot6 \text{ ,,}$

(g) Average turnover period—

$\dfrac{\text{average stock}}{\text{cost of sales}}$ $\dfrac{2,800 + 3,000}{2 \times 5,760} \times 12 = 6 \text{ ,,}$ $\dfrac{3,000 + 2,500}{2 \times 7,500} \times 12 = 4\cdot4 \text{ ,,}$

Earnings rates on [2]—

(h) Total assets—

$\dfrac{\text{net profit}}{\text{total assets (gross)}}$ $\dfrac{535}{9,000} \times 100 = 5\cdot9\%$ $\dfrac{225}{10,800} \times 100 = 2\cdot1\%$

(i) Equity interest—

$\dfrac{\text{net profit} - \text{pref. div.}}{\text{ord. cap.} + \text{res.} + \text{profit}}$ $\dfrac{435}{4,875} \times 100 = 8\cdot9\%$ $\dfrac{125}{5,000} \times 100 = 2\cdot5\%$

(j) Ordinary capital—

$\dfrac{\text{net profit} - \text{pref. div.}}{\text{ordinary capital}}$ $\dfrac{435}{3,000} \times 100 = 14\cdot5\%$ $\dfrac{125}{3,000} \times 100 = 4\cdot2\%$

[1] It is assumed that the debtors and creditors were approximately the same at the beginning and end of last year.

[2] Strictly, these rates should be calculated on average funds employed, &c. In practice it is common to use the year-end figure.

THE LATE MR THOMAS LISTER, M.A., C.A.

By the death on February 26, 1967, at the age of 74, of Mr Thomas Lister, M.A., C.A., The Institute of Chartered Accountants of Scotland, and the accountancy profession in general, has lost an outstanding member.

Mr Lister had decided to retire on March 31 next from the firm of Thomson McLintock & Co., Chartered Accountants, London, whose staff he joined in 1921 and of which he had been a partner since 1931 and senior partner since 1958, and from the firm of Thomson McLintock & Co., Chartered Accountants, Glasgow, of which he was also a partner. It is grievous indeed that he was not spared to enjoy the retirement which he had so richly earned. Deep sympathy is extended to Mrs Lister and to her daughter and two sons in the irreparable loss they have sustained.

Tom Lister, who was admitted to membership of The Society of Accountants in Edinburgh 52 years ago, was elected President of The Institute of Chartered Accountants of Scotland at the Annual Meeting of Members held in March 1959. An excellent account of his career up to that time was given on pages 272/273 of THE ACCOUNTANTS' MAGAZINE of the following month. The impression created—and so very rightly created—by the words there used was of a very busy man of outstanding ability and wide experience, and of great qualities of heart and mind who, over a long period of years, gave unstinting, invaluable service to his Institute and to his profession. Correctly, emphasis was placed on his deep interest in the vitally important matters of the education, training and examination of entrants to the profession and it is appropriate indeed that the

Report on these subjects made to the Council of the Institute in 1956 by the Committee of which he was the natural Convener came to be, and still is, known as the " Lister Report ".

The office of President of the Institute is demanding on time and energy even for one based north of the Border. Tom Lister made light of the extra burden placed on him by the fact that he was resident and practising his profession in London. Deeply sensible as he always was of the unique honour done to him by his fellow members in his election as President—he was the first member located furth of Scotland to be appointed to the Scottish Institute's highest office—he willingly undertook the considerable amount of additional travelling involved for him. Never has the Institute had a more conscientious President: never was he heard to complain of the strain on him. And thus it was that at the end of his year of office it was freely and fully acknowledged that he had met more than adequately all the demands on him, had discharged his manifold duties to the complete acceptance of all the members, and had everywhere enhanced his Institute's standing and reputation, of which he was always a zealous guardian.

Tom Lister's interest in the affairs of the Institute did not diminish when he demitted the Presidential office in 1960. Indeed it continued unabated: since then he has served on various Institute Committees and in fact he attended a meeting of one of these in Edinburgh as recently as February 16.

Few members have given as much of themselves to serve the Institute—none can have given more.

Tom Lister adorned the profession of which he was proud to be a member and in the practice of which he found such pleasure and satisfaction. Apart altogether from recognising his outstanding professional abilities, which included a capacity to grasp quickly the essentials of a problem, no one who was privileged to know him well could possibly fail to be impressed by the utter completeness of his integrity, by his modest bearing despite his high standing in his profession and the width of his knowledge and experience, and by his ready approachability. Serious minded, he had yet a nice sense of humour. He gave devoted service to his church over a long period of years.

Quite simply, Tom Lister was in every sense a good man whose passing will be mourned by all who knew him, and whose like we may not soon see again.

The Late Mr Thomas Lister, M.A., C.A.

Last month's issue contained an appreciation of the late Mr Thomas Lister, M.A., C.A., a Past President of The Institute of Chartered Accountants of Scotland, who died on February 26 in his 75th year. Our printer's timetable however did not permit us to include also details of his long and distinguished service to the Institute and his wider interests.

Mr Lister was educated at the Royal High School, Edinburgh, and at the University of Edinburgh, where he graduated. He was apprenticed to Messrs A. & J. Robertson, Chartered Accountants, Edinburgh, and he passed his final examination with distinction. He was admitted a member (Edinburgh) in 1915.

During the First World War he served in the Royal Artillery. On his return he spent two years in industry. In 1921 he joined the staff of Thomson McLintock & Co., London, of which he later became senior partner.

He was a member of Council of the Institute from 1952 to 1956 and was re-elected in 1958, when he was appointed Vice-President. He was President of the Institute for 1959-60.

Apart from his Chairmanship of the Committee on Education and Training, whose Report in 1956 led to the institution of the Academic Year for C.A. Apprentices, he served on many other Institute Committees. From 1952 to 1954 he was Convener of the London Local Committee, he was a member of the Discipline Committee from 1954 to 1958 and again from 1960 to 1965, of the Taxation Committee from 1958 to 1960 and of the Company Law Committee from 1960 to 1965. He was also a member of Committee and Chairman (1952-54) of the Association of Scottish Chartered Accountants in London and he lectured to the Glasgow and Edinburgh Students' Societies.

Outside the sphere of the accountancy profession Mr Lister included among his activities membership of the Spens Committees which reported on the appropriate levels of remuneration for doctors and dentists under the National Health Service. He was an Extraordinary Director and also a member of the London Board of the Scottish Amicable Life Assurance Society, a Director of the Temperance Permanent Building Society and Chairman of the London Board of Scottish Insurance Corporation Ltd. Among other offices which he held were those of Treasurer of the Edinburgh University Club of London, and he was a member and office-bearer of Ferne Park Baptist Church.

We take this opportunity of endorsing most sincerely the tribute to Mr Lister which was published in last month's issue.

The early 1950s in the UK produced few examples of creative thinking by
accountants. There was no academic community, and practitioners were
concerned mainly with more mundane matters of accounting practice. Thus,
Lister's paper is unusual in terms of its timing and content.

The lecture challenged the conventional system of financial accounting
and reporting. It questioned the conventions of the function, particularly
the influence of the lower of cost or market rule, and the distortion of
profit by the realisation principle. The nub of the paper relates to the
possibility of accounting and reporting unrealised profits. However, the
approach to the latter issue was not described and explained in the present-
day terms of, say, replacement cost or net realisable value accounting.
Instead, Lister's paper concentrated on what he described as the projection
principle.

The Lister approach attempted to report the financial consequences of
transactions until their completion (he used two examples of hire purchase
and civil engineering contracts). Thus, he suggested the reporting of the
profits realised in the current year plus the estimated profits on
contracted work or operations to be completed in future periods. He also
suggested the need to project tax provisions on these future profits.
Lister's reporting would therefore forecast and report all profits on
work to which the entity was already committed.

So far as balance sheet reporting was concerned, Lister questioned
the use of aggregates of historic cost, feeling that the latter did not
reflect a true and fair view. He suggested the revaluation of assets on
a replacement cost basis, with depreciation provided on such revaluations.

ACCOUNTING STATEMENTS—A GENERAL FORMULA

By THOMAS LISTER, C.A.

(Being a Lecture delivered to the Chartered Accountants Students' Society of Edinburgh on 23rd February and to the Glasgow Students' Society on 9th March 1951)

I SHOULD like to put before you this evening some thoughts on the content of accounting statements, and I must begin with a word of caution. The views that I propose to submit will probably not be of much help to you in forming an opinion as to whether accounts have been framed so as to comply with the Companies Act, 1948; they will certainly not lead to a tax computation that either your client or the Inspector of Taxes would accept; they may even leave you doubtful of the distinction between a provision and a reserve. I hope, however, that you will not be afraid of straying from the path of orthodoxy, if I can persuade you that the orthodox, or as I prefer to say, the traditional doctrine is founded on unscientific premises.

I would also ask you to remember that this lecture is a purely theoretical exercise. It may well be that I shall go a long way beyond what you consider possible or acceptable in practice to-day, and, let me admit, I am seeking to be provocative. But the value of a theoretical study is not to be judged by its immediate applications, and practical problems are not likely to be solved satisfactorily except against a background of sound theory.

I make no claim to originality: much of the material of the lecture is to be found in one form or another in the writings of British and American accountants during the past twenty years or so.

My illustrations are not to be taken as models of style. They are designed to bring out sharply the points of the argument, and whatever seems not to be material for that purpose has been condensed as much as possible. Also, as a matter of obvious convenience, the figures used are smaller than life-size.

ACCOUNTING PARTIES

The earliest example of an accounting party is the servant, steward, or agent, whose duty it is to account to his master for the possessions entrusted to him, and for the fruits thereof. It is readily understandable that the emphasis in such a case should be on the agent's intromissions with cash, and that the keynote of the auditor's report on his cash account, or in more elaborate form, his account of charge and discharge, should be " sufficiently vouched and instructed."

But, even in New Testament times, a steward was expected to do more than account satisfactorily for the cash entrusted to him. The servant in the parable of the talents who kept his pound wrapped up in a napkin and in due course repaid in full the money he had received was condemned, whereas there was promotion for those who converted the money into goods and traded.

Even when the principal looks after his own business, there are other parties who are involved. You have all, no doubt, heard of the man who found it necessary to have four separate sets of accounts—one for the bank, one for the Inspector of Taxes, one for his wife, and one for himself. As I have already said, I shall not be concerned with accounts for the Inspector of Taxes, and I shall leave to any of you who care to tackle it the problem of devising a system by which the other three sets of accounts could be prepared from one trial balance.

The most familiar accounting statements nowadays, of course, are Company Accounts, and with the development of joint stock enterprise the emphasis has changed. Stockholders require a report from their stewards—the directors or managers—on the condition of the under-taking; this, if it is to be complete, demands a great deal more than an account of cash intromissions. The keynote of the auditor's report thus now becomes " a true and fair view."

EFFECTS OF UNDERSTATEMENT

It is an elementary principle in any form of scientific work that facts must be ascertained and stated without bias. Let me give you a very simple illustration. You are asked the dimensions of this table and reply, " 4 feet by 2 feet." A measurement is taken and the table is found to be, say, 4 feet 6 inches by 2 feet 2 inches, whereupon you observe, " Oh well, I was on the safe side, anyhow." Any scientist, indeed any school-boy, would laugh at you. But is that necessarily very different from the way in which some facts are customarily recorded in accounting statements ?

Let us look for a moment at the items of a typical Balance Sheet.

Cash should normally raise no question. Debtors are stated after providing for bad and doubtful debts, and creditors may include estimates of unascertained liabilities; in many cases there is a deliberate attempt to ensure that any error is " on the safe side." Stock is taken at cost or market price, whichever is lower, and this usually means that every item which is not worth cost is written down to market price. The probable result is that, irrespective of any general change in the price level, a mixed stock will stand at something less than cost of replacement. As regards fixed assets, it is frequently the policy to write down plant, and sometimes buildings also, to a nominal sum over as short a period as possible.

Let us next consider the Profit and Loss Account. I shall have more to say, later on, about Balance Sheets.

The effect of adopting the valuation rule of " cost or market price if lower " is obviously that unrealised losses are charged against the profit of the year, but unrealised gains are not brought in, and that of course is the intention of the rule. You may, in fact, say that the rule is virtually part of the definition of profit: an unrealised gain is not a profit. It is worth while, however, asking if this results in a satisfactory measurement of profit.

Take the simple case of a wholesale merchant whose purchases include the following:—

> 100 tons of commodity A at £10 a ton,
> 100 tons of commodity B at £20 a ton.

At the close of the year the price of commodity A has risen to £12 a ton and that of commodity B has fallen to £18 a ton, and if he still holds both parcels he is neither richer nor poorer for his purchases. His Profit and Loss Account, however, would show a loss for the year of £200. The error is " on the safe side," but what about the next year, in which, if he sold both parcels, he would show a profit of £200, in addition to his ordinary wholesaler's margin of gross profit ? Is the error " on the safe side " then ?

If he had sold the 100 tons of commodity A after the rise in price and had then bought a further 100 tons at £12 a ton, the loss on commodity B would have been offset by the realised profit of £200, although (apart from the question of wholesaler's margin) his position is in no real sense altered by the sale and purchase.

Now let us look at the case of a manufacturer. Like the merchant, he may find the price of some of his raw materials rising and that of others falling. We may assume that the selling price of the product moves with that of the material. According to the valuation rule as commonly applied, if the price of the material has fallen, the finished stock will be written down, not by the whole fall in the material, but only to the extent that the cost of the finished article exceeds the sale value (less selling expenses still to be incurred); if the price of the material has risen, no profit will be shown until a sale takes place. That is to say, the unrealised

H

profit on the manufacturing process will be brought in, but only if it is offset by a loss on the material.

That is the case of the manufacturer making for and selling from stock. He may, however, be taking orders for forward delivery, and may be prudent enough to buy his materials as he books his orders. Even so, unless individual purchases are linked to individual orders, you may still find that the valuation rule is applied to write down materials that have fallen in price, the result, of course, being to throw up an abnormal profit on the order when it is completed in the following year.

It is possible to carry the matter one step beyond this. Where there is a " futures " market, the covering of raw material requirements may take the form, not of buying and taking into stock the actual goods needed, but of forward contracts. You may in such circumstances find that provision is made against so-called onerous contracts—*i.e.*, contracts to buy at prices which are above the market price at the balancing date, even though they are matched by orders on hand at prices correspondingly higher than the current selling prices. As in the previous examples, this will clearly produce a distortion in the following year's results.

ACCOUNTING FOR UNREALISED PROFITS

I submit to you that, although there may be palliatives, there is only one complete remedy for these distortions, and that is to discard entirely the principle, or rule, of providing for unrealised losses while ignoring unrealised profits, and to accept that if an accounting statement, and more especially a series of accounting statements, is to give a true and fair view of the profits and losses of an undertaking, regard must be paid to the effect of all the transactions of the period, closed or open, completed or uncompleted. To accounts prepared in this unorthodox way I propose, borrowing from Oliver Cromwell, to apply the description " new model."

The merchant's Profit and Loss Account might then take this form:—

EXHIBIT A.
MERCHANT'S PROFIT AND LOSS ACCOUNT

Sales (deliveries) during year			£1000
Cost of Sales—			
Stock at beginning of year (at market value)	£50		
Purchases (deliveries) during year	800		
	£850		
Less Stock at close of year (at market value)	100		
		750	
			£250

Gross Profit—

On deliveries	£225	
On appreciation of stock	25 (a)	
	——	£250
Unrealised Profit on Forward Sales at close of year . .	£100 (b)	
Less Unrealised Profit on Forward Sales at beginning of year	20	
	——	80
Unrealised Loss on Forward Purchases at end of year .	£10	
Unrealised Profit on Forward Purchases at beginning of year	4̶0̶	
	——	−50
		£280
Deduct Expenses of the year		100
Net Profit		£180
of which unrealised ((*a*) and (*b*)) . . .	£125	
realised	55	
	——	£180

The manufacturer's Profit and Loss Account might correspondingly take this form:—

EXHIBIT B.

MANUFACTURER'S PROFIT AND LOSS ACCOUNT—NEW MODEL

Finished Products delivered to customers during the year .		£1000
Cost of Production, including raw materials at prices ruling at dates of sale contracts		900
Manufacturing Profit on Finished Products delivered . .		£100
Materials Account—		
Gains due to price fluctuations—		
on raw material stock	£50 (a)	
on raw material in Finished Products in stock . .	25 (b)	
on raw material in Finished Products delivered .	50	
	——	125
Forward Contracts Account—		
Losses on Forward Purchases of raw materials at close of period	£30	
Profits on Forward Purchases of raw materials at beginning of period	20	
	——	−50
		£175

Net Profit		£175
of which unrealised ((*a*) and (*b*))	£75	
realised	100	
		——
		£175

The same account set out on what I think may fairly be called · orthodox lines would read:—

EXHIBIT C.

MANUFACTURER'S PROFIT AND LOSS ACCOUNT—ORTHODOX BASIS

Finished Products delivered to customers during the year .	£1000
Cost of Production	850
	——
Trading Profit	£150
Deduct Provision for losses on Forward Purchases of raw materials	30
	——
Net Profit	£120

You will observe that the net profit in the orthodox account differs from the realised portion of the net profits in the new model account by the amount of profits on forward purchases at the beginning, which " orthodox " accounting would ignore. A further difference, of precisely the same nature, would of course arise from the valuation of opening stock in one case at current value, and in the other at cost, or market if lower. For brevity, I have not brought this point out in the illustration; in practice, however, the differences arising on physical stocks would in many cases be of more significant amount than differences on forward contracts.

LONG TERM TRANSACTIONS

I want now to consider the presentation of profit and loss accounts of businesses whose transactions normally extend over protracted periods. Examples are hire-purchase trading, shipbuilding, and civil engineering, and I propose to examine the first and last of these.

It is not, I think, possible to say that one method of arriving at the profit of a hire-purchase business is orthodox and all others are un-orthodox; but the very obvious risks of this business have undoubtedly caused accountants to favour the method which defers the profit on the individual transaction longest. The argument runs that the transaction is a contract of hire, with an option to purchase, that the profit therefore is earned only as instalments are collected, and (in the extreme case) that as the overheads are running on anyhow, not even sufficient gross profit should be taken on delivery of the article to cover the selling expenses attributable to the transaction.

If the level of sales, the length of credit allowed, and the profit margin all remained steady, an ultra-cautious measurement of profit, consistently maintained, would not matter. But none of these does remain steady: a growing business opens up new branches, and the additional trade causes a reduction instead of an increase in profit to be shown at first; new hire-purchase contracts decline owing to general trade depression, bad management, or shortage of supplies, and profits apparently rise as old contracts run off; the length of credit to be given may be restricted by law, and the same value of turnover then brings its return over a shortened period, but possibly at a lower rate. A method which unduly defers the taking of profit in these circumstances—all of which are to be found in common experience over the last twenty years—must result in statements of profit which can only be misleading unless accompanied by a full explanation.

A first step would be to depart from caution to the extent of taking credit for a cash profit on the transaction—*i.e.*, treating it as if it were a cash sale coupled with a financing arrangement. Even this goes only part of the way, for the financial profit is secured, subject to the incidence of bad debt losses, on the signature of the hiring contract, and the results for one, two, or possibly three years ahead are accordingly determined already to a substantial extent.

I suggest that a Profit and Loss Account set out thus comes nearer to giving a true and fair view of the profit of a hire-purchase business than one prepared on a deliberately cautious basis:—

EXHIBIT D.

HIRE-PURCHASE PROFIT AND LOSS ACCOUNT—1950

Cash Profit on articles delivered in 1950 on Hire-purchase Agreements	. :		£1000
Financial Profit on above agreements after providing for future interest, costs of collection, and estimated bad debts—			
On instalments due 1950	. . . .	. £100	
On instalments due 1951	. . . .	. 200 (*a*)	
On instalments due 1952	. . . .	. 150 (*b*)	
		——	450
	Carry forward	.	£1450

| | Brought forward | . | £1450 |

Differences between provisions for interest, costs of collection,
and bad debts made in previous years and actual charges for
those items   .   .   .   .   —10

Net Profit £1440
  of which unrealised ((a) and (b)) £350
      realised   .   .   .   ,   .   .   . 1090
                                                    ——
                                                    £1440

In Exhibit E. I have assumed a sequence of events which might be
found in the accounts of many hire-purchase traders: rising turnover
in the later 'thirties, a rapid shrinkage from 1940, and recovery as supplies
began to become available again, with a reduction in the length of credit
and in the margin of gross profit. You will note that, for the sake of
brevity, the recovery in turnover is shown as taking place from 1944
onwards, although in fact it could not have occurred to any great extent
earlier than 1946.

In 1936 and 1937 the deferment basis results in a slight fall in reported
profit, although turnover has been steadily rising; in 1940, when new
business has dropped catastrophically, the time-lag produces a largely
increased profit, and it is not until 1944, when trade has begun to expand
again, that the full effect of the lean years is shown. The contrast with
the results brought out in the " new model " accounts may be left to
speak for itself.

THE PROJECTION PRINCIPLE

The essential feature of the "new model" Profit and Loss Accounts
that we have been considering is that they apply the principle of projection—that is to say, all transactions are carried forward to their completion. In the simple case of the merchant dealing in a " futures "
market, projection does not involve anything more than an assumption
regarding the solvency of the other parties to the transactions. In the
more complicated hire-purchase accounts which I have illustrated there
are, of necessity, more difficult assumptions and estimates to be made,
but I suggest that the difference is one of degree.

I want now to press this idea of projection one stage further and to
suggest to you how it might be applied in the presentation of, say, a civil
engineering contractor's results. A business of this kind might be
engaged at any one time on a small number of large contracts, some of
them extending over several years. If the orthodox principle of bringing

EXHIBIT E.

COMPARISON OF HIRE-PURCHASE TRADING RESULTS ON ALTERNATIVE BASES

	1935	1936	1937	1938	1939	1940	1941	1942	1943	1944	1945
Assumptions—											
Sales, i.e., gross hire-purchase contracts (spread evenly over the year)	£4000	£4500	£5000	£5000	£5000	£2000	£1000	£1000	£1000	£4000	£6667
Gross Profit as percentage of sales	50	50	50	50	50	50	40	40	40	40	40
Period of Credit (years)	3	3	3	3	3	3	2	2	2	2	2
Selling Expenses (20 per cent of Sales)	800	900	1000	1000	1000	400	200	200	200	800	1334
Collecting Expenses, Bad Debts, and Interest ignored											
Cash Collections (deposits ignored)—											
Contracts of year	667	750	833	833	833	333	250	250	250	1000	1667
Contracts of 1st preceding year	1333	1333	1500	1667	1667	1667	667	500	500	500	2000
Contracts of 2nd preceding year	1333	1333	1333	1500	1667	1667	1667	667	250	250	250
Contracts of 3rd preceding year	667	667	667	667	750	833	833	833	333	..	..
	£4000	£4083	£4333	£4667	£4917	£4500	£3417	£2250	£1333	£1750	£3917
Trading Account—											
(a) Deferment Basis—											
Cash Collections	£4000	£4083	£4333	£4667	£4917	£4500	£3417	£2250	£1333	£1750	£3917
Cost attributable to Cash Collections	£2000	£2041	£2167	£2334	£2458	£2250	£1733	£1200	£767	£1050	£2350
Selling Expenses	800	900	1000	1000	1000	400	200	200	200	800	1334
Net Profit	£1200	£1142	£1166	£1333	£1459	£1850	£1484	£850	£366	—£100	£233
(b) New Model—											
Sales	£4000	£4500	£5000	£5000	£5000	£2000	£1000	£1000	£1000	£4000	£6667
Cost of Sales	£2000	£2250	£2500	£2500	£2500	£1000	£600	£600	£600	£2400	£4000
Selling Expenses	800	900	1000	1000	1000	400	200	200	200	800	1334
Net Profit	£1200	£1350	£1500	£1500	£1500	£600	£200	£200	£200	£800	£1333

Total Sales over Period . £39,167

Total Cash Collections . £39,167

Total Net Profit over Period—
(a) Deferment Basis . £10,983
(b) New Model . £10,383

into account only realised profits is accepted, the accounts for any year might, by themselves, be almost meaningless. While the practice is not uniform, it is quite common for sums on account of profit on uncompleted contracts to be brought in. Whether the effect of this is to produce results which really reflect the varying fortunes of the business will depend on the objectivity with which the uncompleted contracts are assessed—in other words, the success with which the temptation to aim at equalising profits has been resisted.

So far, the case is not very different from that of the hire-purchase trader. But the civil engineer's profits are going to depend to a large extent for some years on the contracts which he has taken, even though they may not have been commenced, and it is possible to project them also thus:—

EXHIBIT F.

CONTRACTOR'S PROFIT AND LOSS ACCOUNTS—NEW MODEL

1949	Results of work executed	Estimated Results of work secured and to be executed in years				
		1949	1950	1951	1952	1953
Profit on work executed in 1949—						
On contracts secured in previous years, as estimated at 31st December 1948	£150	—£150				
Differences between estimated and actual results	+5					
On contracts secured in 1949	120					
Estimated Future Profit on contracts secured in 1949			£130	£100	£50	
General Overheads. .	—50		—50	—50	—50	
	£225					
Balances brought forward from 1948 * . .	—270	150	150	80	30	
Balances carried forward .	—£45	..	£230	£130	£30	

* Before General Overheads as regards future years.

1950	Results of work executed	Estimated Results of work secured and to be executed in years				
		1949	1950	1951	1952	1953
Profit on work executed in 1950—						
On contracts secured in previous years, as estimated at 31st December 1949	£280	−£280				
Differences between estimated and actual results	−10					
On contracts secured in 1950	50					
Revision of time schedules	+20			−£10	−£10	
Estimated Future Profit on contracts secured in 1950				50	25	£10
Revision of previous estimates of Profit . .				−15		
General Overheads . .	−55			−55	−55	−55
	£285					
Balances brought forward from 1949 * . .	−45		280	180	80	
	£240		..	£150	£40	−£45
Distributions . .	120					
Balances carried forward .	£120		..	£150	£40	−£45

* Before General Overheads as regards future years.

You will note that this example has been deliberately made rather an extreme one, to demonstrate what a projection of the Profit and Loss Account might tell. The profit which would ordinarily be reported was £225 in 1949 and £285 in 1950, apparently a very healthy increase. If the rule not to take any profit until the completion of a contract had been applied, it is quite possible that the increase of 1950 over 1949 would have been still more marked. But, looking at the projections, we see that the profit in sight at the end of 1949 was £390, compared with only £145 in sight at the end of 1950, and it would appear that while 1951 promises to be a fairly good year the prospects thereafter are almost entirely dependent on work which has yet to be found.

PROJECTION OF TAXATION

There are two important items in the Profit and Loss Account to which I have not yet referred—namely, depreciation and obsolescence, and taxation. It will be convenient, as you will see presently, to leave depreciation until a little later.

Those of you who are old enough will remember that until 1927 trades and professions were assessed to Income Tax on the average of three years' profits. At that time the general practice was to charge against each year the legal Income Tax liability of the year, and it was quite exceptional for any account to be taken of a difference between the actual profit and the assessable profit. When the basis was changed and the Income Tax payable came to be related, normally, to the profit of the preceding year, it was only slowly recognised to be desirable in all cases, and essential in some, that the charge for tax should be related to the profits reported. The current practice, you will appreciate, is an example of projection: the consequence—namely, an Income Tax liability to arise in future on the profits earned in the year under review—is reflected in the accounts of that year.

When the initial allowance was introduced, accounting recognition of the ultimate effect on taxation liability was again rather slow, but it is now generally accepted that the best practice is to make the appropriate adjustments year by year through an equalisation account, so that an amount is charged against profits each year equal to the tax that would be payable in respect of the year's profits if initial allowances were not granted.

All I need say with regard to taxation in relation to the " new model " Profit and Loss Accounts that we have been studying is that in projecting Income Tax (and Profits Tax) charges you must have regard to all the profits, realised or unrealised, that you are admitting into the accounts. Further, you should not stop at profits, but should be prepared to project the taxation relief on losses. Failure to do this would introduce, as far as tax is concerned, the same kind of distortion as does undervaluation of stock or the ignoring of unrealised profits.

The " new model " Profit and Loss Account would be reflected in the Balance Sheet in changed descriptions of certain assets and liabilities, and in the emergence of some unfamiliar items. By now I hope that you will agree there need be nothing alarming in a Balance Sheet like this:—

EXHIBIT G.

CONTRACTOR'S BALANCE SHEET, 31ST DECEMBER 1949

Assets

Current Assets—
Work in Progress, including Profit thereon, less sums received on account	£100		
Expenditure on contracts secured but not commenced .	5		
Trade Debtors, including retentions . . .	40		
Cash at Bank	30		
	--·——	£175	
Fixed Assets—			
Land and Buildings	£500		
Plant	800		
	——	1300	
		£1475	
Suspense Accounts—			
Estimated Future Profit on contracts secured . .	£390		
Income Tax on losses carried forward . . .	20		
	——	410	
		£1885	

Liabilities

Current Liabilities and Provisions—			
Trade Creditors ·	£80		
Provisions for Claims . `	10		
	--——	£90	
Future Taxation—			
Equalisation of Initial Allowances		50	
	Carry forward .	£140	

Brought forward .		£140
Capital and Surplus—		
Share Capital	£1000	
Capital Reserve	400	
	£1400	
Less Profit and Loss Account—Adverse balance .	45	
	£1355	
Estimated Future Profit	390	
		1745
		£1885

THE UNIT OF MEASUREMENT

I would now like to look at the Balance Sheet more generally. Does it really give a true and fair view of the state of affairs?

The accounts of an undertaking may reasonably be expected to show whether it has been preserved intact, has been improved, or has deteriorated. At the beginning of this lecture, in referring to the parable of the talents, I hinted at the distinction between maintaining the money value of the assets and preserving or improving their real value.

A bank, whose business it is to deal in money, may perfectly fairly be said to have maintained its position if the money value of the assets (sterling in the case of a bank established and operating in Great Britain) is preserved. This applies equally to other financial institutions—for example, life assurance offices—who make their contracts, over however long a period they may extend, in sterling. But a manufacturing or trading company invests its capital in land, buildings and plant, and in stocks of goods, and engages itself, for the most part, to deliver goods; if it is to be regarded as an indefinitely continuing concern it is surely material to ascertain whether its real assets have been preserved.

This leads to what I submit is a fundamental question in relation to accounting statements: in what unit of measurement are they to be compiled? During the period from 1819 (when convertibility was restored after the Napoleonic Wars) to 1914, the answer in Great Britain would have been the pound sterling, freely convertible into gold at

£4, 5s. per ounce. And the fluctuations in the quantity of goods and services £1 would buy—*i.e.*, in the value of sterling money—although not by any means negligible, were not so large or so rapid as to suggest that there might be something wrong with the unit of measurement.

Let me remind you very briefly of the things that have happened to the pound since the beginning of the First World War. In August 1914 the Bank of England was empowered to pay its notes in Treasury notes instead of gold, sterling thus being made virtually inconvertible, although we patriotically avoided the word. In 1920 the American exchange was $3.20 to the £, but by January 1925 it had moved to $4.78, and on 27th April of that year we returned to the gold standard at the old rate of $4.87 to the £. In September 1931 we had to leave the gold standard again. The rate fell overnight from $4.87 to $3.75, and by the end of 1932 it had fallen further to $3.30. During 1933 America was also forced to leave the gold standard and by December of that year the rate had risen to $5.10. In the early part of 1934 it reacted to about $4.90, and it was fairly stable around that level until the autumn of 1938 when it fell to about $4.60 during the Munich crisis. There was little further movement until the beginning of September 1939, when it was officially fixed at $4.03, and there it was held throughout the Second World War and for four years thereafter. The devaluation to a rate of $2.80 to the £ in September 1949 is fresh in all our minds.

The relationship of our unit to the dollar or to gold, of course, is not the whole story, and not necessarily even the most important part. The owner of a pound is concerned with what it will buy of the goods and services that he wants.

As you will be aware, many price indices are compiled. For my present purpose I have chosen ' The Statist's ' Annual Index Numbers of Wholesale Prices, partly because the series has been maintained without change of content for a longer period than any other index, and I am indebted to the editor of ' The Statist ' for permission to use this material.

The accompanying graph (Exhibit H.) shows the movements in the purchasing power of the pound sterling, as measured by ' The Statist ' index, between 1849 and 1949. If we take the purchasing power of the pound sterling, in terms of this index, as 20s. in 1914, the equivalent value in 1849 was 23s. This was the year of the California gold rush, and during the next five years the purchasing power fell to 16s. 8d., at which point it remained fairly constant for twenty years. Between the mid-seventies and mid-nineties there was a steady fall in commodity prices, and the value of the pound rose from a " low " of 15s. 4d. in 1873 to a " high " of 27s. 11d. in 1896. The end of the nineteenth century saw the discovery

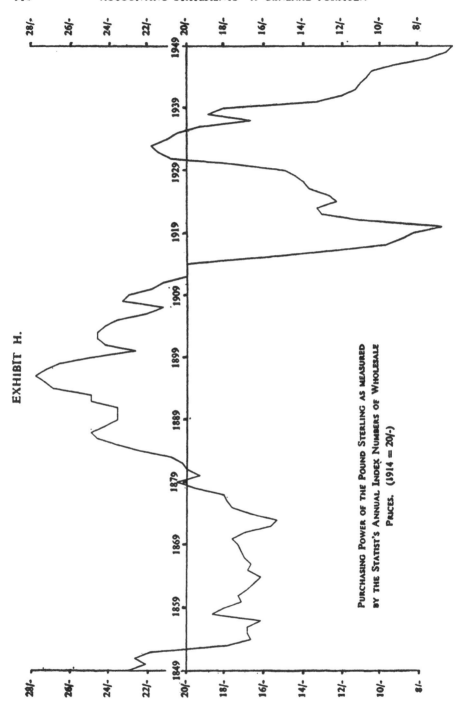

EXHIBIT H.

PURCHASING POWER OF THE POUND STERLING AS MEASURED
BY THE STATIST'S ANNUAL INDEX NUMBERS OF WHOLESALE
PRICES. (1914 = 20/-)

of the vast Rand goldfield in South Africa, and the value of the pound fell again to 20s. in 1914. By 1920 it had fallen to 6s. 9d., almost exactly a third of its pre-war value, but in 1921 came the first post-war slump and it recovered to 11s. When we returned to the gold standard in 1925 it was still only 12s. 8d., and in 1929, just before the Great Depression, 14s. 11d. By 1933 the purchasing power of the pound had risen to 21s. 10d., the highest point in the inter-war years and slightly above the 1914 level. From then on it fell to 18s. 1d. in 1939, 10s. 5d. in 1945, and 6s. 2d. in 1949, which was below even the 1920 figure.

REVALUATION OF FIXED ASSETS AND DEPRECIATION

If you were asked to describe an orange you might, after indicating shape, colour, surface, &c., say that its diameter was approximately the same as that of a cricket ball. That might be accepted as a scientifically sound statement, for the size of a cricket ball is definite within fairly close limits. But if you were to say the diameter was half that of an indiarubber balloon, the statement would be a scientific absurdity, as everything depends on the amount of inflation.

Yet here we are, expressing the opinion that a Balance Sheet shows a true and fair view of the state of affairs, when it may include assets acquired in 1914, 1925, 1939, and 1949, recorded at their respective costs in the pounds sterling of those years, and added together without regard to changes in the amount of goods and services which the pound has commanded from time to time.

I have set out in Exhibit I. the book value and the value adjusted by reference to the wholesale price index of four identical items of plant acquired over the period from 1934 to 1949. For simplicity I have calculated depreciation by the straight line method over twenty years. You will see that the revaluation (after depreciation) exceeds the written-down book value by nearly 50 per cent and, further, that the depreciation for 1950 would be £376 if calculated on book values but £676 on the revaluation. This is by no means an extreme illustration of the effect of rising prices.

Exactly the same can be said of buildings, but owing to their longer life the discrepancy between book value and valuation is likely to be wider than in the case of plant.

The wholesale price index obviously does not give an exact measure of changes in the price of machinery, and if the technique of indices were

EXHIBIT I.

REVALUATION OF FOUR IDENTICAL ITEMS OF PLANT, 1949

1	2	3	4	5	6	7	8
Year of Acquisition	Wholesale Price Index	Cost	Depreciation to 1949 on cost	Written-down book value	Revaluation as new by reference to Wholesale Price Index	Depreciation based on Revaluation	Revaluation allowing for Depreciation
1934	81	£1000	£750	£250	£3,380	£2535	£845
1939	94	1160	580	580	3,380	1690	1690
1944	160	1980	495	1485	3,380	845	2535
1949	274	3380	..	3380	3,380	..	3380
		£7520	£1825	£5695	£13,520	£5070	£8450

to be used to produce revised values of fixed assets, it would be desirable to have one index for buildings and another for plant, and possibly separate indices for different classes of plant. I am not concerned now, however, with the problem of finding appropriate indices; I ask you to accept that, theoretically, they could be made available.

An alternative to the adjustment of fixed asset values by means of a price index is to make an appraisal from time to time. The practical difficulties of time and expense obviously preclude an annual appraisal of fixed assets; this course is often adopted, however, in special circumstances—for example, on a reduction of capital, as a preliminary to a bonus issue of shares or for the purpose of an amalgamation or a flotation. Even where none of these special circumstances existed, a number of companies in this country have made a revaluation following on a major change in the price level, and in some continental countries where inflation has been much greater and more rapid than we have experienced revaluation has been imposed by law.

If you have accepted my premise that a statement can give a true and fair view only if it is drawn up without bias in either direction, you must, I think, agree that either the introduction of a correction to allow for changes in the unit of measurement or a periodical appraisal will result in a better approximation to a true and fair view than is given by a statement based on historical cost alone. I would put the case more strongly than that: I submit that if a Balance Sheet is prepared in sterling or any other currency, ignoring major changes in the value of that currency such as I have described, the result may be a well-performed exercise in book-keeping, but it cannot be regarded as a scientifically acceptable statement of affairs.

Assuming that revised values of fixed assets can be determined from time to time, the amount required to make good the wastage of the year can be calculated in relation to these revised values. This, I submit, is the amount which should be charged as depreciation or provision for renewals in the Profit and Loss Account.

You will note, incidentally, that if accounts are framed on the basis of maintaining the real and not the money value of the undertaking, the significance of the distinction between depreciation and provision for renewal disappears.

There will, in a time of rising prices, be a further factor to be considered—namely, the difference between the renewal provisions created in earlier years and the total provision required on the basis of the latest valuation. This difference has no relation to the results of the year, and it would appropriately be dealt with by an adjustment outside the Profit and Loss Account.

329

In the earlier part of this paper I have discussed various cases in which the full effect of transactions can only be shown by projection. There is one important projection which the introduction of a revaluation demands and to which I should like now to direct your attention. When an item of plant is worn out, the total capital allowances granted for taxation—*i.e.*, initial allowance and annual allowance adjusted by balancing allowance or balancing charge—will equal its original cost less its residual value. If no revaluation has taken place and if depreciation is based on the book value, no difference will arise so far as that item is concerned between the total profit shown in the accounts and the total profit assessable to taxation. If, however, the value is written up, the depreciation charge thereafter will be increased, while the allowance for taxation will not be altered, and so the assessable profit for the period after revaluation will be greater than the profit shown in the accounts. If the plant were sold at the valuation, the new owner would be entitled in due course to full taxation relief on the cost to him, while the original owner would incur a balancing charge. This taxation disadvantage at which the original owner stands is an element that should properly be taken into account in making a revaluation. If Income Tax and Profits Tax together amount to approximately 10s. in the £, it means that only half of the excess of the revaluation over the written-down cost should properly be regarded as appreciation. Alternatively, and better, there should be set aside out of the surplus on valuation a sum equal to the estimated future taxation on the excess of depreciation over capital allowances. Such a provision, you will note, is closely analogous to the provision already discussed in connection with initial allowances, although the latter merely alters the incidence of taxation as between one year and another, without altering the total, while the former—on an upward revision of values—has the effect of relieving the Profit and Loss Account altogether of part of the charge for taxation.

Exhibit J. shows the adjustments arising on a revaluation.

EXHIBIT J.

BALANCE SHEET, 31ST DECEMBER 1950, INCORPORATING
REVALUATION AT 31ST DECEMBER 1949

Plant—

At Cost	. £1000	
Appreciation on revaluation as new—at 31/12/49	. 400	
Revaluation as new		. £1400
	Carry forward	. £1400

Less :   Brought forward   . £1400

   Accumulated depreciation to 31/12/49 on cost .   .   £300
   Adjustment of accumulated depreciation to take account
     of revaluation   120
   Depreciation for year to 31/12/50, based on current
     valuation   70
           .   —— 490

Written-down value at 31/12/50   .   .   .   .   . £910
Current Assets, less Liabilities 600
           £1510

Provision for Future Taxation—
  On Profits £100
  Equalisation of Capital Allowances   .   .   . 80
  On excess of future depreciation charges over
    future Capital Allowances as at 31/12/49 *   . £140
    Less Applied to reduce taxation charge for
     1950 † 10
          —— 130
           —— 310

        Net Assets   .   .   .   · .   . £1200
Represented by:—
Share Capital £1000
Capital Reserve—
  Appreciation on revaluation of plant (as new)   . £400
  Less :
  Required to make good deficiency in
    depreciation provision at 31/12/49   . £120
  Transfer to Provision for Future Taxation
    on disallowable depreciation   .   . 140
        —— 260
          —— 140
Revenue Reserves   60
           £1200

* Revaluation, less depreciation, at 31/12/49   £980
  Cost, less depreciation, at 31/12/49   . 700
       Difference   .   . £280 at 10s. in £   £140

† Depreciation for year to 31/12/50—
  On revaluation £70
  On cost   50
       Difference   .   . £20 at 10s. in £   £10

THE GENERAL FORMULA

We have discussed this evening a number of cases in which, as I have tried to show, the application of traditional accounting principles leads to unsatisfactory results, and I have indicated how in these cases the shortcomings could be remedied. In such instances as the merchant of Exhibit A., the manufacturer of Exhibit B., and the hire-purchase trader of Exhibit E., the solution offered was to project open transactions and bring into account their estimated ultimate outcome. In the plant account of Exhibit I. the problem of a variable unit of value was dealt with by ascertaining its variations, adopting as standard the unit as existing at the date of the statement and expressing all values in terms of that unit.

I submit to you that the technique of projection and the application of price indices are but two special cases of a general principle, and that if valuation is fully accepted as an essential in the presentation of accounting statements of all kinds the anomalies and distortions that stand out so prominently to-day are all capable of removal. In a single word, then, my general formula for accounting statements is valuation.

In the illustrations which I have used, the effect of interest or discount has been left out of account, for the sake of simplicity. I need hardly point out that interest could not properly be ignored in practice; consideration of this aspect of valuation, however, would speedily lead us into calculations which had better be left to another occasion and another lecturer.

The longer the period of projection the more important does the interest factor become, until the extreme case is reached of a life assurance office whose contracts may extend over fifty years or more. The policies being issued in sterling, and the great bulk of the investments usually consisting of fixed interest-bearing securities, problems arising from the changing value of the pound have fortunately not concerned the actuary much; but the valuation Balance Sheet of a life office may, nevertheless, be regarded as an interesting and important application of the general formula. If, therefore, accountants should now turn to valuation to solve their problems, they will only be borrowing a technique that actuaries have been accustomed to use for nearly two hundred years.

I have not touched, so far, on the question of intangible assets. Expenditure on patents, processes, and development generally does not differ in principle from expenditure on tangible fixed assets. The difference lies only in the greater difficulty of determining what expenditure in this category has a continuing value and of estimating how long that value will last.

Pure goodwill is somewhat different. There is no real distinction between goodwill that has been purchased and goodwill that has been built up, nor, for that matter, between goodwill on which a value appears in the Balance Sheet and goodwill of which the value is only to be found in a Stock Exchange quotation. If the application of the formula were to be carried to its limit, goodwill would be valued, like any other asset. You might then have a Balance Sheet showing a total of capital and surplus which—in theory—should precisely correspond to the market valuation of the shares!

It is scarcely surprising that the problems created by an unstable price level should to-day be stated and discussed in terms of inflation. A glance at the graph showing changes in the purchasing power of the pound, however, will remind you that there have been large movements in the opposite direction also, and the necessary adaptations to the case of falling prices would present no great difficulty.

PRACTICAL APPLICATIONS

I should like now to turn for a few minutes to the question whether this theoretical study has any bearing on the presentation of accounting statements in practice.

There are, of course, various legal and other obstacles in the way of applying the formula to its fullest extent. One formidable difficulty is that all reputable societies of accountants forbid their members, on pain of excommunication, to lend their names to published estimates of profits. No objection is made, however, to their taking part in the preparation of forecasts for private guidance, which, to differentiate them from the dangerous kind, may be called budgets, standard cost statements or the like. You will recognise that schemes of standard costing and budgetary control are in fact projections of a special type—that is, particular applications of the general formula.

Although accountants may not report on the estimates of profit inserted in prospectuses, they have for long accepted a moral responsibility to be satisfied that these estimates are honest and reasonable, and the Companies Act, 1948, now provides that their consent has to be obtained to the publication of any report they make, *in the context* in which it appears. This comes very near to making the moral responsibility a legal duty.

The prospectus frequently includes an independent valuation of buildings and plant, which may or may not be written into the Balance Sheet. Whether the old book values are retained or the valuation is substituted, the accountant must direct his mind to the question of depreciation, or provision for renewal, in relation to the true values of the assets.

In connection with prospectuses, therefore, the general formula is already accepted to a large extent in substance, even though it may be in disguise.

In one respect a prospectus, being a representation on which shares or debentures are offered for sale, differs fundamentally from a report to proprietors. It becomes a matter of honesty that any error should be on the side of understatement; note, however, that this refers to the impression given by the document as a whole, and that understatement producing a rising trend of profits when the real trend was the opposite would not be understatement at all.

It is unlikely that resort to periodical appraisal of physical assets will become common. This is partly because of the difficulty of arriving at accurate values, partly on account of the trouble and expense, but largely because of a feeling that the existing price level is too unstable for a revaluation to be justifiable. This last reason is not perhaps a very good one: it is difficult to see why values should not be adjusted after major changes in prices, merely lest further changes may follow, but the revaluations made in 1919 and 1920 and the slump of 1921 are still well remembered.

Very little of a practical nature has yet been done here or in America, so far as I am aware, to develop the use of index numbers for adjustment of fixed asset values. I believe we shall see experiments in this direction, though probably not in published accounts until the possibilities of the method are more widely realised than they are now.

As regards the ascertainment of profit, there are three important points that are brought into prominence in the " new model " accounts: the rejection of the rule that only realised profits can be brought in, the differentiation between profits from operating the undertaking and profits (or losses) from market fluctuations, and the relation of all charges (this applying particularly to depreciation and taxation) to the current price level.

There are exceptions even to-day to the rule concerning unrealised profits. In farming, rubber growing and plantation accounts generally, it is well accepted practice to value harvested crops at the net amount subsequently realised; and stockjobbers bring in the stocks which they hold, and their " short " positions, at market price. I have indicated that while bringing unrealised profits into account it is possible to divide the balance into a realised and an unrealised portion, and it may be that we shall see some modification of the rule on these lines.

The projection of long-term contracts to show their estimated outcome is likely to remain theoretical, so far as published reports are concerned, on account of the many factors which might upset the most careful estimates. The illustration that I gave nevertheless points to the value of a statement of this type for management purposes.

There is no inherent difficulty in differentiating between the normal profit margin of the merchant or the earnings of the manufacturer from the operations he is performing and the gains or losses resulting from the rise and fall in the materials in which he is dealing. The computation might prove troublesome in practice, but even an approximate separation would be informative, and I look forward to some advance in this direction.

Neither accountants nor company directors can feel at all satisfied with the present position regarding depreciation or renewal provisions. I think it will gradually be more generally accepted that the charge for the year should represent the current cost of restoring the wastage of the year; in time it may be that whether or not a revaluation of assets is written into the Balance Sheet, such a charge will be regarded as essential to a true and fair ascertainment of profit.

There is no doubt that the present basis of taxation adds greatly to the difficulty of any departure from traditional methods of arriving at profits. I cannot enlarge upon that topic to-night, and I will only express the hope that the first Tucker Committee and the Royal Commission will realise how wide the implications of our scheme of taxation are, not only as regards the form of accounts but in their bearing on the financial stability of businesses that are taxed on amounts which, under inflationary conditions, may be much more than their real profits.

Notwithstanding the progress in recent years towards more informative accounts, it remains true that the accounts of the majority of well-managed companies are prepared with a bias towards understatement. It is also true that the shareholders of such companies take for granted the existence of this bias, and they would be misled if without notice they were presented with Balance Sheets and Profit and Loss Accounts made up with complete impartiality. That is a consideration to which due weight must be given in practice, and it will undoubtedly help to ensure that any departure from presently accepted principles is very cautious and gradual.

CONCLUSION

If you take the view that the monetary unit is the one stable thing in a world of change, and that the objective of a business enterprise is to preserve and earn profits on the cash capital invested in it, you will not find much to approve in what I have said. On the other hand, you may consider that there is no true profit unless the real assets of the under-taking are being maintained and that the best basis for computing profit is that which enables the fairest comparison to be made of one year with another. If so, you may conclude that a formula which is applicable to statements of affairs, a wide variety of profit statements, prospectus forecasts, standard costing, and actuarial valuations has some claim to the description of a general formula.

Memorial

FRANK SEWELL BRAY

1906–1979

Frank Sewell Bray was born in London on October 12, 1906, joined the firm of Tansley Witt & Co., chartered accountants, of which hé later became senior partner, in the early 1920s, and qualified as an incorporated accountant in 1932 and as a chartered accountant in 1937. Author of numerous books and articles, he became a part-time Senior Nuffield Research Fellow in Cambridge University in 1947, co-editor of *Accounting Research* in 1948, Stamp-Martin Professor in 1952, and Knight Commander of the Order of St. Gregory (a papal distinction) in 1960. He retired in 1977 and died on January 29, 1979.

Such are the bare bones of a career. Unlike most memorialists, I did not have the pleasure and privilege of knowing my subject personally. I write, therefore, as a contemporary accounting historian and as the editor since 1975 of the successor journal to *Accounting Research* (which, through no fault of Bray's, ceased publication in 1958).

That such an excellent and necessary journal as *Accounting Research* should have lasted no more than a decade requires a word of explanation, but one must first go back to the beginning, for Bray's career as accounting practitioner and accounting academic can only be understood in the context of the time and place in which he grew up, both of which may appear strange to many readers of THE ACCOUNTING REVIEW.

LIFE AND TIMES

In the year that Bray was born, the Institute of Chartered Accountants in England and Wales was 26 years old and the Society of Incorporated Accountants and Auditors was celebrating its twenty-first birthday. To become a member of the former, it was necessary to serve articles for five years with a practicing firm at a zero or very small salary and to pay a premium. The financial demands of becoming an incorporated accountant were less and this was the route perforce taken by the young Bray, born into a relatively humble family in southeast London. He would have preferred to become an academic but there the possibilities were even less.

By 1932 Bray was an incorporated accountant and had succeeded so well that Tansley Witt granted him chartered articles at no cost. Gaining honors in both the intermediate and final examinations, he qualified as a chartered accountant in 1937. He was already active within the Incorporated Accountants Research Committee, established in 1935 as the first Research Committee in the British accountancy profession. Bray believed, not without justification, that the incorporated accountants were the intellectual leaders of the profession.

During the 1940s he published his first books (I shall look a little later in more detail at his writings) and worked his way up within his firm, becoming senior partner in 1948.

The late 1940s and the 1950s were a period of intense activity for him. In 1946, he became a member of a sub-committee of the Joint Exploratory Committee set up by the Institute of Chartered Accountants in England and Wales and the National Institute of Economic and Social Research. The Committee eventually produced a rather disappointing and now almost forgotten report entitled *Some Accounting Terms and Concepts* [1951]. More importantly Bray was brought into close contact with the economist J. R. N. Stone (now Professor Sir Richard Stone) who had just become the first director of the newly established Department of Applied Economics at Cambridge University and was at that time and for many years thereafter devoting a good deal of effort to developing the principles of national economic accounting.

Stone has written:

> Frank Sewell Bray was a man passionately interested in accounting ideas which he approached in a scientific spirit. He firmly believed that accounting practice could only be improved within a framework of correct theory based on exact principles. This may conjure up for those who did not know him a formidable image of cold precision. The truth was quite the reverse. He was laughing and open, understanding and generous and took life's disappointments and reverses with philosophical good humour. But behind this easy-going exterior the drive and energy were there to realize many of his hopes for accounting research [1979].

In October 1946 Bray was, while remaining in practice in London, appointed to one of the first two Senior Nuffield Research Fellows in Stone's Department. He remained a Fellow until 1955 when Stone was appointed P. D. Leake Professor of Finance and Accounting and ceased to be director.

In 1946, THE ACCOUNTING REVIEW was 20 years old and the world's only academic accounting journal. There was clearly room for another one. Bray was one of those in 1948 responsible for the establishment of *Accounting Research* and he became its co-editor with Leo Little of the University College of the South West of England (now more briefly known as the University of Exeter and by a happy coincidence the present editorial home of *Accounting and Business Research*). Bray described the new journal, which was sponsored by the Society's Research Committee, in an article he wrote for THE ACCOUNTING REVIEW in 1949:

> And this seems the place to comment upon the need which for some time past has been felt in some circles for a periodical given up to articles on advanced prospects of accounting and those subjects which are intimately associated with it. It is therefore hoped to fill the gap by the publication in Great Britain of a new periodical of standing to be called *Accounting Research*. This journal will be sponsored by the Research Committee of the Society of Incorporated Accountants, and its editorial policy will be directed to keeping close contacts with all branches of the profession and with the universities in all countries. It will be published by the Cambridge University Press twice yearly and the first issue should be ready towards the end of October, 1948.
>
> It will be the policy of *Accounting Research* to publish articles which make a real contribution to the theoretical and practical development of the accounting art, so that the intention is to provide a scholarly medium for making known advanced work undertaken by accountants whether they are engaged in professional practice, as executive officers in industry, or as teachers in universities. Moreover, it is also intended that special regard shall be had to the publication of postgraduate research studies. Thus, those subjects which because of the length at which they need to be treated, or because of the advanced standard of the work they demand cannot be included in the weekly and monthly professional journals will find their natural place in *Accounting Research*.

> If accounting is to reveal itself as having an honourable part in the play of learning and knowledge, then it must allow and expect changing points of view. So too it must encourage the publication of clear and well meditated accounts of new ideas, in order that everyone concerned with the advancement of the profession may understand what those ideas are about, as a precursor to tests of their merits. Just now the accountancy profession is meeting several new points of view—a healthy sign which bodes well for the development of its art—and in Great Britain, at least, the need has been felt for, a medium in which there can be adequate publication of new ideas and methods at a deeper level than is ordinarily possible in the usual periodicals circulating within the profession. It is contemplated that *Accounting Research* will meet this need.
>
> And lastly we should wish to make a particular point of the declared intention of the editors of *Accounting Research* to draw from outside, as well as from inside, the United Kingdom for its contributors, and it is hoped that not only accountants, but economists and statisticians will evince an interest in this new publication. Thus we may hope that it will serve a purpose in the same scheme of things as that expected from the introduction of the universities into the field of professional education and research [1949c, pp. 275–276].

In 1949, Bray was invited by the Commonwealth Institute of Accountants on a lecture tour of seven Australian Universities where, well ahead of developments in Britain, an academic accounting profession was beginning to blossom. A similar tour in Britain at that time would have been unthinkable. As Solomons has recently reminded us [1974, p. 39], from 1932 to 1947 there were *no* full professors of accounting in England and Wales, full time or part time. In 1947 William T. Baxter was appointed to a chair at the London School of Economics (just around the corner from both Incorporated Accountants' Hall and Tansley Witt's office) and in 1955 Solomons himself was appointed to a chair at Bristol University [1974, p. 37].

In 1952, Bray succeeded Bertram Nelson as chairman of the Incorporated Accountants' Research Committee and was appointed Stamp-Martin Professor at Incorporated Accountants' Hall. (The chair was named after Lord Stamp, a distinguished applied economist, and Sir James Martin, a former president of the Society.) Solomons has described this as "a well-intentioned, probably ill-advised and certainly short-lived attempt to promote academic research in accounting outside an educational institution" [1974, p. 29].

It was short-lived because of the integration of the Society in 1957 with the Chartered Institutes. In the long run this was clearly for the good of the British profession, removing as it did elements of unnecessary divisiveness and snobbishness. In the short run it was harmful. The "new climate" in the English Institute [Zeff, 1972, pp. 27–32] was still almost a decade away. The Council of the Institute had scant regard for professors and academic journals. The *Report of the Committee on Education and Training* [ICAEW, 1961], an astonishing document to reread in 1980, preferred correspondence courses to university tuition. For Bray, the merger meant the discontinuance of both his chair and his editorship. The work of the Research Committee also came to an end. His disappointment must have been bitter.

Reasons given for the decision to discontinue *Accounting Research* are varied, ranging from the fact that it had been incurring a loss to the belief by many members of the Institute's Council that its articles, most of which were written by academics, were abstruse and of no practical value [Zeff, 1972, p. 27].

It was, in fact, an excellent journal with a roll call of contributors that any editor would envy. It was typical of *Accounting Research* and of Bray that they were drawn from throughout the English-speaking world and included economists as well as accountants. The contributors to Volume 1, for example, included Bray himself, F. R. M. de Paula of the U.K., G. O. May of the U.S.A., and A. A. Fitzgerald of Australia, and economists such as J. R. N. Stone, G. L. S. Shackle and A. R. Prest. Later volumes included articles from the academic accountants W. T. Baxter, R. J. Chambers (his first article published outside Australia), S. Davidson, H. C. Edey, L. Goldberg, R. L. Mathews, R. Mattessich and D. Solomons and from the economists G. C. Harcourt (his first article), A. T. Peacock, W. B. Reddaway, R. C. Tress and B. S. Yamey.

Even accounting practitioners were well represented (editors of academic accounting journals know how difficult such articles are to get) by E. L. Kohler, W. W. Werntz and Sir Richard Yeabsley.

Louis Goldberg of the University of Melbourne expressed a widely held opinion when he wrote to *The Accountant* in December 1958, expressing grief at the obituary notice of *Accounting Research*:

> Among my personal acquaintances, many accountants—practising as well as academic—looked on *Accounting Research* as one of the very few learned journals in the world in its field. It had established for itself a unique place in accounting as a journal which was open to any kind of article, from whatever source, which gave evidence of original thought or research. It was not subject to the views or outlook of any professional body and its pages embodied the spirit of the open mind [1958].

Bray wrote little on accounting matters in the 1960s, his last important work in the field being a chapter on "Accounting Postulates and Principles" [1966].

He devoted himself increasingly to the business of his firm but remained active in other spheres. He acted, for example, as chairman for the Centre for Interfirm Comparison which had been established in 1959 by the British Institute of Management in association with the British Productivity Council.

A sincerely religious man, he had been for many years financial adviser to a number of Roman Catholic Dioceses and Religious Orders. He was a member of the independent committee of inquiry set up by the National Council of Social Service, under the chairmanship of Lord Goodman, to examine the effect of charity law and practice on voluntary organizations. The committee made a number of important recommendations on, *inter alia*, charity taxation, accounts and audit [NCSS, 1976] an area which is beginning to generate a surprising amount of interest in Britain.

In his retirement, Bray hoped to write a study of Fénelon, for whose work, especially the *Discourse on Prayer* and the *Treatise on the Existence of God*, he felt a deep regard. He did not live to fulfill this task. After a short illness he died on January 29, 1979, in his 73rd year. He is survived by his wife and son.

WRITINGS

It is time now to look in more detail at Bray's writings. He wrote eight books between 1944 and 1957: *Design of Accounts* (with H. B. Sheasby) [1944]; *Precision and Design in Accountancy* [1947], a collection of his early writings; *Farm Accounts* (with C. V. Dawe) [1948]; *Social Accounts and the Business Enterprise Sector of the National Economy* [1949a]; *The Measurement of Profit*

[1949b]; *The Accounting Mission* [1951], based on lectures given during his Australian tour; *Four Essays in Accounting Theory* [1953]; and *The Interpretation of Accounts* [1957], based on lectures he gave as Stamp-Martin Professor. *The Accounting Mission* is currently available in the "Accounting Classics Series" series edited by Robert Sterling. The others are out of print.

Bray had a writing style all his own, which occasionally baffles the reader. He was, for example, capable of writing such an extraordinary sentence as:

> Throughout this discussion we have sought to emphasise the importance of identifying the generic distinction between capital and current with those *actual* transactions, measurable in terms of units of money, which are promoted by the economic traversal of an enterprise along the paths of temporal periods intentionally limited for the purpose of recurrent survey, and in so doing we have commended a substitution of the adjectival use of the word capital by the term resting [1949b, p. 14].

Four themes recur throughout his writings:

(1) an emphasis on an academic and philosophical approach, on theory and on the importance of research;
(2) an emphasis on design, form, and standardization;
(3) an emphasis on the links of accounting with economics, especially in the field of national income accounting; and
(4) problems of profit measurement and accounting for inflation.

Philosophy, Theory and Research

Bray began his writing career with letters to the *Incorporated Accountants' Journal* (renamed *Accountancy* in 1938). As early as May 1932, he was writing to the editor that "I, in common with many other students, have spent the last nine years of my life in receiving instruction in technical accountancy, added to which my office duties and responsibilities have been in a similar direction; as I grow older [he was then 25], I desire to develop a philosophic outlook" [1947, p. 108]. In the January 1934 issue, he was arguing, in another letter, that "Many distinguished accountants have contributed to our professional knowledge, but so far there does not appear to have been any attempt at organised research, a development of fundamental importance in the field of scientific inquiry" [1947, p. 112].

Bray's mature ideas on research are set out in the lecture he gave at the University of Sydney on October 20, 1949. He argued that the least practical thought of today is often the most practical in execution tomorrow and that a hankering after short-term results depresses rather than gives birth to ideas. He stressed the need for fundamental and long-term research as especially necessary for a subject which "has moulded itself upon the solution of expedient issues." "I look for the day," he concluded, "when . . . accounting research schools are securely established in all our Universities. And to my professional brethren I would say: see to it, and press for it, that such research schools, if they should ever chance to come into being here, are made secure upon the foundation of Chairs of Accounting" [1951, pp. 59, 66].

In one of his Stamp-Martin lectures, he argued that "in the history of the professions it has often transpired that new ideas, even when they seem to lie at some distance from main interests, eventually become matters of vital concern with great utilitarian significance" [1957, pp. 86–87].

Bray was one of a small number of British academics expressing such ideas in the 1950s. Few practitioners were listening, alas! Bray's friend W. Bertram Nelson was one of the exceptions, pointing out with some penetration that "An estrangement between the practice and theory of any profession is always a waste of time" [ICAEW, 1961, p. 84].

Design, Form and Standardization

Bray believed strongly in order, precision, design, uniformity, and standardization. The elements of uniformity were information, classification, choice and use of terms, and conventions of measurement [1947, pp. 87–88].

Design of Accounts [Bray and Sheasby, 1944], described by de Paula [1948, p. 119] in a review as "an invaluable contribution to our professional knowledge and technique," is almost entirely devoted to specimen forms of accounts, drawn up on the principles of clarity, arrangement in groups under headings, unambiguity, ease of comparison, and compliance with statutory requirements. *Farm Accounts* [Bray and Dawe, 1948] also lays great stress on specimen forms. By far the greater part of *Social Accounts and the Business Enterprise Sector of the National Economy* [Bray, 1949a] is taken up with accounts and statements.

Standardization of, or uniformity in, the main forms of account he regarded as essential. It was necessary to think out "a few really fundamental forms" which would be capable of adoption to all problems as they arose, whether of management or stewardship [Bray, 1953, p. 72]. These forms he found, as we shall see later, in the economic relationships set out by Keynes and transposed into accounting terms by Stone and others.

Bray's regard for form is unusual for a British accountant but not for a continental European. He was obviously influenced by H. W. Singer's analysis of *Standardised Accountancy in Germany* in a book of that name published for the National Institute of Economic and Social Research by the Cambridge University Press [1943]. Curiously enough, however, Bray apparently never discussed the example of the French national accounting plan, the first and second editions of which were published in 1947 and 1957 [CNC, 1965].

Bray clearly believed that a set of formal accounts could be derived which would apply to every entity:

> [T]he Keynesian identities . . . give birth to a series of fundamental accounts which are just as relevant for firms or companies as for the nation as a whole. . . . they are not only fundamental but universal as well, and . . . they contribute the key to all accounting designs [Bray, 1953, p. 25].

He believed in a "pure theory of accounting which seeks to apply universal concepts of structure, form and measurement to any and every economic activity which requires to be viewed by means of accounts. In short, an invariant pattern exemplifying such a view of economic activity as points to an effective use of resources" [Bray, 1954, p. 138]. These he set out as follows [Bray, 1957, p. 34]:

I. Current

(a) Operating activity   Real

(b) Income   Real
                                                                  ± Financial items
                                                                  ± Transfers
                                                                  ± Disposable income
(c) Outlay   Disposable income
                                                                  = Consumption
                                                                  + Saving

II. Source and Use of Funds (Capital Changes)

(a) Saving and internal operating provisions
(b) Real asset formation
(c) Valuation changes
(d) Financial incomings and outgoings, and changes in monetary claims.
(The ultimate resolution of the accounting identity: Saving = Investment)

III. Capital

Real wealth and net monetary claims.

The accounts illustrating these are, for a company, the profit and loss account; "sources, earmarkings and utilization of funds" *i.e.*, a funds statement (Bray often called this a "resting account"); and a balance sheet.

Although he recognized that consumption was not relevant in company accounting, Bray never really considered whether forms which derive from Keynesian economic identities (form I represents the *ex post* relationship between income, consumption, and investment, II the equality of *ex post* savings and investment for a period and III the equality of *ex post* savings and investment at a point in time) are relevant for any other purpose than preparing the accounts of the nation as a whole. Why should the accountant not draw up a profit and loss account simply to serve the needs of shareholders?

But for Bray national accounting was dominant:

> A mature system of national accounting must ultimately call for some aggregation of private accounting results, and there must be no impediments occasioned by lack of uniformity in private accounting practices. Thus, as national accounting develops, private accounting will need to devise some conforming uniformity not only in relation to the *design* of private accounts, but also to the principles of income measurement and asset valuation [1946, p. 483].

In some ways, on the other hand, Bray never shook off the effects of his long practical training in double entry bookkeeping. His essay on "Accounting Principles" begins with the acute and well-expressed observation in paragraph 1 that:

> The rules of an acquired skill, when brought to the settled tendency of habit and committed to textbooks, are very apt to be mistaken for fundamental doctrines when they are still little more than the discrete boundaries of an empirically constructed technique [1953, p. 2].

But in paragraph 13 we are told that the familiar idea of double-entry is quite fundamental to all accounting theory [1953, p. 4].

Economics and National Economic Accounting

Bray saw many reasons why accountants should study economics:

(a) in order to determine the accountant's position in the scheme of things (as he put it in the letter of May 1932 already quoted and in a letter to *The Accountant* of October 9, 1933). This was his "cultural" reason [1947, pp. 108, 111];
(b) because in his view financial accounting statements were "statistical documents in the field of applied economics"ı [1949a, p. 27] and "chronicles of economic dealings" [1951, p. 3]; and
(c) because a study of the use of accounting forms for national economic purposes should force accountants to re-examine and call into question the adequacy of conventions which were subconsciously set to the service of traditional ends [1949b, p. 55].

He also saw a good reason why economists should take an interest in accounting:

the accounting approach to the presentation of information on economic transactions is the best means so far employed in explanation of national income statistics and . . . it is by far the best method of affirming those economic identities which lie at the heart of the new economics [1951, p. 21].

Bray's concern for national economic accounting and economic thinking led him to propose, well ahead of his time, not only that economists should make more use of the accountant's traditional financial statements but that accountants should adopt new forms themselves, *viz.* what are now known in the UK as source and application of funds statements and statements of added value.

Bray called for a redesigned profit and loss account "to give a reasonably clear idea of the output value added by a company as achieved through its input allocations of labour and capital" and also stated that "Information on the source and use of industrial finance would be greatly facilitated if companies could be induced to publish a summary account of their capital incomings and outgoings, much as the best companies do in America" [1953, pp. 41, 43].

Bray collaborated on a number of occasions in his writings with economists; for example, in his book *Farm Accounts* [Bray and Dawe 1948], which he wrote with C. V. Dawe of the University of Bristol, and in an article with Richard Stone [1948].

Profit Measurement and Accounting for Inflation

Bray began, for all his interest in economics, as a supporter of the traditional accounting conventions of profit measurement. In a letter to *The Economist* of May 17, 1944, in reply to letters from the economist Singer, he concluded that if Singer could suggest a better basis for drawing accounts than that which relied on the accounting principle of historical cost, he for one would be very glad to know it [1947, p. 113]. In July, 1945, in correspondence with Singer he expressed himself strongly:

. . . I am not inclined to favour the view that replacement values, or values resulting from the application of index numbers should be substituted for recorded costs in the keeping or main statement of accounts.
I feel that historical costs are in point of fact the only real objective dependable data available for the construction of accounting records [1947, p. 121].

He did envisage, however, a second section of the profit and loss account in which adjustments could be made [1947, p. 122].

Not very convincingly, he argued that the historical cost principle was fairly implicit in company legislation and that therefore accountants were obliged to retain the principle in the legal accounting documents they are called upon to formulate [1947, p. 124]. Early in 1945, he expressed the view that the prime basis for the preparation of accounting documents could not be anything other than monetary cost and that economists would have to take out of accounts prepared on this basis that evidence which they required and readjust it in line with their conception of economic theory [1947, p. 37]. He expressed the differing approaches well when he wrote that economists regard a fixed asset as a production good while accountants tend to regard it as a delayed consumption good [1947, p. 59]. In 1946, he thought it might be possible to give economists something of what they wanted by a supplementary valuation of a fixed asset by adjusting the original cost by a general price index.

It was Bray's appointment as a part-time Senior Nuffield Research Fellow in the Department of Applied Economics at Cambridge which appears to have changed his views. The changeover can be seen in his Cambridge monograph *Social Accounts and the Business Enterprise Sector of the National Economy* [1949a] where the main text favors the conventional accounting valuations of cost or lower market value for inventories while the appendix recommends that both opening and closing inventories should be shown in the operating account at "last cost" prices.

His book on *The Measurement of Profit* [1949] is disappointing. As A. R. Prest pointed out in a review [1950], Bray does not add much to our fundamental knowledge of the nature of income and capital, being content to summarize the views of Pigou and Hicks, without attempting to push their analyses further. Bray did, however, clearly recognize, while so many of his fellow accountants failed and continued to fail so long to recognize, that the existing accounting conventions conceived in an era of relative monetary stability had lost their force [1949, p. 55]. Bray made no substantive contribution to inflation accounting, but he was well aware of the problems and of the urgency of tackling them.

In Conclusion

Bray moved in the three worlds of economics, accounting practice, and academic accounting. What were his contributions to each of them? Stone has written that Bray confirmed economists in their belief that:

> there was nothing wrong in what they were doing from an accounting point of view. On details, accountants might be able to point to situations that the economists had not really thought about and suggest solutions, but the accounts they would incorporate into a social accounting system would not differ materially from those proposed by economists [1979].

Bray was clearly a success as a practitioner (under his leadership, Tansley Witt became one of the top 20 firms in the U.K., but his immediate impact on practice was small. It is only recently that the British accounting profession has tackled inflation accounting, funds statements, and value added statements. To what extent Bray helped to create a climate in which such practices would eventually be accepted is hard to gauge.

Finally, Bray was not in the mainstream of British academic accounting either personally or in the ideas he espoused. The London School of Economics, not Cambridge, has been the breeding ground of British academic accounting. Cambridge University has confined its teaching and research to macroaccounting and has virtually ignored microaccounting.

Nor have British accounting academics accepted the primacy of national accounts. For most of Bray's life they stressed the needs of shareholders. Today, they are emphasizing the differing needs of the various user groups.

Bray's influence, then, was indirect rather than direct. He helped to make academic accounting possible rather than creating it himself. His most important contribution, I suggest, and I acknowledge my own bias, was his editorship of *Acvounting Research*.

R. H. Parker

REFERENCES

Bray, F. Sewell, Review of H. W. Singer, *Standardised Accountancy in Germany*, in *Economic Journal* (September 1946), pp. 482–484.
———, *Precision and Design in Accountancy* (Gee & Co., 1947).
———, *Social Accounts and the Business Enterprise Sector of the National Economy* (Cambridge University Press, 1949a).
———, *The Measurement of Profit* (Oxford University Press, 1949b).
———, "The English Universities and the Accounting Profession," THE ACCOUNTING REVIEW (July 1949c), pp. 273–276.
———, *The Accounting Mission* (Melbourne University Press and Cambridge University Press, 1951; Scholars Book Co., 1973).
———, *Four Essays in Accounting Theory* (Oxford University Press, 1953).
———, "Accounting Dynamics," *Accounting Research* (April 1954) pp. 133–153.
———, *The Interpretation of Accounts* (Oxford University Press, 1957).
———, "Accounting Theory and Company Law," *Journal of Business Law* (1959), pp. 18–25, 154–162.
———, "Accounting Postulates and Principles," in Morton Backer, (ed.), *Modern Accounting Theory* (Prentice-Hall, 1966), pp. 28–47.
———, and C. V. Dawe, *Farm Accounts* (Oxford University Press, 1948).
———, and H. Basil Sheasby, *Design of Accounts* (Oxford University Press 1st ed. 1944, 2nd ed. 1947, 3rd ed. 1949, 3rd ed. rev. 1956).
———, and Richard Stone, "The Presentation of the Central Government Accounts," *Accounting Research* (November 1948).
Conseil National de la Compatabilité (CNC), *Plan Comptable Général* (Paris, 1965).
de Paula, F. R. M., "Design of Accounts," in his *Developments in Accounting* (Pitman, 1948, repr. Arno Press, 1978), pp. 119–122.
Goldberg, L., "The Demise of *Accounting Research*," Letter to *The Accountant* (13 December, 1958).
Institute of Chartered Accountants in England and Wales (ICAEW), *Report of the Committee on Education and Training* (1961).
Joint Exploratory Committee, *Some Accounting Terms and Concepts* (Cambridge University Press, 1951).
National Council of Social Service (NCSS), *Charity Law and Voluntary Organisations* (Report of the Goodman Committee) (1976).
Prest, A. R., Review of F. S. Bray, *The Measurement of Profit* in *Accounting Research* (July 1950), pp. 458–459.
Singer, H. W., *Standardised Accountancy in Germany* (Cambridge University Press, 1943).
Solomons, David (with T. M. Berridge), *Prospectus for a Profession. The Report of the Long Range Enquiry into Education and Training for the Accounting Profession* (Advisory Board of Accountancy Education, 1974).
Stone, Richard, Letter to R. H. Parker, 25 June 1979.
Zeff, Stephen A., *Forging Accounting Principles in Five Countries* (Stipes Publishing Company, 1972).

F. Sewell Bray, 'Auditing Theory' (1954-5)

Bray was one of the best-known UK practitioner-academics. Mainly identified
with writings on accounting theory, he produced this paper for the Students'
Society in 1954. It is one of the few examples in the literature of
accounting where accounting theory is linked with auditing theory.

The approach to auditing advocated by Bray centred on the need for the
auditor to take a general rather than a particular view of fairness. He
cited the improved systems of control within business as one reason for
this change, and illustrated the point with the accounting issue of
distinguishing revenue and capital transactions. In fact, he outlined the
audit problems associated with three different types of transaction - real
(concerning operating and trading activities), financial (relating to
financial matters), imputed (largely concerning accounting allocations),
and non-monetary (not involving any movement in cash resources). In doing
this, he indicated the varying degrees of difficulty facing the auditor
evidencing the fair view (the difficulty increasing in the order given
for the transactions).

Thus, Bray saw the auditor tending to take a general approach to
evidencing his opinion, and having to cope with transactions with varying
support from evidential material. Despite this, he envisaged the audit
function moving towards a more objective basis with the aim of attesting
the objectivity and reliability of financial information. The main
problem was, in his opinion, the difficulty of establishing the degree
of audit care and skill needed to attest in this way. Finally, he
advocated a movement towards efficiency or management audits.

The essay is much different in its approach and content from the
earlier ones in this volume, and such comparisons reveal the extent to
which audit thinking had changed during the history of the Students'
Societies.

AUDITING THEORY

By F. SEWELL BRAY, F.C.A., F.S.A.A.
Stamp-Martin Professor of Accounting

(Being the substance of a Lecture given to the Chartered Accountants Students' Society of Edinburgh on October 22, 1954)

AUDITING is an ancient practice bearing its own particular witness to the theological doctrine of original sin. It has always been directly concerned with matters of stewardship and accountability. The dishonest or careless steward was brought to a halt at the audit of his accounts. Away back in the past an auditor was a hearer; entries in accounts were read to him, and as an independent arbiter he approved or disapproved as he heard them. Thus, those who had the charge of other people's resources were required to give voice to their stewardship.

In principle, an audit is, and always has been, an independent third party examination of monetary and other records concerned with income and wealth. At first, and by the nature of things, this independent examination was a highly detailed affair very much preoccupied with the *bona fides* of incomings and outgoings. It persisted right up to my own time as an articled clerk, but with the development of accounting theory and practice, especially in the last thirty years, auditing ideas and methods have tended in part to move away from this meticulous inspection of an entity's recorded incomings and outgoings. Larger enterprises now have better control over the multitudinous transactions passing through their books of account. Almost imperceptibly, auditing theory has been brought to recognise the regularity and system which exists in economic life, and when it is not so much concerned with deliberate fraud it takes its cue from accounting theory and looks to the evidence supporting the presentation of a fair view of the epitomised transactions of an accounting entity both over time and at a defined point in time. The structure and form of accounts allied to significant disclosure, the existence of assets and liabilities, and the measurement of classified aggregates, have become as important, if not more important, than mere accountability for a complete series of individual items of incoming and outgoing in succession.

Lord Justice Morris lecturing on *The Spirit of Justice* said recently that " The lawyer must seek to distinguish between the particular and the general. He has learned that the rules of a code of laws or of a legal system must as far as possible be uniform, certain and of general application." [1] Equally the auditor must distinguish between the particular and the general. When auditing was absolutely concerned with the detailed examination of records then the particular was predominant. Nowadays, it is falling into place behind the general. And what are we to understand by the general in auditing? I suggest that the general theory of auditing must follow those general rules of an accounting system which as far as possible are uniform, certain and of general application.

In *Four Essays* [2] I set out what I considered to be some of the general principles of a formal accounting system. I will touch on them here and comment as I go on their special relevance to auditing theory. There are two general economic concepts fundamental to the practice of accounting; they are *periodic income* and *wealth*. This involves a fundamental sifting of transactions into the categories of current and capital, or, if you prefer, those which end up in the profit and loss account and those which end up in the balance-sheet. A modern auditor must take steps to see that this differentiation has been properly thought out, and carried out. Ofttimes this is a bothersome problem when we are dealing with expenditure. I give an example. It is not always easy to determine what borderline expenditure connected with fixed assets should be capitalised. Quite apart from verifying the mere *bona fides* of the outgoing, the auditor must consider whether such expenditure has added to the value of the asset, and whether it results in benefits which are deferable over time. He should inquire if such a particular outgoing has done anything to *increase the life* of the asset to which it is related, or to promote an increase in its *efficiency*, as measured either by output capacity and/or improved product quality. If the expenditure has merely kept the asset in *working* order then it is a current cost.

Apart from the distinction between current and capital, transactions in accounts may be classified as real, financial, imputed and non-monetary. Without going into much detail, real transactions mainly refer to purchases and sales of goods and services, recorded at the times of transfers of title, at the prices then obtaining. Financial relates to transactions in debts and claims. Imputation refers to those transactions which do not arise from exchanges between entities, *e.g.* depreciation, and rent

[1] *The Spirit of Justice*, by the Rt. Honourable Lord Justice Morris. Haldane Memorial Lecture delivered at Birkbeck College, 1954.

[2] *Four Essays in Accounting Theory*, Oxford University Press, 1953, and see also *The Formal Principles of Public Company Accounting*, Reprint No. 3, published by the Incorporated Accountants' Research Committee for the Stamp-Martin Professor of Accounting.

charges for owner-occupied buildings. Non-monetary means transactions in kind, *e.g.* directors' benefits received otherwise than in cash. As a matter of detail you should all be familiar with the auditing of real and financial transactions. You should know the kind of documents which are required to evidence real transactions, but you must always remember to investigate records of the physical movement of the goods which pass against the entries in the accounts. Financial transactions should give little cause for difficulty providing you remember that some transactions in debts and claims are limited by constitutional considerations. The auditing techniques relevant to both real and financial transactions are commonplace, and are to be found in any generally accepted text-book.

Imputed transactions call for the exercise of judgment and belong to another category, although I am afraid that for your present purposes I cannot guide you much beyond the accepted conventions. Thus, a modern auditor will need to be convinced that a proper method of depreciating fixed assets has been consistently followed from one period to another. He should satisfy himself that it conforms to a reasonable pattern of experienced technical factors, and if price factors have been taken account of he should judge their propriety and view the matter from the standpoint of an adequate disclosure in the final accounts. Rent charges for owner-occupied buildings can be tested by reference to net annual values. Non-monetary transactions are not so easily verified. For one thing, the physical records are apt to be imperfectly kept and therefore are not usually acceptable without the support of substantiating answers to careful inquiries. Then again, there is a pricing problem which can only be dealt with if the auditor has some knowledge of, or calls for information on, the prices of similar goods which have been the subject of actual *exchange* transactions on a market around the same time.

I return to the bearing of accounting theory on auditing theory, and I want to bring to your notice two very simple propositions which are at the bottom of all final accounts required to be audited. The first says that in a given time period income is devoted to consumption expenditure and saving. The second says that saving is resolved in capital formation. We rarely find that companies and suchlike enterprises constituted for profit come within the ranks of final consumers, although occasionally professional auditors are concerned with the spending accounts of persons and estates. If we rule out consumption expenditure from the general run of commercial auditing, we are left with concepts of income, saving and capital. A proper accounting structure for a commercial enterprise will be generally expressed in a set of formally related accounts: a profit and loss account to measure period income, an appropriation account to show transfers of income and the measurement of saving, sometimes a " sources and utilisation of funds " statement primarily to show the application of saving, and a balance-sheet to measure capital as a stock. I do not need to remind you of the importance of income measurement to an auditor who is concerned to see that the legal and financial constraints on income distribution have been properly observed. Quite apart from the intrinsic auditing principles of justification and verification, the modern auditor is getting in the situation where he is expected to take some responsibility for the structure and form of final accounts, and the conceptual measurements which such accounts are meant to give, although as things stand at present such things are very largely matters of convention and statute. It is usually said that accounts are matters of stewardship prepared for shareholders and proprietors, and as a consequence an auditor's responsibility to third parties who have incidentally relied upon those accounts lies in the grey land of legal obligation. I can see the day coming, however, when accounts based on the kind of theory I have been putting to you will put the practice of auditing on a much more objective basis, such that an auditor will be expected to attestt he objective reliability of the accounts and their conceptual measurements, but this is still some way off.

As we all know, companies are the most important entities with which the modern auditor has to do, and the Companies Act, 1948, has some rather vital regulations on the subject. The auditors' report must be attached to any circulated or published copies of the accounts. This report is addressed to members on the accounts examined and on all balance-sheets, profit and loss accounts and group accounts, laid before the company. In general it states whether the auditors have obtained all necessary information, whether proper books have been kept, whether the balance-sheet and profit and loss accounts are in agreement with the books, whether they present a true and fair view of the company's affairs, and whether they give the information required by the Act. As Professor Gower has recently pointed out, the disclosure philosophy regarded as the fundamental principle of investor protection, only works if the information disclosed can be safely taken as accurate. " Unless checked by some independent authority this cannot be relied on; so far as the accounts are concerned the auditors are this independent authority." [1]

Although the Companies Act is clear on the nature of auditors' duties we are still confronted with a measure of uncertainty in regard to the care and skill which they are to exercise in carrying out their duties.

[1] *The Principles of Modern Company Law*, by L. C. B. Gower, p. 450 (London: Stevens & Sons Ltd., 1954).

We all remember the famous judgment of Lopes, L.J., in the *Kingston Cotton Mill* case, but the reported cases referred to in our text-books are for the most part old and it is doubtful if they can be wholly relied upon for guidance in the future. The general principle is plain. An auditor must act with that skill, care and caution which a reasonably competent, careful and cautious auditor would use. Professional standards are rising, and notwithstanding the dictum in the *Kingston Cotton Mill* case Professor Gower suggests that "it is coming to be accepted that an auditor should not rely wholly on the honesty and accuracy of others even as regards taking stock, and that he should at least satisfy himself that it has been taken on sound principles and, probably, that he should carry out a spot check of at least one sample item." [1] It is not difficult to see the anomaly in a meticulous vouching of petty cash expenditure when stock valuations have been cursorily regarded.

I spoke earlier about regularity and system in economic life, a regularity and system which is well marked in a firm's accounting methods. This leads me to the related subjects of internal control and sampling tests. We know that the end of an audit is only achieved by a responsible and orderly examination of records, but if a modern auditor of a reasonably large-scale undertaking is to exhaust the possibilities of bringing to light *all* cases of dishonesty and fraud then he must attempt a thoroughly detailed examination, not missing out anything. For the great majority of such concerns this would involve a prohibitive cost, a cost which would be out of proportion to the benefits achieved. It has therefore come about that the modern auditor of sizeable enterprises has first to proceed by acquiring a personal familiarity with the procedures and methods of the accounting system; he must know their functions and their limitations, he must assure himself that they are so designed as to control errors and irregularities and he must know that they are working as they were planned. [2] If he is thoroughly satisfied on the adequacy and effectiveness of the system he can then resort to sampling tests, but he should never forget that the implications of such entries as he does meticulously examine must be carefully thought about before they are passed. He must especially see to it that the control elements of the system of accounting are such that undisclosed transactions are well-nigh impossible, and while we are on this question of undisclosed transactions we all know how necessary it is to consult the minute-books of companies. In recent

[1] *The Principles of Modern Company Law*, by L. C. B. Gower, p. 452.
[2] Cf. the references to " Proper Evaluation of the Examinee's Existing Internal Control for Reliance Thereon by the Auditor " in *Generally Accepted Auditing Standards*, Special Report by the Committee on Auditing Procedure of the American Institute of Accountants (1954).

D

years there have been a number of statistical suggestions involving
sampling methods as applied to auditing test checks. It seems to me that
these methods very largely relate to the discovery of errors and
irregularities in recording, and therefore I regard them as more peculiar
to internal control or internal auditing than to the independent audit.
I quote from some remarks which I made about this to a conference of
statisticians at Oxford in 1952:—

" A certain amount has been written about sampling methods as
applied to auditing test checks. In this context I must record my view
that fraudulent entries, or a lack of entries presupposing fraud, in books
of account, usually turn up when and where they are unsuspected, with
all the characteristics of the unexpected. I am, therefore, sufficiently
old-fashioned to prefer the examination of a selected series of entries
which is both complete and continuous in itself, in order to secure that
nothing at random has matured within that range. I am inclined to think
that the selection of the period is more a matter of auditing experience
than of technical analysis, though I do see that a sequential sampling
plan used systematically has advantages where the records of large
industrial entities are made the subjects of continuous audits. The trouble
is that apart from mere mechanist slips, slips which should be virtually
non-existent in these days of highly developed recording, no error is
really acceptable to an auditor as an *error* until its motive has been
thoroughly probed." [1]

In a recent publication of the American Institute on *Generally
Accepted Auditing Standards*, it is said that an extensive insight into a
system of control can be obtained by investigating a series of related
transactions: " For example, review of the data supporting the various
steps arising from a certain requisition for materials, including the
preparation of the purchase order, the record of the receipt of the material,
the approval of the voucher for payment, payment therefor, and tracing
the transactions to the particular accounts, is often more revealing than
the examination of vouchers or checks for a specified period of time." [2]

A great deal of judgment is required of the independent auditor in
selecting adequate samples of entries for testing the validity of a firm's
accounts. For example, the modern auditor should pay attention to the
system in force for plant construction authorisation and the system for
operating budgets; and I should not regard it as outside his province

[1] *Four Essays in Accounting Theory*, p. 52 (Oxford University Press, 1953).
[2] *Op. cit.*, p. 33.

to call for the budgets relevant to the period of his audit. In most cases inventories present problems, and whilst it may be very necessary to restrict oneself to sampling procedures in this context, it is plainly quite inadequate to apply such techniques to the verification of investments.[1] Where verification and checking is a difficult matter because of the complexities of recording, then it is essential that the independent auditor should concentrate his attention at this point.

Internal check and control are especially related to the subject of mechanised accounting. You may remember that the Report of the Mechanised Accounting Sub-Committee of the Taxation and Financial Relations Committee of The Institute of Chartered Accountants in England and Wales made the point that " Audit checks should, more than ever, be directed to testing the principles of the accounting system (including the internal check) and its practical operation. If the principles are sound and applied effectively, the auditor will be able to dispense with a considerable amount of detailed routine checking. The soundness and efficiency of the control system are of much greater importance than the mechanical operation of the machine or the hole in a card. If it is established by means of test-checks that the control records do prove the arithmetical accuracy of the ledgers, then it becomes possible for the auditor to vouch, by means of code references, direct from prime documents to the ledgers instead of through the intermediary of a day-book. Direct vouching in this way has distinct auditing advantages, particularly in vouching the private and nominal ledgers." [2]

It should be especially remembered that transactions which do not lend themselves to the normal routine of the accounting system should receive special attention from the independent auditor. While we are on the subject of mechanised systems I think we should notice one of its most serious dangers. Again I quote from the Report of the Mechanised Accounting Sub-Committee: " There is also a danger—one of the most serious dangers in any mechanised system—of prime documents or punched cards being miscoded and resulting in the transactions being guided from the start through the wrong channel, a type of error which may be difficult to locate. In general, it will be found that an internal check must be imposed in some form on all or most of the postings, particularly in regard to allocation, but to a large extent this can be achieved by breaking down the controls into suitable subsections, thus narrowing the risk of errors remaining undetected."

It has been said in some quarters that modern auditing is almost

---

[1] *Op. cit.*, p. 35.
[2] *Mechanised Accounting and the Auditor*, March 1949, p. 16.

wholly devoted to questions of stewardship, that this in itself is a negative affair and that the modern auditor should develop positive techniques which will enable him to give an opinion on the efficiency with which the accounting entity has been conducted. Efficiency audits may or may not prove a desirable development, but I should like to say that in my judgment there is nothing very unusual about them, only their name. Investigations have always been a common feature of professional work, but I suggest they are different in category from the kind of audit which is required by the Companies Act, 1948, and they should not be thought of in the same context. In the normal stewardship audit " scrutiny of vouchers and records and the follow-up and explanations of abnormal items remain the foundation of the audit procedure." [1] Verification and a careful regard for methods of valuation, within the limits of accepted principles and conventions, are still the keynotes of modern auditing standards.

[1] *Mechanised Accounting and the Auditor*, March 1949, p. 19.

James R. Leitch, CA

James Leitch was born in 1905. He was indentured with Grahams Rintoul Hay Bell and Company, Chartered Accountants, and was admitted to membership of The Institute of Chartered Accountants of Scotland in 1928. In 1929, he joined Deloitte Plender Griffiths and Company, Chartered Accountants, in London. For the next twenty years he remained with this firm until he was appointed in 1948 as Comptroller of Associated Commercial Vehicles Ltd. (a company which merged with British Leyland Ltd. in 1962). Between 1958 and 1970, Mr Leitch was appointed to the board of directors of this company and its main subsidiaries. In 1970, he retired as Comptroller and in 1972 retired from all business activities.

Mr Leitch served on several committees of the Scottish Institute, and during the 1950s he gave several papers relating to the problems of accountants in industry (including one to the Second Summer School of the Institute).

James R. Leitch, 'The Accountant and Inflation: Changing Price Levels'
(1956-7)

The final lecture reproduced in this collection is one which examines the
case for abandoning the use of historic cost accounting and, instead,
adopting replacement costs. It is a questioning paper which seeks to
establish that accountants produce financial statements which are an
improvement on those produced in the conventional way.

Leitch's method of analysis was to examine individual asset categories,
and discuss the possible application of replacement costs in each. With
buildings, he identified the problems of non-identical replacement and
situations where replacement was not contemplated. He suggested any changes
in replacement cost could be noted in the statements without a formal
accounting. He next examined plant, and covered most of the main problems
being discussed today in relation to current cost accounting (non-identical
replacement; the relevance of government indices; and technological change).
The difficulty of substituting a factual figure with a hypothetical one was
felt by Leitch to warrant a note in the directors' report but not a change
in the method of accounting for plant. In addition, he felt replacement of
fixed assets was a financing problem, and depreciation was aimed at the
recovery of original cost. If management wished to fund higher replacement
costs it could make appropriate transfers to reserve.

Leitch continued his criticism of replacement cost accounting ideas in
the area of inventory, suggesting that the use of standard costs to determine
cost of sales would be a reasonable approach. His paper reflects the view
which exists to a considerable extent in industry today that the use of
replacement costs during a period of inflation does not necessarily produce
improved financial information for report users.

THE ACCOUNTANT AND INFLATION: CHANGING PRICE LEVELS

By J. R. LEITCH, C.A.

(Being a Paper read to the Glasgow Chartered Accountants Students' Society on December 18, 1956)

THE subject of the accountant and inflation undoubtedly represents one of those problems which ought to interest every accountant in the country and to which every accountant ought to be prepared to make some contribution. The inflationary spiral which has been in force since the end of the war has posed problems which are, as yet, unsolved.

My thesis is that although, in a period of changing prices, I do not deny that conventional accounting based on original cost may be open to criticism, I am not at all satisfied that the alternative methods put forward by economists, statisticians and others are practical in their application and would not give rise in the minds of the layman to " confusion worse confounded " in the understanding of accounts. Before we discard the conventional method of accounting, let us be quite certain that we substitute a better one.

I would like to deal with some of the practical problems arising from the discarding of conventional accounting, particularly as they would affect the engineering industry.

During the Sixth International Congress of Accounting held in London in 1952, there were, I believe, eight papers delivered on the subject of " Fluctuating Price Values " and the diverse views and opinions expressed were almost as numerous. At that Conference, as to-day, one of the main bones of contention was the plea that in the balance sheet the replacement cost of fixed assets should be shewn, instead of the original cost, and the treatment of depreciation thereon. I have deliberately omitted the word " historical." At the moment fixed assets are generally shown in the balance sheet at original cost—*i.e.*, the price the owners paid for them. Now let us first examine the argument for substituting replacement cost as regards buildings.

BUILDINGS

It will, I think, be generally agreed that buildings, be they factory or other business premises, are not held for re-sale but primarily for the purpose of earning profits for their owners whether they be individuals or private or public companies. The asset, no doubt, may wear itself out in so doing. The life of a building, however, may be expected to extend over a few decades and, provided it is properly maintained out of revenue, may extend well beyond the notional 50 years life allowed by the Revenue authorities on certain classes of buildings. I am suggesting that there are many factory premises in perfectly good condition to-day which were erected more than 50 years ago. Assuming for the moment that depreciation charged in the accounts of a business owning factory premises has been based on a 50 year life, the amount so charged against revenue is sufficient to cover that part of the original cost of the premises which is considered to have been used up over its life in helping to produce the final product.

Under the present accounting procedure buildings are shown in the balance sheet at the original cost to the owner, and whether we like it or not it is a statement of fact. It is suggested that there be substituted an amount which represents what these buildings would now cost to replace. Let us for a moment consider a company having a number of factories scattered throughout the country: these factories have been erected over a period of years extending from 1920 to the present day and are all held for the purpose of earning profits. The company has no thought of replacing these factories—they might well be in a perfectly good state in forty or fifty years' time—and even if it had the question might well be asked: Will we replace them with identical buildings? The company might well consider extending and enlarging the factories, but there is no suggestion that the cost of such extension should be something that should be provided out of revenue in the year in which the extensions took place or that the profit and loss account should be charged with the extensions. Would any useful purpose be served by reducing the profits of this company in order to provide the enhanced cost of replacing buildings which might well have, as already stated, a further forty or fifty years' life when, in fact, such replacement is not even contemplated? Would any useful purpose be served by writing up the value of these factories to present day replacement costs and, presumably, adjusting it each year thereafter and creating a capital reserve, if you bear in mind that replacement cost is a matter of opinion? At the moment, by showing the factories at original cost in the balance sheet, we are dealing with facts and I see no reason why we should be drawn into the land of "make believe" by putting some other value on them which is only a matter of opinion and certainly enters the realms of " fancy ", particularly when replacement is not contemplated.

It is argued, of course, that the owners of the business should be given some indication of what it would cost to replace the present factories. I have no objection at all to this being done, but I cannot appreciate why the value should be shown in the balance sheet as if it were the intention to sell or replace the factories.

The only circumstance in which factories would be replaced would be the occurrence of a disastrous fire, and it seems to me quite logical for the buildings to be insured at an estimated cost of replacement. The furthest I, personally, would be prepared to go in this matter would be to show, by way of a note attached to the accounts or mention in the directors' report, the amount for which the buildings are insured against fire. The owner or owners would then have a straightforward statement of what it would cost to replace buildings in certain circumstances.

PLANT AND MACHINERY

Now let me turn to plant and machinery. This asset, as in the case of buildings, is not held for re-sale, but primarily for earning profits and it wears itself out in so doing. There is, however, a difference of degree between buildings and plant in that the working life of plant and machinery in many businesses is comparatively short—an average, perhaps, of ten to twenty years—and is often affected by the fact that industry is always striving for greater efficiency through the use of more up-to-date methods of production. It is undoubtedly true that the cost of necessarily replacing plant and machinery is rising each year owing to inflation, and it is also true that if there is going to be continuity of the business it is necessary to provide funds or to retain working capital for the enhanced cost of replacement.

Under the present accounting procedure, plant, like buildings, is shown in the balance sheet at the original cost to the owner. It is said that this method should be abandoned and that instead—

(1) plant and machinery should be shown in the balance sheet at the cost of replacement and that the difference between original cost and the cost of replacement should be carried to capital reserve, and accordingly,

(2) the amount set aside for depreciation in the profit and loss account should be calculated on replacement cost instead of original cost.

362

I will deal with the question of depreciation later, but at the moment I would like to make one or two comments on the use of replacement cost in the balance sheet.

The replacement of these assets is usually a continuing process. Perhaps no more than 10 per cent of the total plant and machinery is normally replaced in a single year. It should not be imagined that each piece of plant is earmarked for replacement on a certain date, neither should it be thought that it will be replaced by an identical article—in all probability it will not. Industry is always looking for more up-to-date methods of production and most new plant is capable of doing a better job than the plant it replaces. The decision whether to replace plant is mainly governed by whether or not the new plant is capable of earning so much more than the old that its capital cost can be recovered quickly. The important element in these days is the time factor and a piece of plant producing two units per hour might well be replaced by a machine producing four units per hour. Almost certainly such new plant will cost more, but unless its operating costs are double the old, its earning capacity will be proportionately greater than the plant it replaces. The increased cost, therefore, is not entirely attributable to the enhanced cost of replacement but contains a considerable element of improvement. It is assumed, by the advocates of replacement costs, that reasonably accurate estimates can be made of the cost of replacement as and when replacement is necessary. Is it known what replacements will take place? The theory put forward by economists, statisticians and others, is that indices of price levels should be used which give an indication of the replacement cost of plant. They argue that the replacement cost of plant ought to be shown, whether plant is to be replaced or not in the year following the date of the balance sheet. The value so placed on the plant is itself subject to variation each year if it is intended to maintain a replacement cost value. This, in effect, means a revaluing of plant, etc. each year, based presumably on an index of price levels. I doubt whether any Government index of prices could possibly be correctly applied to different types of plant used in a variety of businesses, nor could it possibly be up-to-date. I am not sure how it is proposed in practice to discount the actual cost of new machines to allow for the considerable element of improvement derived from the replaced plant. It must also be remembered that a period of ten years or longer might well elapse before replacement was considered, and by that time new ideas might alter the nature of replacement.

I feel, therefore, that it is undesirable to substitute a hypothetical figure in the balance sheet for that of original cost. It may be the economist's dream—but it would certainly be the accountant's nightmare! Again, I have no objection to some indication being given to the owners of a business of the cost of replacing plant and machinery at present day prices and would suggest that, as in the case of buildings, the value placed on these assets for fire insurance purposes should be mentioned in the directors' report or by way of a note attached to the accounts.

DEPRECIATION

Now to deal with the question of depreciation. It seems to me that the fundamental idea behind the provision of depreciation is inclined to be lost when considering the theory of replacement cost. In pre-war days, when we had a stable currency, the fact that amounts written off for depreciation approximated to the amount required to replace the assets may have helped to confuse the issue. The idea behind a provision for depreciation is to write off an asset over its working life, for which purpose there is included in the cost of sales, not only the cost of material and labour and expenses incurred, but also that part of the original cost of the assets employed which is considered to have been used up in manufacturing the product sold. If this view is accepted it will be seen that the setting aside of amounts towards the enhanced cost of replacement, although it may be closely related to depreciation, is really a separate problem. All expenditure incurred by a business, be it capital or revenue, in manufacturing a product or in giving a service, must be recovered either when it is incurred or over a number of years, otherwise the business would simply cease to prosper. Depreciation represents the recovery—deferred over a number of years—of actual expenditure incurred; in my view, depreciation does not represent and never has represented, any more than this.

The problem of the eventual replacement of assets or the re-equipping of factories entails a survey of future expenditure, some of which may not be incurred for a period of five, ten, fifteen years or longer. Is it suggested that even before such expenditure is undertaken or envisaged a charge must be made against the current year's profits to recover it?

Since the war the decreasing purchasing power of the pound has undoubtedly made the problem of replacing plant and machinery a very difficult one, particularly in view of high taxation. When the replacement cost advocates assume that amounts required to be set aside for this purpose are in fact additional depreciation to be charged against profits of the current year, they are taking it for granted that accurate estimates can be made of the cost of replacement after discounting the improvement element.

May I repeat that, in my view, the fundamental error is the misconception of the nature of depreciation, possibly due to the fact that before the war the depreciation provided to recover expenditure actually incurred did provide a sum sufficient to buy an identical piece of plant at the same price.

Even then, however, plant was being replaced by better plant; but as the additional cost was, perhaps, of less consequence, and as taxation was not at to-day's high level, the problem of financing that additional cost did not give rise to anxiety. The nature of depreciation has not changed, but there has arisen this new problem of financing the enhanced cost of the future replacement of fixed assets. It seems to me that the problem is one of assessing the extra capital required for the future replacement of these assets. This capital can be provided from the savings of the business concerned or by the introduction of new capital and to that extent, in my view, it has nothing to do with depreciation. Prudent business managements recognise that they must retain sufficient savings to face the enhanced cost of purchasing new plant and machinery. Accountants also have generally advised industry not to distribute the whole of the profits but to conserve their resources by placing to reserve an estimated amount to cover this future expenditure.

In some cases where the asset values have not been written up to replacement cost, an amount is often specifically set aside in the profit and loss account and is variously described as—

(a) " Additional depreciation to cover replacement cost ";
(b) " Depreciation proportion of increased replacement cost "; or
(c) " Amount retained out of profits to finance replacement of assets at rising prices."

There are two problems to be considered:—

(i) The treatment of the item in the profit and loss account;
(ii) The treatment in the balance sheet.

Generally speaking, where a description is used in the profit and loss account similar to that mentioned in (a) and (b) the amount has been charged against profits, but where the description has been similar to (c) the amount has been shown as an appropriation of profits.

H

Where do you put it in the balance sheet? In my view you must create some sort of a reserve, which implies that the "enhanced depreciation" is not a charge against profit but an appropriation of profit. In all balance sheets I have examined where this item appears it has been treated as a capital reserve. I am not enamoured, therefore, of the suggestion that such amounts should be charged against the profit and loss account, and I still hold the view that any amount so set aside is an appropriation of profits and not a charge against them. If the business concern agrees to earmark the reserve in some special way no harm will be done, although I am not an advocate of cluttering up a balance sheet with all sorts of reserves of one kind or another. It seems to me that the general reserve of a business, together with the unappropriated profits, represents the savings set aside over the years for the very purpose of being able to finance future expenditure required in keeping up-to-date its fixed assets.

STOCK

I turn now to the problems of inflation as it affects stock-in-trade. The effect of inflation on stock is somewhat different from that on fixed assets. The reasons, I suggest, are that fixed assets normally have a life extending far beyond a single accounting period and that the effect of inflation makes itself very apparent whenever comparisons with original and current costs are made, e.g. when buildings or plant are replaced or extended, or when insurable values are revised, or when assets are sold. On the other hand the stock of material of a manufacturing business is constantly turning over even within a single accounting period. The problem of absorbing the current cost of material in cost of sales is, I suggest, of far greater concern to industry than the problem connected with the depreciation of fixed assets. In most industries direct material purchases—for the purposes of this paper I am ignoring productive labour cost—represent a far higher proportion of the total cost of sales than does depreciation. As I see it, the industrial accountant has two major difficulties to overcome:—

(1) His Management will require, as early as possible, estimates of the amount by which their trading results and product costs will be affected by the increased prices payable for material.

(2) In preparing interim or annual accounts he will need to recover

the actual cost of output from his factory although knowledge of the *cost of that production* will not necessarily *be of future value to his Management.*

My own experience with a firm manufacturing complex products containing many thousands of different parts has shown that the most practical solution to both the difficulties is offered by a standard costing system disclosing a variance on the value of material as and when it is purchased. Most raw material spends several months in the factory after it has been purchased before it becomes the finished product and the variance factor allows a reasonably accurate estimate to be made of the cost of output several months ahead. Moreover, the fact that both input and output of material stocks are valued at standard cost enables the stock account to be maintained correctly. The variance thrown up on purchases is written off to cost of sales at the time when it is assumed the material is actually incorporated in the products sold. Undoubtedly there is a time lag varying between three and six months according to the number of times stock turns over within a single account-ing period. This time lag, however, is not as serious as it may seem, because the current product costs are known and are taken into account in the fixing of selling prices or future sales policy.

There is now to be considered the valuation of the stock in the balance sheet. In recent years there has been a plea for the substitution of the LIFO method of valuation as opposed to the generally accepted method of cost or market value—market value being defined as net realisable selling price—used in this country. LIFO is not a departure from original cost but makes use of the convention that the last goods to come into stock may be regarded as the first to go out. This means, in effect, that raw materials are charged to production on the last in first out principle, thereby ensuring that production has been charged with the current cost. It follows, therefore, that the stock valuation at the close of any accounting period will be based on the cost of the very earliest purchases. It will be appreciated that in times of rising prices such stock valuation will be below cost and also below current replacement value. On the other hand, when prices are falling the value of stock at any one accounting date will be above that of original cost and also above current replacement costs. LIFO is in fairly common use in America, where it is accepted as a recognised basis. In this country it has not yet been so accepted and is not recognised by the taxation authorities as a method of valuing stock. There is little doubt that LIFO does result in an under-valuation of realisable assets and, whilst I do not deny that

LIFO may have its uses, I consider that, where stocks are being constantly turned over, a system which assumes that a basic stock is held but never used cannot truthfully record what has actually happened. The advocates of this system are, of course, much more concerned to see that the charge to production for the consumption of raw materials is the current replacement cost; the stock valuation at the end of an accounting period is of secondary consideration.

It must also be borne in mind that, as in the case of fixed assets, it should not be assumed that stock will be replaced. In many industries changes in the design of products or in the pattern of demand for them may result in considerable changes in the quantity and variety of stocks on hand at the beginning and end of any accounting period. The danger in the LIFO method of valuation of stock is that if stocks run down profits will be overstated because the charge to production for the consumption of raw materials is at the price the stock originally cost, which, certainly in a period of rising prices, bears no relation to reality. In other words, profits may well be understated while stocks are being built up and overstated when stocks are running down.

TAKE-OVER BIDS

It has been suggested in some quarters that take-over bids indicate how grave can be the consequence of antiquated values. Let us examine this proposition. I imagine that the individual organising such a bid looks first at the price at which the company's shares are quoted on the Stock Exchange, in the hope that he can buy a good business at a low price. The Stock Exchange quotation is, however, affected by the dealings of the normal investor and such a person usually takes into account four factors when considering a purchase of shares. These factors are:—

(a) Earnings yield on quoted price of shares;
(b) Dividend yield;
(c) Profit earned; and
(d) Asset value.

In my opinion the above is the order of importance of these factors to the normal investor. In other words, the Stock Exchange price is very much more sensitive to the profits earned, etc., than to the valuation of assets. After all, assets have little value to the investor if they cannot earn profits.

Although the take-over bidder is concerned with the quoted prices of the shares, he will also be concerned to a greater extent than the normal investor with the value of the assets. In the case of a manufacturing company the fact that assets are written up to replacement costs does not make the concern more efficient, nor does it allow it to declare a higher dividend or show a better profit cover for that dividend. I have already indicated that the owners of the business should be given some indication of the current worth of the assets by way of a note, or preferably in the directors' report.

In my view the take-over bidder is often tempted to acquire the business with a view to putting the assets to more fruitful uses because of the low price of the shares on the Stock Exchange, brought about either by insufficient earnings in relation to the assets employed or *by dividend restriction.* If a company is well managed and its earnings are sufficiently high in relation to the assets employed and provide adequate cover for a reasonable dividend, then the price of its shares on the Stock Exchange should be such that they will not attract a take-over bidder; on the other hand, the company which possesses valuable assets and whose earnings are low and dividend cover small will obviously attract the take-over bidder. Is this a bad thing? In my view, most take-over bids arise from the inefficient use of assets; if these assets could be used to better purpose, then from the point of view of industrial efficiency there is no reason why this should not be done. I hope I have indicated that take-over bids are not, in themselves, a justification for the introduction of replacement costs for assets in the balance sheet.

TAXATION

In 1951 and 1952 the Royal Commission on the Taxation of Profits and Income held public sessions at which one of the principal topics was accounting in periods of inflation. The Commission were pressed to consider the adequacy of the taxation allowance for depreciation of fixed assets on the grounds that such depreciation should be based on replacement costs. The matter, to my mind, was well summed up by Mr W. S. Carrington, a Chartered Accountant and a member of the Commission, who said " Is not the problem—stripped of much of the wool that surrounds it—shall the taxpayer be allowed relief on the building up of liquid resources required to purchase the plant, or shall he be allowed relief when he spends the money, or shall he be allowed relief over the period of use of the new asset that he has bought? "

The Commission also considered the LIFO valuation of stock and some very pointed questions were put to those advocating the adoption of this method for tax purposes.   The Chairman, Lord Radcliffe, commenting on the theory of replacement cost accounting, stated that it was implicit in the theory, that a business should be able to maintain a constant volume of trading activity out of tax free resources.   No matter how a business expanded and contracted—what was the standard to show the precise volume of business which ought to be maintained?

If you accept these views, it seems to me, in effect, that you would immediately become involved in attempting to define the normal productive capacity of each particular business—I suggest a most difficult task.

The Chairman also stated that a marked depreciation in the purchasing power of the pound created a need for more money in business apart from taxation.   The real problem was to say from what source this additional capital was to come.   Must it come from tax free gain . . .?

Changes in the purchasing power of money are not limited to industry. Other sections of the community are affected and have a right to be considered.   It seems to me that in claiming allowances for depreciation, etc., on the basis of replacement cost, industry is putting forward a plea for special consideration.

It is difficult to visualize just where the loss of revenue to the Exchequer could be made good if replacement costs were allowed as a charge against profits.   Presumably other sections of the community would be required to bear the burden and it might well be asked whether this would be fair and equitable to those concerned.

GENERAL

I mentioned at the beginning of this paper that there was a great diversity of opinion on this whole subject.   There are those who advocate the writing up of fixed assets to replacement cost and those who do not. There are those who would substitute depreciation on a replacement cost basis but not deal with the question of stock, and on the other hand there are those who would deal with stock but not with depreciation.   There is a difference of opinion among replacement cost advocates as to the basis of the depreciation charge.   Some advocate the basis of current replacement costs and others the use of indices current since the asset was originally bought. As I have already stated, I have seen no adequate attempt to deal with the fact that the assets are seldom replaced in identical form. A company may well have equity shareholders, holders of preference shares, debenture holders, as well as trade creditors, beneficiaries under profit sharing schemes—all of whom have an interest in the profits of the company. In the space at my disposal it is not possible to deal with the position as affecting these classes.

I do not deny that the difficulties created in industry by the decline of the purchasing power of the pound are disturbing, but, as one writer has put it, "I see great difficulties and complexities in the way of the adoption of a new conception of profit." I am extremely doubtful whether the discarding of the use of original cost and the substitution of other alternatives is practicable and possible of general application throughout industry. In fact, at times I doubt the basis upon which the new ideas of profit are founded. I read an article recently by Professor F. W. Paish, Professor of Economics at the University of London, in which he gave the following example:—

> " Let us take a gentleman who for his livelihood sells matches in the street. We will assume that he had 1s. for which he bought a packet of a dozen boxes of matches, which, on the following day, he retails at 2d. a box. Thereby he secures a gross turnover of 2s. and a profit of 1s. But one day when he goes to replace his packet of matches, he finds that the price has gone up to 1s. 6d.; so he has to pay 1s. 6d. to replace his stock. What is his profit now? If you start from the 1s. and finish with the 2s. at which he sold them, there is a profit of 1s. but if you start from the point when he had already bought his packet of matches, he starts with a packet of matches and nothing and finishes up with a packet of matches and 6d. so that clearly his profit is 6d."

The truth is, of course, that every business starts with money and I should have imagined that the trader in matches might well have said to himself, " I started with a shilling, I now have sixpence plus a dozen boxes of matches which cost me 1s. 6d. and could certainly be sold for that price. Therefore, my total worth is now 2s. Where did I get the extra shilling from? Capital to start—1s., capital to end up—2s." What is the difference? I suggest the difference represents his profit on his trading. The manner in which he deals with that profit is an entirely different question, that is, whether he distributes it or retains it. If he distributes it all he may have to borrow to continue his business, but the fact remains in my view that he has still made 1s. profit.

There are quite a number of practising accountants who advocate the principle of replacement costs as having always been the correct and realistic procedure to be applied. I often wonder whether they have the courage of their convictions and do, therefore, qualify in their report as auditors and in prospectuses, the truth and fairness of profits arrived at on the basis of original cost. Perhaps, of course, they feel that the consequent cessation or curtailment of reasonable dividends, the effect thereof on market quotations and on ability to raise fresh capital, might not be beneficial to the national economy and fair to shareholders. It would be very interesting to know to what extent precept and practice go hand in hand. It may be, of course, that after all, the view is taken that profits or losses arrived at on either basis can be accepted as true and fair.

CONCLUSION

I am fully aware of the great number of points connected with fluctuating price levels that I have not touched upon here, but I think you will agree that to attempt to deal extensively with such a subject in one short paper would be nothing short of ridiculous. I have tried to point out some of the practical problems which can arise if conventional accounting methods are discarded. It may be that the ultimate solution is to prepare accounts on the present accepted lines and to supplement them either by giving additional information in the Chairman's speech, or directors' report, or in a note attached to the balance sheet as to the possible cost of the estimated additional capital required for future replacement of assets after taking into account the provisions which have already been made.

I have expressed certain views on the matter, but these views are not necessarily right and you may not agree with them. May I express the hope that whatever your views may be, I have stimulated your thoughts on this very important problem.